SAINT LOUIS DAYS
SAINT LOUIS NIGHTS

A culinary tour
of the Gateway City

Presented by
Junior League
of St. Louis...
*Improving the Community
Through Trained Volunteers*

DESIGN BY:
*Hawthorne / Wolfe Corporate
Communications Consultants, Inc.*

COVER PLATE BY:
Susan Garson

PHOTOGRAPHY BY:
John Watson

CONCEPT BY:
Matthew J. Fister

J unior League of St. Louis is part of an international organization of women committed to promoting voluntarism and to improving the community through the effective action and leadership of trained volunteers. Its purpose is exclusively educational and charitable.

Junior League of St. Louis reaches out to women of all races, religions and national origins who demonstrate an interest in and commitment to voluntarism.

Junior League of St. Louis donates more than 375,000 volunteer hours annually to the community through a focus on "Women Working for Tomorrow's Community," which is achieved in the following areas of concentration:
-    Women's Well Being
-    Today's Families
-    Supporting our Youth

For current programs offered, please visit our website at www.jlsl.org.

Copyright© Junior League of St. Louis
First Edition - December 1994 - 10,000 copies
Second Edition - January 1995 - 10,000 copies
Third Edition - July 1996 - 10,000 copies
Fourth Edition - April 1998 - 10,000 copies
Fifth Edition - July 2001 - 5,000 copies
Sixth Edition - October 2003 - 7,000 copies
ISBN # 0-9638298-2-3
Library of Congress Card Catalog
(LCCN): 94-078292

WIMMER
COOKBOOKS

ConsolidatedGraphics
1-800-548-2537

TABLE OF CONTENTS

ORIGINAL COOKBOOK COMMITTEE

Joan Shelton Hagedorn-Ball, Sharon Etzel Boranyak, Susan Moreland Cocking, Mary Lagen Corrigan, Kathryn Cooper Cornwell, Linda MacCarthy Finerty, Susan Maupin Gausnell, Randi Kotas Hanpeter, Marianne Kramer Haskins, Barbara Hinshaw Kemery, Sally Ward Ledbetter, Colleen Frawley Mehan, Gay Young Moppert, Dorothy Markwort Rhodes, Linda Fendler Sperberg

PAST CHAIRS

1992 - 1994 Linda Fendler Sperberg

1994 - 1995 Mary Lagen Corrigan

1995 - 1996 Sally Ward Ledbetter

1996 - 1997 Betty Miller Amelotti

1997 - 1998 Sharon Anderson Ward

1998-1999 Chair Carey Johnson
*   Vice Chair, Millicent Dohr, Becky Eggman*

1999-2000 Chairs, Millicent Dohr, Becky Eggman
*   Vice-Chairs, Tracee Holmes, Lisa Price*

2000-2001 Chairs, Lisa Price, Laurie Zeveski
*   Vice Chairs, Susan Hoffman, Todd Higley*

2001-2002 Chairs, Susan Hoffman, Sara Owens
*   No Vice Chairs*

2002-2003 Chair, Lisa Lineback
*   Vice Chair, Darcy Snodgrass*

2003-2004 Chair, Darcy Snodgrass
*   Chair Elect, Sabrina Heiman*

4

FOREWORD

The title *Saint Louis Days...Saint Louis Nights* symbolizes the diversity of culinary specialities prepared in St. Louis kitchens. Since its humble beginning as a French fur trapping outpost more than 300 years ago, the city has attracted people with wonderfully rich ethnic traditions. St. Louis cuisine, which is as varied as day and night, has been strongly influenced by this melting pot of nationalities and customs. The incredible array of outstanding restaurants which covers the metropolitan area proves St. Louisians love to eat.
The food is a unique mix of old and new, basic and elaborate.
It includes everything from Midwestern meat and potatoes to the re-nowned Italian specialities from "the Hill," to the latest trends in fine cuisine.

St. Louis' famous culinary firsts include the ice cream cone and hot dog, which both originated from the 1904 World's Fair; toasted ravioli created by the Italian chef on "the Hill" who accidentally knocked a plate of ravioli into a pan of hot grease; and the sinfully rich Gooey Butter Cake that came from the German bakers in South St. Louis.

The *Saint Louis Days...Saint Louis Nights* committee has attempted to present the best of St. Louis' own special and diverse cuisine in this cookbook. We hope that you enjoy what we have selected as you prepare the unique recipes that make up *Saint Louis Days...Saint Louis Nights.*

THE JUNIOR LEAGUE OF ST. LOUIS: 80 YEARS OF COMMUNITY SERVICE

The Junior League of St. Louis (JLSL) has a proud history of addressing the needs of the St. Louis community. Founded in 1914 by just 25 members, today it is the fifth largest member of the Association of Junior Leagues International (AJLI) with 2,400 members.

The JLSL commitment to community began in 1917 when it established the **Occupational Therapy Workshop** for disabled persons in St. Louis. This independent agency, now known as **Vocational Counseling**

and Rehabilitation Services, still provides valuable support to the area's handicapped.

In 1945, the JLSL created the **Forest Park Children's Center,** a home and program for emotionally disturbed children which later, in 1955, merged with **Edgewood Children's Center.** Today this facility plays a vital role in the community serving children and families in need.

In the 1960s, the JLSL collaborated on the establishment of museums at the **Academy of Science in Oak Knoll Park** and the creation of the **Arts and Education Council and Fund.**

In 1964, the JLSL started the **Junior Kindergarten,** a preschool program for disadvantaged children. It was later replicated nationwide to become the **Head Start** program.

Teen Outreach, started by the JLSL in 1982, is an after-school program whose goals are to discourage teenage pregnancy and encourage partici-pants to graduate from high school. This JLSL model program is now administered nationally by the AJLI.

In 1986, the **St. Louis Crisis Nursery** was begun. The **Crisis Nursery,** a program which focuses on the prevention of child abuse and neglect, is currently being studied by other Junior Leagues across the country that are interested in starting similar programs.

In 1994, the JLSL initiated **TOTAL (Teen Opportunities To Achieve in Life)**. TOTAL is a school-based community collaboration composed of educational, health, social service, and volunteer organizations from the private and public sector, dedicated to the empowerment of teens and their families.

As the JLSL enters the new millenium, the focus is **'Women Working for Tomorrow's Community.'** The JLSL will pursue this vision as it continues a 90-year tradition of helping others through its own initiatives; through collaborations with other organizations; and by lending support and trained volunteers to community projects already in existence.

Indulge in savory appetizers before accompanying friends to the theater. St. Louis offers a rich array of performing arts including the Muny Opera, Dance St. Louis, Opera Theatre of St. Louis, the St. Louis Symphony Orchestra, the Repertory Theatre, Riverport Amphitheatre, County Pops, the Black Repertory Theatre, and much more.

• • •

Charlie Gitto's

Charlie Gitto has made a career of serving outstanding Italian food to the people of St. Louis, as well as national celebrities and sports figures. His restaurant career began as a busboy in 1945. Family-owned and operated since 1974, Charlie Gitto's On The Hill and Charlie Gitto's Downtown Pasta House are favorite lunch and dinner spots for Italian epicureans.

MEDITERRANEAN-STYLE CALAMARI

Yield: 12 servings

5   pounds **squid**, cleaned
      Juice of 2 **lemons**
½   cup **olive oil**
3   cloves **garlic**, minced
12   flat **anchovies**
1   medium **white onion**, diced
2   tablespoons **capers** (non pareilles)
25   **Greek black olives**, pits removed
2   tablespoons fresh chopped **parsley**
¼   cup **red wine vinegar**
2   tablespoons **sugar**
      Cracked **red pepper**
      Salt and **pepper**
1½   cups **chicken bouillon**
1   cup meatless **tomato sauce** (or ½ cup tomato paste)

- Place squid into boiling water, adding juice of 2 lemons. Boil on medium heat about 10 minutes.
- Strain and then cool squid by rinsing with water.
- Leave tentacles the way they are, but cut the squid tubes into pieces about the size of a nickel in width.
- Heat a large skillet, and then add olive oil and garlic.
- Add the anchovies to the garlic in the skillet. Sauté until anchovies dissolve.
- Add diced onion and sauté until medium-brown.
- Add capers, olives, parsley, vinegar, sugar, red pepper, salt, and pepper. Cook on high about 5 minutes.
- Finally, add the cut up squid and tentacles, and then the bouillon and tomato sauce. Cook on medium about 30 minutes.

You can serve this flavorful calamari immediately, or chill in the refrigerator for a day and serve cold. Either way, you'll find this a tasty dish to enjoy before many a meal.

Melenzane Rypiena from Giovanni's

Yield: 4 servings

4   medium-sized **eggplants**
12   **plum tomatoes**
     Salted water
2   tablespoons **olive oil**
2   cloves **garlic**, minced
1   ounce fresh **basil**, chopped
     Salt
     Pepper
½   pound **anoletti pasta**
2   ounces **Pecorino Romano cheese**, grated

- Hollow out each eggplant with spoon, leaving 1-inch thickness inside eggplant.
- Level bottom of eggplant to allow level standing base.
- Sauté eggplant evenly in oil for 1 minute on each side.
- Remove eggplant and allow to drain.
- Cook plum tomatoes in lightly salted water for 15 minutes; then remove and peel skin.
- Process tomatoes through food mill and set aside.
- Sauté olive oil and garlic for 1 minute; add tomatoes and basil.
- Add salt and pepper to taste.
- Cook over medium heat for 15 minutes.
- In boiling, lightly salted water, cook anoletti for 5 minutes, leaving slightly al dente (pasta will finish cooking during baking process).
- Drain pasta; add to tomato sauce.
- Stuff eggplant with pasta and tomato sauce.
- Top with Pecorino Romano cheese.
- Bake for 5 minutes at 350° and serve.

RIDDLE'S CRAWFISH-STUFFED MUSHROOM CAPS

Yield: 2 dozen

Crawfish Stuffing:

4	tablespoons chopped **green onions**
¾	cup (1½ sticks) **butter**
1	pound cooked **crawfish meat**
⅓	of **White Sauce** recipe
½	cup **half-and-half**
1	**egg yolk**
2	tablespoons **dry sherry**
1½	teaspoons **cayenne pepper**
½	teaspoon **salt**
¼	to ½ cup **bread crumbs**
24	large **mushroom caps**

White Sauce:

¼	cup (½ stick) **butter**
¼	cup **flour**
¾	cup **chicken stock**
¾	cup **half-and-half**
⅛	teaspoon **salt**
⅛	teaspoon **pepper**

- Sauté green onions in 6 tablespoons of the butter. Add crawfish meat and cook over medium heat to warm through.
- Add ⅓ of White Sauce recipe, then add half-and-half, mixing well. When mixture is hot, quickly beat in egg yolk.
- Add sherry, cayenne, and salt. Simmer 3 to 5 minutes.
- Stir in bread crumbs. Remove from heat and cool.
- Meanwhile, sauté mushroom caps in remaining butter until just cooked through.
- Preheat broiler.
- Stuff crawfish mixture into caps and heat through under broiler.

White Sauce:
- Cook flour briefly in butter to make a roux.
- Slowly whisk in stock and half-and-half.
- Season with salt and pepper.
- Cover with plastic wrap and refrigerate until ready to use.

Chef Andy Ayers shares this favorite of Riddles Penultimate Cafe & Wine Bar on the University City Loop.

RIDDLE'S BLUE CHEESE-TABASCO® STUFFED MUSHROOMS

Yield: 3 to 3½ dozen

3   pounds large **mushrooms** (about 40 total)

1   cup chopped **green onions**

1   cup (2 sticks) **butter**

8   ounces **blue cheese**, crumbled

¼   teaspoon **salt**

¼   teaspoon **pepper**

½   to ¾ cup **bread crumbs**

2   to 3 tablespoons **Tabasco® sauce**

- Carefully remove stems from mushrooms. Set aside caps.
- Finely mince stems, using chef's knife or food processor with s-shaped blade.
- Sauté the minced stems and green onions in 6 table-spoons of the butter.
- Add blue cheese and stir to melt over medium heat. Some lumps may remain. Add salt and pepper, continuing to stir.
- Add bread crumbs, mixing well, until consistency is appropriate for stuffing.
- Stir in Tabasco® to taste.
- Cool stuffing.
- Meanwhile, sauté mushroom caps in remaining butter. Cool and then stuff.
- This much of preparation can be done a day ahead.
- Just before serving, reheat stuffed caps at 425° until heated through.

A popular new item at Riddles Penultimate Cafe & Wine Bar, from Chef Andy Ayers.

GREGORY'S MINI PIZZAS

Yield: 30 2½-inch pizzas

6 ounces **cream cheese**, softened

6 ounces **goat cheese**

2 ounces **sun-dried tomatoes**, reconstituted and minced

1 small **eggplant**, diced into ¼-inch pieces

2 tablespoons **olive oil**

1 teaspoon **oregano**
Salt and **pepper** to taste

2 **12-inch thin pizza shells** (available in freezer section or deli section as part of a "pizza kit" in most supermarkets)

1 cup **pine nuts**, lightly sautéed in butter

1 cup chopped **scallions**

1½ cups grated **Provel cheese**

- Combine cheeses and tomatoes in mixer until smooth. Reserve.
- Sauté eggplant in olive oil. Season with oregano, salt, and pepper. Cool down and reserve.
- To prepare mini pizza shells, cut out about 30 2½-inch round shells from the 2 prepared shells. You may use a biscuit cutter or cut around a small dry measuring cup. (If you make your own pizza dough, make sure it is thin.)
- Spread each pizza shell with cheese spread and lay out on ungreased baking sheet.
- Top each pizza with the following in this order: sautéed eggplant, pine nuts, scallions, grated Provel cheese.
- Bake pizzas in 425° oven until cheese is melted and slightly golden.
- Serve hot.

Gregory Mosberger of Gregory's Creative Cuisine, Inc., developed this unique pizza recipe — a favorite among his catering customers.

CROSTINI
WITH ROASTED RED PEPPER SPREAD

Yield: 4 dozen

2   7-ounce jars **roasted red peppers**, drained

2   tablespoons extra virgin **olive oil**

2   tablespoons minced fresh **Italian parsley leaves**

1   tablespoon fresh **lemon juice**

2   teaspoons **capers**, drained

1   medium **garlic** clove, smashed and peeled

1   **baguette loaf** of bread
     Olive oil to brush on bread

1   bunch fresh **basil leaves**, shredded into ⅛-inch strips

- Arrange drained peppers on a double layer of paper towel. Let dry while preparing recipe.
- Combine next 5 ingredients in a food processor bowl; process until capers and parsley are very finely chopped. Or, chop finely with large knife.
- Add drained peppers and process, using on/off pulses, until peppers are coarsely chopped. Or, use a knife to chop peppers, then add to parsley mixture.
- Store spread in covered container in the refrigerator for up to 5 days. Bring to room temperature at least 30 minutes before serving.
- Preheat oven to 350°.
- Slice bread into ¼-inch slices.
- Place on baking sheet and brush tops lightly with olive oil.
- Bake until edges are light brown and centers are crisp, about 10 minutes. Or, sauté in a little olive oil or butter until both sides are golden.
- Spread roasted red pepper mixture on each slice of crostini.
- Top with fresh basil leaf.

This fabulous, easy appetizer will certainly add color to your table! Can be halved easily.

CREAMY CHEESE DIP WITH GARDEN CRUDITÉ

Yield: 1 cup

5½ ounces soft, mild **goat cheese**

2 tablespoons **olive oil**

3 tablespoons minced **radish**

2 tablespoons minced **green onion**

Additional minced or grated **radish** for garnish

- Combine cheese and oil with fork until well blended.
- Fold in minced vegetables.
- Crudités may include blanched asparagus tips or snow peas, or red pepper strips, baby corn, or radishes.

This delicate dip is also good on thinly sliced baguette.

CHUTNEY CHEESE SPREAD

Yield: 6 to 8 servings

1 8-ounce package **cream cheese**, softened

4 ounces **Cheddar cheese**, grated

¼ teaspoon **salt**

¾ teaspoon **curry powder**

4 tablespoons **dry sherry**

¾ cup **chutney**

Green onions, chopped

- Mix cheeses, salt, curry powder, and sherry.
- Mold into circle on plate.
- Refrigerate for at least 1 hour before serving.
- Just before serving, spread chutney on top of cheese mold and garnish with green onions.
- Serve with bacon-flavored crackers.

The chutney topping makes this an attractive appetizer.

WRAPPED ASPARAGUS

Yield: 3 dozen

36 medium **asparagus**

36 slices **prosciutto ham**
(4 inches long)

4 ounces **blue cheese**,
crumbled

Dressing:

½ cup **balsamic vinegar**

½ cup **vegetable oil**

½ cup **olive oil**

½ teaspoon **salt**

½ teaspoon **pepper**

½ teaspoon **lemon juice**

½ teaspoon **basil**

- Trim asparagus to 4 to 6 inches and peel end with a potato peeler.
- Place asparagus in a microwaveable container with ½ cup water. Cover tightly with plastic wrap.
- Microwave on high 2½ to 3 minutes.
- Remove asparagus and plunge into icy water. Drain and dry.
- Wrap each asparagus with a slice of prosciutto.
- Arrange asparagus on a large, flat platter with a lip around the edge.
- Sprinkle blue cheese over top of asparagus.
- Mix dressing ingredients in a jar with lid and shake to mix.
- When ready to serve, pour dressing over top of asparagus.

If you need to cut the prosciutto, use a scissors—much easier since the ham is so thin.

GOAT CHEESE TORTE
WITH SUN-DRIED TOMATO TAPENADE

Yield: 6 servings

1   8-ounce package **cream cheese**, softened
2   ounces **blue cheese**
½   8-ounce jar **sun-dried tomato tapenade**
4   ounces **goat cheese**
    Assorted **crackers**

- In a food processor, or by hand, mix ¾ package cream cheese with blue cheese.
- Spread on a plate to make a 4-inch circle.
- Top with 2 ounces of tapenade.
- In food processor, or by hand, mix remaining cream cheese with goat cheese.
- Spread on top of first layer.
- Top with 2 to 3 ounces of tapenade.
- Serve with assorted snack crackers.

Easy to make. You can find sun-dried tomato tapenade in most supermarkets.

SHRIMPLY DELICIOUS

Yield: 4 to 6 servings

6   ounces **light cream cheese**, softened
1½   tablespoons **horseradish**
1½   tablespoons grated **Parmesan cheese**
1   pound jumbo **shrimp**, steamed
½   cup finely chopped fresh **parsley**
     Cocktail sauce

- In a mixing bowl, combine cream cheese, horseradish, and Parmesan cheese. Mix with a fork.
- Peel and devein shrimp. Cut lengthwise partially but not completely through the entire length and the back of the shrimp, making a pocket.
- With a table knife or small spatula, spread cream cheese mixture into the pocket.
- Roll the back of the shrimp with the cream cheese into the parsley.
- Arrange shrimp on a platter.
- Serve with cocktail sauce.

SHRIMP PÂTÉ

Yield: 10 to 12 servings

1   pound **shrimp**
¼   cup finely chopped **onion**
3   tablespoons **lemon juice**
4   tablespoons **butter**
1   8-ounce package **cream cheese,** softened
4   tablespoons **mayonnaise**
1   teaspoon **garlic salt**
1   teaspoon snipped, fresh **parsley** or **parsley flakes**

- Boil shrimp in lightly salted water. Save one shrimp for garnish.
- Peel, clean, devein, and mince shrimp.
- Mix remaining ingredients with a food processor or mixer on high.
- Fold in shrimp by hand.
- Pack mixture into a crock or appropriate serving container.
- Refrigerate at least 6 hours.
- Garnish with one remaining shrimp, and parsley.
- Serve with plain crackers.

SOUTHERN PRIZE SHRIMP DIP

Yield: 6 servings

1   8-ounce package **cream cheese**, softened
    Juice of 1 **lemon**
2   pounds cooked **shrimp**, peeled, deveined, and coarsely ground
7   **green onions**, minced
¼   cup (approximately) **mayonnaise**
    Tabasco® sauce
    Worcestershire sauce
    Salt and **pepper**

- Soften cream cheese with lemon juice.
- Add shrimp and green onion to cream cheese.
- Add enough mayonnaise to give consistency for dipping with crackers.
- Season to taste with Tabasco® and Worcestershire sauces, and salt and pepper.

This dip is wonderful with a variety of crackers, including rye and savory crackers. Also good with veggies.

PESTO SHRIMP IN A BLANKET

Yield: 24 appetizers

12 cooked, peeled extra-large **shrimp**

12 slices **white bread**

¼ cup **unsalted butter**

1 clove **garlic**, finely chopped

1 tablespoon, plus 1 teaspoon **pesto sauce**

1 teaspoon finely grated **lemon peel**

¼ teaspoon **salt**

¼ teaspoon ground **black pepper**

- Cut each shrimp in half across width.
- Stacking bread 4 high, cut off crusts with serrated bread knife.
- Using a rolling pin, roll each bread slice flat.
- In a small bowl, beat butter until soft and smooth.
- Stir in garlic, pesto sauce, lemon peel, salt, and pepper. Beat until smooth and well blended.
- Spread 1 side of each slice of bread with butter mixture and cut each slice in 2 triangles.
- Place a shrimp in center of each bread triangle. Fold 2 points to center and secure with a toothpick.
- Arrange on a grid in a grill pan; broil under a moderately hot grill until bread is lightly browned.
- Serve immediately.

CRAB RANGOON SPREAD WITH WON TON CRACKERS

Yield: 40 appetizers

20   **won ton squares**

3   to 4 tablespoons **butter**, melted

    Grated **Parmesan cheese**

1   8-ounce package **cream cheese**

2   tablespoons **milk**

¼   teaspoon **garlic powder**

6   ounces **crabmeat** or **crab-flavored seafood** (if canned, rinse and drain)

1   tablespoon chopped **parsley** or **green onion**

    Sweet-and-sour sauce (optional)

- Preheat oven to 375°.
- Lightly brush cookie sheet with melted butter.
- Cut won ton squares in half.
- Arrange rectangles in prepared pan. Brush with melted butter and sprinkle with Parmesan cheese.
- Bake 5 to 7 minutes until golden brown.
- Cool on paper towels.
- Repeat with remaining won ton squares.
- Place cream cheese in glass bowl and soften in microwave oven on high power 1 to 2 minutes.
- Stir in milk and garlic powder.
- When well blended, stir in crabmeat and parsley.
- Heat 1 to 3 minutes longer until thoroughly heated.
- Spread mixture in shallow serving dish.
- Top mixture with sweet-and-sour sauce, if desired.
- Serve heated spread with won ton crackers.

A wonderful new way to serve a classic favorite!

VEGETABLE DIP À LA RUSSE

Yield: 2¼ cups

1   cup **sour cream**
1   cup **mayonnaise**
¼   cup **chili sauce**
1   tablespoon cream-style **horseradish**
1   teaspoon **Worcestershire sauce**
     Dash of **salt**

- Mix well and store in refrigerator.

A quick-to-fix dip that tastes great!

VEGETABLE MEDLEY DIP

Yield: 8 to 10 servings

1   8-ounce can chopped **black olives**
1   8-ounce can **green chili peppers**, chopped
2   large **tomatoes**, chopped
4   to 5 **green onions**, chopped
1   teaspoon **vegetable oil**
1½   tablespoons **vinegar**
     Salt to taste

- Combine all ingredients and store in refrigerator 1 day before serving.
- Serve with tortilla chips (nonfat chips, if desired).

This low-fat dip is especially good when tomatoes are in season.

SWISS CHEESE SPREAD

Yield: 2 cups

8   ounces **Swiss cheese**, shredded
4   tablespoons **mayonnaise**
¼   teaspoon **salt**
2   **green onions**, finely chopped

- Mix shredded cheese with enough mayonnaise to hold cheese together (about 4 tablespoons).
- Add salt and green onions, and mix well.
- Serve in bowl with crackers.

This spread is a great at any party.

Spinach Pesto

Yield: ⅔ cup

1   cup fresh **basil leaves**, firmly packed

½   cup fresh **spinach leaves**, torn

¼   cup grated **Parmesan** or **Romano cheese**

¼   cup **pine nuts**, **walnuts**, or **almonds**

2   cloves **garlic**

2   tablespoons **olive oil**

- In a blender or food processor, combine basil, spinach, cheese, nuts, and garlic.
- Cover and blend until it forms a paste.
- Stop machine and scrape the sides several times.
- Add oil, gradually blending to consistency of soft butter.
- Transfer to storage container.
- Freezable up to 1 month.

Excellent spread for toasted baguettes.

Fruit Kabobs with Amaretto Dip

Yield: 6 servings

1   3-ounce package **cream cheese**, softened

3   tablespoons **sour cream**

3   tablespoons **powdered sugar**

1½   tablespoons **amaretto liqueur** (or ¼ teaspoon almond extract)

6   **wooden skewers**, 8 inches long

12   small to medium **strawberries**, trimmed

12   **green grapes**

6   1-inch pieces of freshly cut **pineapple**

- Combine cream cheese, sour cream, powdered sugar, and amaretto. Cream for 1 minute or until smooth.
- Refrigerate until ready to serve.
- Place strawberry, grape, pineapple, grape, strawberry on each skewer.
- When ready to serve, place all skewers on a platter with the dip in a bowl. (Or, for salad or brunch dish, place one skewer and a spoonful of dip on each plate.)

Beautiful, delicious, and easy! For a low-fat version, try low-fat cream cheese and sour cream.

CARAMEL APPLE DIP

Yield: 8 to 10 servings

14 ounces **caramels**
1   8-ounce package **cream cheese**, softened
½   cup **brown sugar**
2   tablespoons **granulated sugar**
1   teaspoon **vanilla**
¾   cup chopped **dry-roasted nuts**
    Apple slices

- Gradually melt caramels in microwave, stirring every 30 seconds until soft. Watch closely — caramels burn easily.
- Stir in cream cheese, the sugars, vanilla, and nuts.
- Dip apple slices into caramel mixture.

This dip keeps in refrigerator several weeks.

BACON ROLL-UPS

Yield: 20 servings

¼   cup **margarine**
½   cup **water**
1½ cups **herb stuffing mix**
1   **egg**, slightly beaten
¼   cup mild or hot **bulk pork sausage**
½   pound sliced **bacon**

- In a small saucepan, melt margarine in water.
- Place the stuffing mix in a large mixing bowl.
- Add margarine/water mixture to stuffing mix.
- Add egg and sausage; blend thoroughly.
- Chill 1 hour for easier handling.

- Shape into small oblongs about the size of a pecan.
- Cut bacon slices into thirds.
- Wrap each piece of stuffing mixture with bacon and secure with toothpick.
- Place on rack on shallow pan.
- Bake at 375° for 35 minutes or until brown and crisp. Turn halfway through cooking.
- Drain on paper towels and serve hot.

These hearty appetizers can be made a day ahead and refrigerated. You can also freeze them before baking; just thaw and bake as directed.

BRIE IN PASTRY

Yield: 12 servings

1   sheet **frozen puff pastry**
     (Pepperidge Farm®)

1   16-ounce wheel **Brie cheese**

¼   cup sliced, toasted **almonds**

¼   cup chopped **parsley**
     (optional)

1   **egg**, beaten with
     1 teaspoon **water**

- Thaw pastry 20 minutes.
- Roll sheet out on a lightly floured surface to a 15-inch circle.
- Preheat oven to 400°.
- Slice Brie in half horizontally and layer with almonds and parsley.
- Reassemble Brie and place in center of pastry.
- Brush pastry edges with egg wash and pull up sides to enclose Brie.
- Place seam side down on ungreased baking sheet. If desired, decorate top with pastry scraps (twisted rope figure criss-crossing top or leaf shapes).
- Brush with egg wash.
- Bake 20 minutes. Let stand 10 minutes before serving.

This is an easy and delicious recipe that makes a beautiful presentation!

Brie with Herbs in Bread

Yield: 6 to 8 servings

1 **French baguette loaf** of bread (about 10 ounces)

¼ cup virgin **olive oil**

3 tablespoons dry **white wine**

1 teaspoon coarsely ground **black pepper**

2 cloves **garlic**, peeled and chopped (about 1 teaspoon)

1 piece of ripe **Brie cheese** (about 10 ounces)

3 tablespoons chopped **chives**

1 cup coarsely shredded **basil leaves**

1½ cups loose coarsely shredded **sorrel leaves** (can substitute other herbs or eliminate this ingredient, if not available)

- Cut baguette in half lengthwise and sprinkle cut surface of each half with oil, wine, pepper, and garlic, dividing ingredients evenly between two halves.
- Trim Brie to remove any crust and cut into ¼-inch slices, preferably large and thin.
- Spread half of herbs on cut surface of bottom half of loaf; arrange cheese slices on top. Spread remaining herbs on top of Brie. Place top half of bread loaf on top to re-form loaf.
- Press bread halves firmly together and roll as tightly as possible in plastic wrap, then in aluminum foil. (If tightly wrapped, the bread absorbs the juices better.)
- Press loaf between two baking sheets and refrigerate with 3 to 5 pounds of weight (a can or jar) on top for 4 to 5 hours before cutting in slices to serve.

You may serve this appetizer cold or at room temperature.

CRANBERRY-GLAZED BRIE

Yield: 20 servings

3   cups fresh **cranberries**
       (12-ounce bag)
¾   cup packed **light brown
       sugar**
⅓   cup **water**
⅛   teaspoon **dry mustard**
⅛   teaspoon ground **cloves**
⅛   teaspoon ground **allspice**
⅛   teaspoon ground **ginger**
1   whole large (15-ounce)
       Brie cheese round
       Assorted crackers
       Apples and **pears**, cut in
       sections and dipped in
       lemon juice

- Combine cranberries,
  brown sugar, water,
  and spices in heavy
  nonaluminum saucepan.
- Cook over medium heat
  until most of the berries
  pop, stirring frequently (5 to
  6 minutes). Consistency
  should be fairly thick and
  jam-like.
- Cool to room temperature.
- Cut circle in top of cheese
  rind, leaving ½-inch border
  around the rim.
- Carefully remove center
  circle of rind from the
  cheese. Do not cut through
  sides of rind.
- Wrap sides of cheese in foil.
  Place cheese on cookie sheet.
- Put cranberry mixture in
  middle of cheese.
- Bake at 350° for 12 to
  15 minutes, or until cheese
  softens inside.
- Serve warm with crackers,
  apples, and pears.

HONEY-ALMOND BRIE

Yield: 8 servings

1   1-pound wheel **baby Brie
       cheese**
       Honey, enough to cover
       top of Brie
2¼   ounces sliced **almonds**

- Place Brie cheese on micro-
  wave-safe dish.
- Cover Brie with honey.
- Place almonds on top of
  Brie.
- Heat in microwave until
  cheese begins to melt, about
  60 seconds on high.
- Serve with crackers.

Incredibly easy, but tasty appetizer!

Salsa Riviera

Yield: 4 cups

2   large **tomatoes**, seeded and diced

½   **cucumber**, pared, seeded, and diced

½   cup diced **red onion**

¼   cup diced yellow or green **bell pepper**

2   tablespoons seeded and finely chopped **jalapeño pepper**

½   teaspoon **oregano**

¼   teaspoon **salt**

- In medium bowl, combine all ingredients.
- Cover and chill at least 2 hours to blend flavors.
- Serve as dip with tortilla chips.

Excellent in the summer with fresh tomatoes!

Black Bean Salsa

Yield: 12 servings

2   15-ounce cans **black beans**, drained and rinsed

1   16-ounce can **white shoe peg corn**, drained

6   tablespoons fresh **lime juice**

6   tablespoons **olive oil**

1½   teaspoons ground **cumin**

½   cup **red onion**, chopped fine

¼   cup chopped fresh **cilantro**

½   teaspoon **salt**

1   cup peeled and chopped **tomato**

Chopped **jalapeño pepper** (optional)

- Combine everything except tomatoes.
- Cover and refrigerate overnight.
- Add the chopped tomatoes just before serving; you may also want to drop in a little more lime juice and add a little chopped jalapeño pepper.
- Serve with tortilla chips.

This is an incredibly good appetizer with white or blue corn chips. It's also great as a side dish served on Bibb lettuce.

"Show-Me" Guacamole

Yield: 6 to 8 servings

2   ripe **avocados**
2   tablespoons grated **onion**
2   teaspoons **lemon juice**
¼   cup grated **Cheddar cheese**
¼   cup diced **tomato**
¼   cup **sour cream**
¼   teaspoon **salt**
½   teaspoon **garlic powder**
1   to 2 teaspoons **hot sauce** (not picante)

- Peel and mash avocados.
- Add all other ingredients.
- Adjust taste by adding more salt, garlic powder, and hot sauce.
- If you are making the guacamole ahead of serving time, put the avocado pit in the dip to keep it from turning brown.
- Cover with plastic wrap so that wrap touches surface of guacamole. Seal the edges.

Southwestern Tomato Salsa

Yield: 4 to 6 servings

3   **green onions**, chopped
1   4-ounce can chopped **black olives**
1   4-ounce can diced **green chili peppers**
3   tablespoons **olive oil**
½   tablespoon **vinegar**
1   teaspoon **salt**
1   teaspoon **garlic salt**
½   teaspoon ground **cumin**
2   large **tomatoes**, chopped

- Mix all ingredients except tomatoes.
- Add tomatoes just before serving.

A flavorful way to enjoy summer tomatoes at their peak!

BAJA-DERVES

Yield: 3 dozen

1½ cups (6 ounces) shredded **sharp Cheddar cheese**

1 4-ounce can diced **green chili peppers**, drained

1 2¼-ounce can sliced pitted **ripe olives,** drained

¼ cup sliced **green onion**

¼ cup **mayonnaise**

6 ounces boneless **chicken breasts**, cooked and coarsely chopped

36 round **tortilla chips**

- In a large bowl, combine cheese, chili peppers, olives, onion, and mayonnaise.
- Gently fold in chicken.
- Arrange tortilla chips on ungreased cookie sheet.
- Top each chip with a rounded teaspoon of the cheese mixture.
- Bake at 350° until cheese melts. Serve immediately.

Especially good using mesquite-grilled chicken.

BAKED JALAPEÑOS

Yield: 50 appetizers

25 **jalapeño peppers**

1 8-ounce package **cream cheese**

12 ounces shredded **Cheddar cheese**

1½ teaspoons **Worcestershire sauce**

4 slices **bacon**, cooked crisp and cut into small pieces

- Cut jalapeños in half, lengthwise, and remove the seeds.

- Place jalapeños in boiling water for up to 10 minutes (the less time, the hotter and crisper the jalapeño).
- Mix cream cheese, Cheddar cheese, and Worcestershire sauce.
- Fill each jalapeño half and top with a small piece of bacon.
- Place on baking sheet and bake at 400° until cheese is bubbly, about 5 minutes.

Excellent! For true hot pepper fans, boil the peppers no longer than 5 minutes.

MEXICAN FUDGE

Yield: 6 to 8 servings

8 ounces grated **Cheddar cheese**

8 ounces grated **Monterey Jack cheese**

3 **eggs**

½ cup thick and chunky **salsa**

- In a large bowl, mix cheeses together.
- Put half of mixture in bottom of greased 9 x 9-inch glass pan.
- In a separate bowl, mix eggs and salsa together. Pour on top of cheese in pan.
- Add remaining cheese on top and bake at 350° for 30 minutes.
- Cool and cut into squares.

You can serve this party favorite warm or cold. An easy choice when you have to "bring an appetizer."

HOT BEEF DIP

Yield: 12 servings

2 6- to 10-ounce packages **Buddig pressed beef**

½ cup **sour cream**

1 medium **onion**, chopped

1 cup chopped **pecans**

1 8-ounce package **cream cheese**

¼ cup chopped **green pepper**

- Chop beef and other ingredients into small chunks.
- Combine all ingredients in a small baking dish.
- Bake at 350° for 15 minutes.
- Serve with crackers.

Different and good!

MUSHROOM STRUDEL

Yield: 16 servings

6 tablespoons **butter**

1 pound **mushrooms**, chopped

2 tablespoons chopped **shallots**

  Salt and **pepper**

½ teaspoon **tarragon**

2 tablespoons **red wine**

½ cup **sour cream**

½ cup (1 stick) **butter**, melted

4 to 6 sheets **phyllo pastry**, thawed

1 cup fine dry **bread crumbs**

- In a large skillet, melt 6 tablespoons butter and sauté mushrooms and shallots.
- Cook over medium-low heat until mushrooms are tender.
- Add seasonings, tarragon, and wine. Continue to cook over low heat until most of the wine is absorbed.
- Stir in sour cream and remove from heat.

- Let mixture cool for about 15 minutes. (This can be refrigerated overnight and brought to room temperature before continuing.)
- Meanwhile, melt butter.
- Brush 1 sheet of phyllo pastry with melted butter and sprinkle with 1 tablespoon bread crumbs. Add about 3 tablespoons of mushroom mixture on one side of the pastry, 1 inch from the edge. Roll up like a jelly roll. Place on top of another buttered phyllo sheet. Roll up, use butter to dampen ends, then tuck ends inside.
- Repeat above step, using the rest of the mushroom mixture.
- Place strudels on cookie sheet and bake at 325° for 30 to 40 minutes until light brown.
- Cool strudels about 15 minutes. Slice into 1½-inch slices to serve.

An elegant appetizer!

BLUE CHEESE TOASTS

Yield: 6 servings

1	**baguette loaf**, sliced about ¼ inch thick
8	strips **bacon**, cooked, drained, and chopped
1	tablespoon ground **sage**
½	teaspoon ground **white pepper**
6	ounces **Saga blue cheese**, softened
3	tablespoons unsalted **butter**, softened

- Preheat broiler.
- Arrange bread on baking sheet.
- Broil bread slices until lightly toasted.
- Top each slice with some bacon; add sage and pepper.
- Combine cheese and butter, and then spread over bread slices.
- Broil until cheese bubbles.
- Serve warm.

Can be made without the bacon.

CRISPY CHEESE BARS

Yield: 3½ dozen

1	loaf thinly sliced **white bread**
8	ounces **sharp Cheddar cheese**, grated
6	slices **bacon**, cooked crisp and chopped fine
2	ounces **almonds**, diced
1	cup **mayonnaise**
2	teaspoons **Worcestershire sauce**
	Salt and **pepper**

- Mix all ingredients except bread.
- Spread mixture on bread; cut each slice of bread into 3 strips.
- Put strips on cookie sheet and freeze.
- Remove strips from cookie sheet and place in freezer bag. Store in freezer.
- When ready to use, take out desired amount of strips from freezer. Place frozen strips on cookie sheet.
- Bake at 400° for 10 minutes until brown.
- Serve hot.

HOT CHEESE PUFFS

Yield: 40 rounds

4	ounces **cream cheese**, softened
¾	teaspoon minced **onions**
¼	cup **Hellmann's® mayonnaise**
1	tablespoon dried chopped **chives**
⅛	teaspoon **cayenne pepper**
⅛	cup grated **Parmesan cheese**
½	small loaf **Pepperidge Farm® white bread**

- In a bowl, combine all ingredients except bread. Mix well.
- Cut bread into 1½-inch round circles.
- Spread each round with cheese mixture.
- Arrange rounds on cookie sheet.
- Bake at 350° for 15 minutes, or until slightly browned.
- Serve hot.

Using a small round cookie cutter, you can cut 4 rounds at a time. To freeze, cut bread and spread cheese mixture. Bake when ready to serve, but lengthen baking time to about 20 minutes.

SUN-DRIED TOMATO TAPENADE APPETIZER

Yield: 2 dozen

12	**mini bagels**, sliced in half lengthwise
1	8-ounce jar **sun-dried tomato tapenade**
1	8-ounce package **feta cheese** (or goat cheese)
1	bunch fresh **basil**
	Pine nuts (optional)

- Spread tapenade on bagel halves.
- Sprinkle bagels with crumbled feta cheese and chopped basil. Top with pine nuts, if desired.
- Place bagels on cookie sheet and toast at 400° for 10 minutes.

A tasty appetizer, and so simple to make! Tapenade is found in the produce or pasta section of most supermarkets.

PALMIERS WITH MUSTARD AND PROSCIUTTO

Yield: 10 to 12 servings

1   18 x 11-inch sheet frozen **puff pastry**

3   tablespoons **honey mustard** (or Dijon)

4   ounces thinly sliced **prosciutto ham**

1   cup grated **Parmesan cheese**

1   **egg**

2   teaspoons **water**

- Spread mustard over puff pastry.
- Arrange prosciutto evenly over mustard to cover all the pastry.
- Sprinkle with Parmesan and lightly press into prosciutto with rolling pin.
- Starting at long edge, roll up pastry like a jelly roll to middle of dough. Then, roll up the other side the same way. (May be refrigerated at this point.)
- Slice pastry into ½-inch slices.
- Line cookie sheet with parchment paper to absorb excess butter (or place pastry on paper towels after baking).
- Place pastry slices on cookie sheet. Refrigerate for 15 minutes.
- Beat egg and water. Brush on top of each slice.
- Bake at 400° about 20 minutes, or until puffed and golden.
- Serve warm or at room temperature.

An elegant-looking appetizer with a delightfully tangy taste!

GLAZED PARTY SALAMI

Yield: 20 servings

1½ to 3 pounds **hard salami**

1 7½-ounce jar **Dijon mustard**

1 10- to 12-ounce jar **orange marmalade**

1 to 2 loaves party **rye bread**

- Choose hard salami that would lay nicely on party rye.
- Slice salami almost through in thin slices (matching bread slices), leaving spine along one side.
- Mix together mustard and orange marmalade.
- Pour mixture over salami in baking dish.
- Marinate in refrigerator 24 hours or longer.
- Bake at 250° about 3 hours, basting every ½ hour. Check that edges do not burn.
- Serve salami on platter with marinade poured over top. With sharp knife, finish cutting through the spine of the salami.
- Let guests place salami slices on top of party rye.

TOMATO CHEESE PIE

Yield: 8 servings

1 9-inch **pie crust**, unbaked

3 medium **tomatoes**, cut into wedges

½ teaspoon **salt**

½ teaspoon **pepper**

½ teaspoon ground **basil**

½ teaspoon ground **oregano**

¼ cup chopped **chives**

½ cup **mayonnaise**

¾ cup shredded **mozzarella cheese**

¾ cup shredded **Cheddar cheese**

- Bake pie crust in preheated 425° oven 5 minutes.
- Remove pie crust. Reduce oven temperature to 400°.
- Fill pie shell with tomato wedges. Sprinkle salt, pepper, basil, oregano, and chives over tomatoes.
- In a mixing bowl, combine mayonnaise and cheeses.
- Carefully spread cheese mixture evenly over tomatoes, making sure cheese extends to all edges.
- Bake at 400° 20 to 25 minutes, or until crust is golden.

PINE NUT PESTO CHEESECAKE

Yield: 10 to 12 servings

Crust:

½	cup dry **Italian bread crumbs**
2	tablespoons grated **Parmesan cheese**
1	tablespoon finely chopped toasted **pine nuts**
2	tablespoons **butter**, melted

Filling:

2	8-ounce packages **cream cheese**, softened
1	cup **sour cream**
½	cup grated **Parmesan cheese**
3	**eggs**
¼	cup finely chopped toasted **pine nuts**
3	tablespoons fresh **basil**, chopped
2	tablespoons sliced **green onions**
½	teaspoon **garlic powder**
¼	teaspoon **white pepper**
¼	teaspoon **salt**

- Lightly grease 9-inch springform pan.
- In small bowl, combine all crust ingredients; press into bottom of pan.
- In mixing bowl, beat cream cheese until smooth; beat in sour cream and Parmesan until smooth.
- At low speed, add eggs, then stir in remaining ingredients.
- Pour filling into crust-lined pan.
- Bake at 375° for 30 to 40 minutes until set.
- Cool on wire rack.
- Refrigerate 3 hours or overnight.
- Remove sides of pan from cheesecake. Garnish it with fresh sprigs of basil.
- Serve with crackers or bagel chips.

This cheesecake has a wonderful flavor. It freezes well, too. Easy to take to a party.

BACON AND ONION CHEESECAKE

Yield: 8 to 10 servings

7   slices **bacon**, diced

1   medium to large sweet **onion**, chopped

1   clove **garlic**, minced

15   ounces **ricotta cheese**

½   cup **cream**

2   tablespoons **flour**

½   teaspoon **salt**

¼   teaspoon **cayenne pepper**

2   **eggs**

½   cup chopped **green onions**

- In skillet cook bacon until crisp; remove to paper towels.
- Pour off all but 1 tablespoon of drippings.
- Cook onion and garlic in bacon drippings until tender, about 5 minutes.
- In a bowl, combine ricotta, cream, flour, salt, and pepper, blending until smooth.
- Add eggs, one at a time; blend until smooth.
- Stir in bacon, cooked onion mixture, and green onions.
- Lightly grease a 9-inch springform pan.
- Pour batter into pan; bake at 350° for 40 minutes or until center is set.
- Cool on a wire rack.
- Serve at room temperature with assorted crackers.

PUB-STYLE CHEESE PUFFS

Yield: 4 servings

1   thin **baguette**, 8 inches long

⅓   cup **chutney**

⅓   cup grated **Cheddar cheese**

¼   cup crumbled **blue cheese**

6   cherry **tomatoes**, halved

⅓   cup **alfalfa sprouts** or **radish sprouts**

- Remove the ends of baguette.
- Slice remaining baguette into twelve ¾-inch slices; place on baking sheet.
- Spread chutney evenly over one side of each slice.
- In a small bowl combine cheeses; then top slices with cheese mixture.
- Place one cherry tomato half on top of each slice.
- Place baking sheet in oven and broil until cheese is bubbly.
- Remove from oven and garnish with sprouts just before serving.

HOT SPINACH DIP

Yield: 10 to 12 servings

2	tablespoons **oil**
1	medium **onion**, chopped
2	small **tomatoes**, peeled, seeded, and chopped
2	tablespoons canned chopped **green chilies**
1	10-ounce package **frozen spinach**, thawed and squeezed dry
2	cups grated **Monterey Jack cheese**
1	8-ounce package **cream cheese**, cut into ½-inch pieces
½	cup **half-and-half**
1	tablespoon **red wine vinegar**
	Salt and **pepper**, to taste

- Sauté onion in oil about 4 minutes.
- Add tomatoes and chilies and cook 2 minutes.
- Transfer mixture to large bowl and mix in remaining ingredients.
- Spoon into 9-inch deep-dish pie pan or shallow baking dish.
- Bake at 400° for 30 to 35 minutes until bubbly.
- Serve with corn chips or toasted pita triangles (Brush pita triangles with butter, season with lemon-pepper and chili powder. Bake at 400° on top third of oven for 6 to 8 minutes.)

The seasoned pita chips add a nice touch to this savory dip.

Spinach Parmesan Dip

Yield: 10 to 12 servings

1   10-ounce package **frozen chopped spinach**

1⅓ cups grated **Parmesan cheese**, divided

1   large **onion**, chopped

1   clove **garlic**, chopped

4   ounces **cream cheese**, softened

1   cup **mayonnaise**
    Salt and **pepper**

3   fresh **hot peppers**, red or green, chopped or sliced thin (optional)

1   teaspoon **paprika**

- Defrost and squeeze excess water out of spinach.
- Mix together spinach, 1 cup Parmesan cheese, onion, garlic, cream cheese, and mayonnaise.
- Season mixture with salt and pepper to taste.
- Place in greased casserole dish. Top with thinly sliced peppers, if desired, and remaining ⅓ cup Parmesan cheese; sprinkle with paprika.
- Bake at 350° for 20 minutes until hot and bubbly.
- Serve with crackers.

Sour Cream and Caviar Potato Bites

Yield: 8 servings

8   **red potatoes**, scrubbed

3   tablespoons melted **butter**
    Salt
    White pepper

½   cup **sour cream** or **crème fraîche**

½   cup **caviar**

- Preheat oven to 400°.
- Cut away ends of potatoes. Cut each potato in ½-inch rounds.
- Brush baking tray with some of the melted butter and arrange potatoes on tray.
- Brush tops with melted butter and season with salt and pepper.
- Roast 20 minutes.
- Turn and brush tops with melted butter. Season with salt and pepper.
- Roast 15 minutes longer.
- Drain on paper towels.
- Arrange on serving platter.
- Spread a little sour cream on each slice and spoon ¼ teaspoon caviar in the center.
- Serve immediately.

BRANDY SLUSH

Yield: 24 8-ounce servings

7   cups **water**
1½   cups **sugar**
1   12-ounce can frozen
     lemonade concentrate
1   12-ounce can frozen
     orange juice concentrate
1½   cups **brandy**
     7-Up®

- Boil water and sugar. Cool.
- Add lemonade, orange juice, and brandy.
- Freeze 24 hours or longer.
- To serve, fill glasses half-full with slush mixture, then fill with 7-Up®; stir.

Can be served in an ice bucket to keep cold.

ORANGE JULIUS

Yield: 4 8-ounce servings

1   6-ounce can frozen **orange juice concentrate**
1   cup **milk**
1   cup **water**
1   teaspoon **vanilla**
½   cup **sugar**
10   to 12 **ice cubes**

- Put all ingredients into blender container. Blend 30 seconds at high speed.

Good with vodka, too!

WHISKEY SOUR SLUSH

Yield: ½ gallon

¾   cup **sugar**
1   12-ounce can frozen
     lemonade
1   6-ounce can frozen **orange juice concentrate**
2   cups brewed **tea**
5½   cans (6-ounce) **water**
2½   cans (6-ounce) **whiskey**

- Mix all ingredients together (using the orange juice can to measure the water and the whiskey) and put in closed container in the freezer, at least 1 day before serving.
- Stir occasionally throughout period prior to serving. This time is needed for the mixture to reach a "slush" consistency.

Great drink for a large party.

EGG NOG

Yield: 40 4-ounce servings

12   jumbo **eggs**, separated
2¼   cups **granulated sugar**
1   pint **Ronrico® Gold Label rum**
1   quart **Christian Brothers® brandy**
2   quarts **milk**
3   pints **whipping cream**
1   cup **powdered sugar**
1   **nutmeg** to grate

- Beat egg yolks and granulated sugar until mixture forms ribbons.
- Add rum and brandy slowly with electric mixer on low.
- Beat in milk and 2 pints of whipping cream.
- In separate bowl, beat 6 egg whites and half of powdered sugar until stiff and glossy.
- Gently fold egg whites into rum mixture.
- Beat remaining egg whites and powdered sugar.
- In a separate bowl, whip the remaining pint of whipping cream.
- Fold together egg whites and whipped cream. Glob on top of Egg Nog that has been put into a chilled punch bowl.
- Grate nutmeg over the egg whites to sprinkle lightly.

This recipe is from a Cordon Bleu chef. Always a holiday hit!

HOLIDAY WASSAIL

Yield: 5 quarts

1   **orange**
1   **lemon**
1½   teaspoons **whole cloves**
3   3-inch **cinnamon sticks**
½   cup **sugar**
1   gallon **apple cider**
2   cups **orange juice**
1   cup **lemon juice**

- Peel orange and lemon, carefully, to keep rinds intact.
- Insert cloves in each strip of rind.
- Combine rinds, cinnamon, sugar, and apple cider in a large Dutch oven; bring to a boil.
- Cover, reduce heat, and simmer 10 minutes.
- Remove from heat and cool completely, about 1½ hours.
- To serve, add orange and lemon juices to mix, and thoroughly heat.

BRUNCH and BREADS

Plan a hearty Sunday
brunch and then enjoy
a leisurely afternoon
visiting places of interest
around St. Louis. Stroll
through the lush landscapes
of the Missouri Botanical
Garden or view the magnifi-
cent art of the Cathedral of
St.Louis, which boasts the
largest collection of mosaics
in the world.

• • •

Cafe Balaban

An anchor in the culinary-rich Central West End since 1972, Cafe Balaban was a pioneer in St. Louis continental cuisine and bountiful brunches. When choosing the site for Sunday brunch, Cafe Balaban tops the list. In addition to outstanding menu selections for brunch, lunch, and dinner, Cafe Balaban's wine list has held the Wine Spectator "Award of Excellence" since 1987. Executive Chef and Partner David Timney shares this popular item from Cafe Balaban's varied menu.

AVOCADO AND CRAB COCKTAIL

Yield: 8 servings

4   **avocados**, peeled and diced

1   pound cooked and chilled **crabmeat**

1   cup **Mayonnaise** (can substitute commercially prepared)
    Salad greens

Mayonnaise:

4   **egg yolks**

1   tablespoon **Dijon mustard**

2   ounces **tequila**

3   ounces **Rose's® lime juice**
    Juice from 2 **limes**

3   cups **vegetable oil**

1   cup **olive oil**

4   ounces crusted **pine nuts**

3   ounces chopped **chives**
    Pepper, to taste

- Fold crabmeat with avocado and Mayonnaise.
- Place on a bed of greens.
- Serve well chilled.

Mayonnaise:

- In a small mixer, ribbon the yolks and mustard.
- Slowly add the oils and liquid ingredients.
- Add the pine nuts, chives, and pepper.

St. Louis Gooey Butter Cake

Yield: 9 servings

Crust:

1	cup all-purpose **flour**	
3	tablespoons **sugar**	
⅓	cup **butter** or **margarine**	

Filling:

1¼	cups **sugar**	
¾	cup **butter** or **margarine**	
1	**egg**	
1	cup all-purpose **flour**	
⅔	cup **evaporated milk**	
¼	cup **light corn syrup**	
1	teaspoon **vanilla**	
	Powdered sugar	

Crust:

- In mixing bowl, combine flour and sugar. Cut in butter until mixture resembles fine crumbs and starts to cling.
- Pat into the bottom and sides of a 9 x 9 x 2-inch greased baking pan.

Filling:

- In mixing bowl, beat sugar and butter or margarine until light and fluffy.
- Mix in egg until combined.
- Add alternately flour and evaporated milk, mixing after each addition.
- Add corn syrup and vanilla. Mix at medium speed until well blended.
- Pour batter into crust-lined baking pan.
- Sprinkle with powdered sugar.
- Bake at 350° for 25 to 35 minutes or until cake is nearly set. Do not overcook. Cool in pan.

Gooey Butter Cake originated in St. Louis in the 1930s. According to legend, a thrifty German baker added the wrong proportions of ingredients into his cake batter. It turned into a gooey, delicious mess that is now a St. Louis tradition. Recipe courtesy of Fred and Audrey Heimburger of Heimburger Bakery.

CINNAMON SPONGE COFFEE CAKE

Yield: 12 servings

3 **eggs**
1 cup **granulated sugar**
1½ cups sifted **flour**
1½ teaspoons **baking powder**
¾ cup **milk**, scalded
½ cup (1 stick) **butter**, melted
½ cup **powdered sugar**
½ rounded teaspoon **cinnamon**

- Beat eggs until thick and lemon colored.
- Gradually beat in the sugar. (The secret is lots of beating!)
- Sift together flour and baking powder; add to eggs and sugar.
- Using lowest speed of mixer, add milk all at once. (Batter will be thin.)
- Pour batter into greased and floured 9 x 13-inch pan.
- Bake at 350° for 30 to 35 minutes.
- Remove cake from oven; spoon melted butter over hot cake.
- Combine powdered sugar and cinnamon; sift over cake. (Powdered sugar and cinnamon amounts may be varied to taste.)

NUT COFFEE CAKE

Yield: 12 servings

2 cups **sugar**
1 cup (2 sticks) **butter** or **margarine**
4 **eggs**, separated
1 teaspoon **vanilla**
3 cups **flour**
3 teaspoons **baking powder**
1 cup **milk**
1 cup **walnuts** or **pecans**, ground
Powdered sugar

- Cream together sugar, butter, egg yolks, and vanilla.
- Sift together the flour and baking powder; add to creamed mixture.
- Add milk and nuts.
- Beat egg whites until stiff, and fold into batter mixture.
- Pour into greased tube pan (angel food cake pan).
- Bake at 350° for 1 hour.
- Cool cake in pan about 20 minutes.
- Invert cake and remove from pan.
- Sift powdered sugar on top of cooled cake.

JUNIOR LEAGUE OF ST. LOUIS
CINNAMON ROLLS

Yield: 2½ dozen

1   tablespoon **active dry yeast** (about 1½ packages)
¼   cup warm **water** (105° to 115°)
5   tablespoons **butter**
1   cup **milk**
½   cup **sugar**
1   teaspoon **salt**
1   **egg**
4   cups **flour**
½   cup (1 stick) melted **butter**

Cinnamon Mixture:

1   cup **sugar** (or to taste)
4   teaspoons **cinnamon**

- Sprinkle yeast into the water in a glass measuring cup; set aside to foam.
- In a small saucepan, melt the 5 tablespoons butter in milk; add sugar and salt.
- Pour the warmed milk mixture from the pan into a large mixing bowl. Mix in the egg and flour. Use an electric mixer with a pastry hook or paddle, or mix by hand with a wooden spoon.
- Add the yeast mixture to the dough. Dough will be sticky. (You may need to add up to ½ cup more flour for ease in handling.)
- Cover the bowl with a damp cloth. Let dough rise in a warm place about 1½ to 2 hours.
- Meanwhile, prepare a 9 x 13-inch pan by brushing with a small portion of the melted butter or by spreading the butter with paper towel.
- Punch dough down. Roll out dough onto a lightly floured surface, ¼ inch thick.
- Spread on about half of the remaining melted butter, and half of the cinnamon mixture.
- Cut strips of dough 3 inches wide and 3 inches long. Roll into cigar-shaped rolls 1 inch wide and 3 inches long.
- Dip rolls into melted butter and then roll them in cinnamon mixture.
- Arrange rolls, seam sides down, into pan. Rolls should touch each other without being crowded.
- Bake at 350° for 25 to 30 minutes.

To make lighter rolls, let them rise a second time before baking. For gooey rolls, drizzle additional butter and sprinkle more cinnamon mixture before baking.

TRADITIONAL PIZZA DOUGH

Yield: 4 servings

2⅔ cups **bread flour**
1 teaspoon **salt**
1 teaspoon active **dry yeast**
1 teaspoon **sugar**
¾ cup warm **water** (110°)
1 tablespoon **olive oil**

- Sift flour and salt into a medium bowl.
- In a small bowl, combine yeast, sugar, and ¼ cup water; let sit until frothy.
- Add yeast liquid, remaining water, and oil to flour.
- Mix to a soft dough; knead on a floured surface 10 minutes until smooth.
- Place dough in a greased bowl; cover with plastic.
- Let rise in a warm place 45 minutes or until doubled in size.
- Punch down dough and knead briefly.

- Oil a 12-inch pizza pan. Place dough on pan; press out to edges of pan with your knuckles. Pinch up edges to make a rim.
- Use dough as directed in recipe.

Pizza Variations:

- Herb or Nut Pizza Dough: Knead 2 tablespoons chopped fresh herbs (or one tablespoon dried herbs) into dough. If preferred, knead 1 ounce chopped walnuts into dough.
- Whole Wheat Pizza Dough: Use 2¼ cups whole wheat flour and ¼ cup wheat germ. Add extra water as required to form a soft dough.
- Cornmeal Pizza Dough: Use 2¼ cups bread flour and ⅓ cup cornmeal. An excellent pizza dough for Four Cheese Pizza or your own creation!

FOUR CHEESE PIZZA

Yield: 4 servings

1   recipe **Traditional Pizza Dough**
2   tablespoons **olive oil**
2   ounces **mozzarella cheese**
2   ounces **Gorgonzola cheese**
2   ounces **fontina** or **Gruyère cheese**
½   cup grated **Parmesan cheese**
     Salt and **pepper**
     Chopped **green onion** and grated **Parmesan cheese**

- Brush dough with 1 tablespoon oil.
- Cut the first 3 cheeses into small cubes. Scatter over dough.
- Sprinkle with Parmesan cheese; season to taste.
- Drizzle with remaining oil.
- Bake at 425° for 20 minutes until cheese is melted and dough is crisp and golden.
- Garnish with green onion and additional Parmesan cheese.

Pizza can be varied by adding sliced tomatoes, green peppers, mushrooms, and black olives under cheese layers. Or create your own variations!

SOFT PRETZELS

1   package active **dry yeast**
1½   cups warm **water**
1   teaspoon **salt**
1   tablespoon **sugar**
4   cups **flour**
1   **egg**, beaten
      Coarse salt

- Dissolve yeast in warm water in large mixing bowl.
- Add salt and sugar.
- Blend in flour to form dough.

- Knead dough until smooth. Form into desired shapes.
- Place on lightly greased cookie sheet.
- Brush pretzels with egg. Sprinkle with salt.
- Bake at 425° for 12 to 15 minutes.

Children absolutely love to help with the mixing and shaping! Add variety by adding food coloring to flour or salt!

PARMESAN POPOVERS

Yield: 6 servings

¼   cup **Parmesan cheese**, freshly grated

1   cup **milk**

1   cup all-purpose **flour**

1   tablespoon **butter**, melted

¼   teaspoon **salt**

2   large **eggs**

- Place oven rack on next-to-lowest shelf. Preheat oven to 450°.
- Grease 6 deep muffin or popover pans and sprinkle with Parmesan; set aside.
- In medium bowl, combine milk, flour, butter, and salt.
- Beat in eggs just until blended (over-beating will reduce volume).
- Fill cups ¾ full.
- Bake 15 minutes. Reduce heat to 350° (do not open door) and bake 20 minutes more.
- Carefully remove popovers with spatula and serve immediately.

Easy to make, and elegant!

FOOLPROOF POPOVERS

Yield: 6 servings

1   cup **milk**

1   cup **flour**

2   **eggs**

½   teaspoon **salt**

- Put all ingredients in mixing bowl.
- Stir with spoon until dry ingredients are moist. Disregard lumps.
- Pour into 6 greased, cold custard cups, half-full.
- Place in cold oven.
- Set the oven for 450° and the timer for 30 minutes. Don't peek.
- When the bell rings, serve immediately.

These popovers are great with roast beef or steak, and so easy!

KAMISH BREAD

Yield: 1 loaf

½   teaspoon **salt**
2   teaspoons **baking powder**
3   cups **flour**
1   cup **vegetable oil**
1   cup **sugar**
3   **eggs**
2   teaspoons ground **cinnamon**
2   teaspoons **vanilla**
2   cups chopped **pecans**
     Sugar and **cinnamon**

- Sift together salt, baking powder, and flour; set aside.
- Mix oil and sugar together and beat (by hand) for a minute.
- Add eggs, cinnamon, and vanilla to the oil and sugar mixture.
- Add liquid ingredients to flour mixture.
- Add pecans and stir in (don't overmix).
- Put dough on greased cookie sheet and shape it like a loaf of bread, but half the height of normal bread (elongated).
- Bake at 350° for 20 minutes.
- Remove bread from oven. Slice it and return to oven. Turn the oven off. Keep bread in oven until it cools.
- Mix together more cinnamon and sugar; sprinkle over top of bread.

BRIX BREAD

Yield: 16 slices

½   cup (1 stick) **butter**
1   tablespoon **prepared mustard**
1   tablespoon **poppy seeds**
1   loaf **French bread** (16-ounces), sliced (not all the way through)
½   pound **bacon**, cooked and crumbled
1   bunch **green onions**, chopped
4   ounces **Swiss cheese**, shredded

- Heat butter, mustard, and poppy seeds.
- Spoon mixture between bread sections.
- Sprinkle bacon, green onions, and cheese between bread sections.
- Wrap in foil if you wish, and bake at 350° for 20 to 30 minutes.

STUFFED FRENCH BREAD

Yield: 12 to 16 servings

3   small loaves **French bread**, cut into 4-inch pieces

1   cup **mayonnaise**

½   cup chopped **parsley**

2   8-ounce packages **cream cheese**, softened

1   0.6-ounce package **Italian salad dressing mix**

1   2-ounce jar **pimientos**, drained and chopped

- Mix together all ingredients except bread.
- Hollow out bread pieces, leaving about a 1-inch crust.
- Stuff bread with filling.
- Refrigerate until ready to serve.
- Slice and arrange on tray.

Try warming before serving.

APPLE CHEDDAR WALNUT BREAD

Yield: 8 to 10 servings

2   cups self-rising sifted **flour**

⅔   cup **sugar**

1   teaspoon ground **cinnamon**

½   cup coarsely broken **walnuts**

2   **eggs**, slightly beaten

½   cup (1 stick) melted **butter** or **salad oil**

1½   cups finely chopped, peeled **apples**

4   ounces **sharp Cheddar cheese**, shredded

¼   cup **milk**

- Grease well a 9 x 5 x 3-inch loaf pan.
- In a large bowl, combine flour, sugar, cinnamon, and nuts.
- In a separate bowl, mix remaining ingredients; add to flour mixture.
- Stir until just blended; batter will be lumpy.
- Spoon batter into prepared loaf pan.
- Bake at 350° for 60 to 70 minutes, or until done. (Test center with toothpick.)
- If top of loaf starts getting too brown, cover with foil during last 15 minutes of baking.
- Remove from pan immediately and cool on wire rack.

NORTHWESTERN SCONES

Yield: 8 servings

¼ cup (½ stick) **butter**

2 cups **flour**

¼ cup **sugar**

3¼ teaspoons **baking powder**

¾ cup **cream** or **half-and-half**

2 tablespoons grated **orange zest** (optional)

- Cut butter into flour until crumbly.
- Mix sugar with baking powder. Add to flour and butter mixture.
- Add enough cream to moisten (about ¾ cup).
- If desired, add orange zest.
- Knead briefly; divide into 2 circles, each 1 inch thick.
- Cut circles into quarters.
- Bake on ungreased baking sheet in 400° oven for 15 minutes.

POPPY SEED BREAD

Yield: 2 loaves

3 cups **flour**

1½ teaspoons **salt**

1½ teaspoons **baking powder**

3 **eggs**

1½ cups **milk**

1⅓ cups **vegetable oil**

2¼ cups **sugar**

1½ teaspoons **vanilla**

1½ tablespoons **poppy seeds**

1½ teaspoons **almond extract**

1½ teaspoons **butter flavoring**

Glaze:

¼ cup **lemon juice**

¾ cup **powdered sugar**

½ teaspoon **butter flavoring**

½ teaspoon **almond extract**

½ teaspoon **vanilla**

- Mix ingredients in bowl with mixer on medium for 2 minutes.
- Pour into 2 greased and floured 9 x 5 x 3-inch loaf pans.
- Bake 1 hour at 350°, or 325° for glass loaf pans.
- Let bread cool only 5 minutes.
- Pour glaze over bread while it is still hot.
- Cool completely before removing bread from pans.
- Store in refrigerator.

Glaze:

- While bread is baking, mix glaze ingredients together until sugar dissolves. Set aside.

APRICOT BREAD

Yield: 1 loaf

1	cup **dried apricots**
2	cups **flour**
2	teaspoons **baking powder**
1	teaspoon **salt**
½	teaspoon **baking soda**
1	cup **sugar**
2	tablespoons **butter**, softened, or **shortening**
1	**egg**
¼	cup **water**
½	cup **orange juice**
½	cup **walnuts**, chopped

- Soak apricots 30 minutes in enough warm water to cover.
- Mix flour, baking powder, salt, and baking soda.
- Mix sugar, butter, and egg; add to dry ingredients.
- Stir in water and orange juice with dry ingredients.
- Drain apricots, then quarter.
- Blend apricots and nuts into flour mixture.
- Grease 9½ x 5½ x 3-inch loaf pan and line bottom with waxed paper and grease again.
- Pour in batter and let stand 20 minutes to let rise slowly.
- Bake at 350° about 45 to 65 minutes until toothpick comes out dry.
- Remove from pan and take paper off immediately.

Top seller during days of Early Rising Bread Co.

ZUCCHINI BREAD

Yield: 2 loaves

3 cups all-purpose **flour**

2 teaspoons **baking soda**

1 teaspoon **salt**

½ teaspoon **baking powder**

1½ teaspoons ground **cinnamon**

¾ cup **walnuts**, finely chopped

3 **eggs**

2 cups **sugar**

1 cup **vegetable oil**

2 teaspoons **vanilla extract**

1 teaspoon **lemon extract**

2 cups **zucchini**, coarsely shredded

1 8-ounce can **crushed pineapple**, well drained

- Combine flour, soda, salt, baking powder, cinnamon, and nuts; set aside.
- In a large mixing bowl, beat eggs lightly; add sugar, oil, vanilla, and lemon extract; beat until creamy.
- Stir in zucchini and pineapple.
- Add dry ingredients, stirring only until dry ingredients are moistened.
- Spoon batter into 2 well-greased and floured 9 x 5 x 3-inch loaf pans.
- Bake at 350° for 1 hour or until done.
- Cool for 10 minutes before removing from pans; turn out on rack and cool completely.

Great by itself or with cream cheese spread!

PUMPKIN BREAD

Yield: 3 loaves

3	cups **sugar**
4	**eggs**, unbeaten
1½	teaspoons **salt**
1	teaspoon ground **cinnamon**
1	teaspoon ground **nutmeg**
⅔	cup **water**
1	cup **vegetable oil**
1½	16-ounce cans **pumpkin**
3½	cups **flour**
2	teaspoons **baking soda**

- Mix sugar, eggs, salt, spices, water, and oil thoroughly.
- Add pumpkin and blend well.
- Add flour and baking soda and mix well.
- Pour into 3 greased loaf pans and bake at 350° for about an hour.

A wonderfully fragrant bread as it bakes!

GRANDMA'S PUMPKIN TEA BREAD

Yield: 2 loaves

3	cups **sugar**
1	cup **vegetable oil**
3	**eggs**
2	cups (16 ounces) canned **pumpkin**
3	cups **flour**
½	teaspoon **salt**
½	teaspoon **baking powder**
1	teaspoon ground **cloves**
1	teaspoon ground **cinnamon**
1	teaspoon ground **nutmeg**
1	teaspoon **baking soda**
	Nonstick **cooking spray**

- In a mixing bowl, blend together sugar and oil; add eggs and pumpkin.
- In another bowl, blend together dry ingredients.
- Add dry ingredients gradually to liquid ingredients and blend.
- Pour batter into two 9 x 5 x 3-inch loaf pans, lightly sprayed with nonstick cooking spray.
- Bake at 350° until done (about 1 hour). Do not overbake.

This old family recipe is a holiday favorite.

CHEDDAR CHEESE CHIVE MUFFINS WITH OZARK SMOKED HAM

Yield: 36 mini sandwiches

2 cups unbleached all-purpose **flour**

1 tablespoon **baking powder**

1 teaspoon **light brown sugar**

¾ teaspoon **salt**

⅛ teaspoon **cayenne pepper**

1 **egg**

1 cup **milk**

¼ cup (½ stick) **unsalted butter**, melted

1¼ cups grated **sharp Cheddar cheese**

½ cup chopped **chives**

6 tablespoons **honey mustard**

½ pound **Ozark smoked ham**, sliced ⅛ inch thick

- Preheat oven to 400°.
- Lightly butter 36 miniature muffin cups (3 tins).
- Sift together first 5 ingredients.
- In another bowl, whisk together egg, milk, and melted butter.
- Stir the liquid ingredients into the flour mixture, just until blended.
- Fold in the cheese and chives.
- Spoon batter into muffin cups, filling each ⅔ full.
- Bake about 18 minutes; remove from oven and cool on rack.
- Slice muffins in half and spread bottom lightly with mustard.
- Top with 2 or 3 small slices of ham. Replace top half of muffin.
- Arrange on a serving tray and serve.

These delicious mini-muffin sandwiches are great for a brunch buffet or can be a meal by themselves. The muffins can be frozen or made 2 days ahead and stored in an airtight container.

DIJON AND DILL MUFFINS

Yield: 12 muffins

1½	cups	**whole wheat flour**
½	cup	**all-purpose flour**
¾	teaspoon dried	**dillweed**
2	teaspoons	**baking powder**
¼	teaspoon	**salt**
1	cup	**skim milk**
¼	cup	**vegetable oil**
3	tablespoons	**Dijon mustard**
1	**egg**, beaten	
	Nonstick	**cooking spray**

- Combine first 5 ingredients in large bowl; stir until blended.
- Make a well in center of batter.
- Combine milk, oil, mustard, and egg in the center of the well; stir with a whisk.
- Slowly whisk together dry ingredients and liquid ingredients, just until moistened.
- Spoon batter into muffin tins coated with cooking spray, filling ⅔ full.
- Bake at 400° for 20 minutes or until browned.

A great muffin to serve with chicken or fish.

Brown Sugar Applesauce Muffins

Yield: 2 dozen

1	cup (2 sticks) **butter**, softened
1	cup **brown sugar**
1	cup **granulated sugar**
2	**eggs**
2	cups **applesauce**
3	teaspoons ground **cinnamon**
2	teaspoons ground **allspice**
1	teaspoon ground **cloves**
½	teaspoon **salt**
2	teaspoons **baking soda**
4	cups **flour**
½	cup **raisins**
½	cup **nuts**

- Cream butter and sugars.
- Add eggs and remaining ingredients.
- Pour into greased muffin pans or paper liners.
- Bake at 375° for 12 minutes.

A healthy, fragrant, wonderful muffin.

Six-Week Raisin Bran Muffins

Yield: 3½ dozen

1	15-ounce box **raisin bran cereal**
3	cups **sugar**
5	teaspoons **baking soda**
5	cups **flour**
2	teaspoons **salt**
1	cup **pecans**, chopped
4	**eggs**, beaten
1	cup **vegetable oil**
1	quart **buttermilk**

- Mix dry ingredients together.
- Add beaten eggs, oil, and buttermilk. Mix well.
- Put in large container and cover. Store in refrigerator up to 2 months.
- When baking, fill greased muffin or paper liners ⅔ full.
- Bake at 400° for 12 to 20 minutes.

Great to always have in refrigerator when company pops in.

DOELLING HAUS MUFFINS

Yield: 12 muffins

2   cups **flour**
1   cup **sugar**
¾   teaspoon, **baking powder**
2   **eggs**, beaten
1   cup **sour cream**
⅓   cup **orange marmalade**
1   tablespoon **butter**, melted
1½   teaspoons **vanilla**
     Sugar, to taste

- Grease muffin cups with shortening.
- Stir together dry ingredients.
- Combine the rest of the ingredients until all are moistened.
- Add sugar if marmalade is too tart.
- Fill muffin cups ⅔ full.
- Sprinkle sugar lightly on top.
- Bake at 400° for approximately 20 minutes.
- Serve with butter and marmalade.

Serve with Eggs Florentine, Eggs Benedict, or favorite brunch entrée.

PECAN MINI MUFFINS

Yield: 24 muffins

½   cup (1 stick) **butter**
2   **eggs**
1   cup **dark brown sugar**
½   cup **flour**
1   teaspoon **vanilla**
1½   cups chopped **pecans**
     Nonstick **cooking spray**

- Melt butter, then cool.
- Add eggs and brown sugar to butter and mix by hand.
- Add flour, vanilla, and nuts and mix by hand again.
- Spray small tins with nonstick cooking spray and fill to top.
- Bake 20 minutes at 350°.

Super easy and fabulous. Great for breakfast or luncheons. Also good at Thanksgiving or Christmas.

SOUR CREAM CORN BREAD

Yield: 12 servings

3	**eggs**
½	cup **corn oil**
1	teaspoon **salt**
½	16-ounce can **creamed corn**
1	cup **sour cream**
12	ounces **corn muffin mix** (1½ boxes of **Jiffy® mix**)

- Whip together eggs, corn oil, and salt.
- Add creamed corn, sour cream, and muffin mix.
- Pour batter into 9 x 13-inch pan.
- Bake at 375° for 35 minutes.

Soooo good!

CORN BREAD MEXICAN

Yield: 20 to 30 servings

1	cup **flour**
1	cup **cornmeal**
¼	teaspoon **salt**
4	teaspoons **baking powder**
1	cup (2 sticks) **margarine,** softened
1	cup **sugar**
4	**eggs**
1	16-ounce can **creamed corn**
½	cup grated **Monterey Jack cheese**
½	cup grated **Cheddar cheese**
1	4-ounce can **diced green chili peppers**, drained (optional)

- Preheat oven to 350°.
- Sift flour, cornmeal, salt, and baking powder.
- In another bowl, cream margarine and sugar; add eggs and mix well.
- Add corn, cheeses, chili peppers, and flour mixture; stir until blended.
- Pour batter into greased 9 x 13-inch pan. Place in oven.
- Immediately lower oven temperature to 325°.
- Bake 1 hour.

Wonderful with chilies and soups. Or on its own!

CORN FRITTERS

Yield: 6 servings

3   **eggs**, separated
6   **ears of corn**, grated or
     1 16-ounce can **creamed
     corn**
1   scant cup **flour**
1   teaspoon **paprika**
1   tablespoon **sugar**
1   teaspoon **salt**
2   teaspoons **baking powder**
     Cooking oil

- Beat egg yolks.
- Add corn, flour, paprika, sugar, and salt.
- In a separate bowl, beat egg whites until stiff.
- Fold egg whites into flour mixture and then baking powder.
- Drop batter into hot oil and deep-fry until golden brown.

FOUR CHEESE SANDWICHES

Yield: 4 servings

4   **whole wheat buns**
4   **green pepper rings**
4   **tomato slices**
4   slices **Swiss cheese**
4   slices **Colby cheese**
4   slices **Provolone cheese**
4   slices **Muenster cheese**
     Alfalfa sprouts

Garlic Dressing:

1   **egg**
½   cup **mayonnaise**
¼   cup **oil**
⅛   cup **cider vinegar**
½   teaspoon **lemon juice**
1   clove **garlic**, crushed
¼   teaspoon **salt**
⅛   teaspoon **pepper**

- Place buns open on cookie sheet.
- On bottom half of bun, stack pepper slice, tomato slice, and 1 slice of each cheese.
- Melt under broiler.
- Remove from oven. Add sprouts and dressing.

Garlic Dressing:

- Mix ingredients in blender for 1 minute.

CHEESE GRITS SOUFFLÉ

Yield: 4 to 6 servings

1	cup quick-cooking **grits**
2	cups boiling **water**
2	cups **milk**
5	tablespoons **butter**
3	**eggs**
½	cup **cream**
½	pound **sharp Cheddar cheese**, grated
	Paprika

- Cook grits in boiling water and milk according to package directions.
- Add butter and stir until melted.
- In mixing bowl, beat eggs until frothy; add cream.
- Stir eggs and cream mixture into grits. Fold in half of cheese.
- Pour mixture into a greased casserole. Top with remaining cheese. Sprinkle with paprika.
- Bake at 350° for 1 hour.

Great for brunch!

GRANOLA

Yield: 11 cups

6	cups old-fashioned **oatmeal**
1	cup sweetened **coconut**
1	cup **Grape-Nuts® cereal**
¾	cup mixed nuts (**cashews, almonds**, and **pecans**)
½	cup **sunflower seeds**
¼	cup **brown sugar**
½	cup **vegetable oil**
½	cup **honey**
⅓	cup **water**
1½	teaspoons **salt**
1½	teaspoons **vanilla**

- Combine first 5 ingredients.
- Combine other ingredients and pour over cereal mixture.
- Mix to coat well.
- Spread on greased baking sheets.
- Bake at 300° for 30 minutes.
- Stir every 5 minutes. Cool.
- Store in airtight container.

So much better than store-bought granola. Good with raisins, too.

BAKED OATMEAL

Yield: 6 to 8 servings

½ cup **vegetable oil**

½ cup **sugar**

2 **eggs**, beaten

1 cup **milk**

3 cups old-fashioned **oatmeal**

¼ teaspoon **salt**

- Combine ingredients.
- Transfer to greased 15 x 10 x 1-inch pan.
- Bake uncovered at 350° for 30 to 40 minutes, or until liquid has disappeared and oatmeal is slightly golden.
- Garnish with favorite fruit, honey, milk, etc.
- Refrigerate any leftovers.

Leftovers reheat wonderfully well.

NORWEGIAN PANCAKES

Yield: 6 servings

4 **eggs**

2½ tablespoons **butter**

2 tablespoons **sugar**

¼ teaspoon **salt**

1 cup **flour**

2 cups **milk**

Fresh fruit spread or **jam** (optional)

Maple or **flavored syrup** (optional)

Powdered sugar (optional)

- Beat eggs at high speed.
- Melt butter and set aside.
- Add sugar and salt to eggs and blend. Stir in butter.
- Alternately add flour and milk, blending until mixture is consistency of thick cream.

- Pour ¼ cup batter into preheated, buttered skillet with nonstick coating.
- Pick up skillet and roll batter around so bottom of skillet is evenly coated.
- As edges "ruffle" and turn golden, loosen with spatula.
- Flip quickly in order not to rip pancake.
- When golden, fold into quarters or roll into quarters.
- May be kept warm on a plate in a 200° oven uncovered.
- Serve with fresh fruit on top or inside, and sprinkle with powdered sugar, or top with whipped cream.
- Or, serve as a traditional breakfast item with maple or flavored syrups.

PUFFY APPLE PANCAKE

Yield: 6 servings

6	**eggs**
1½	cups **milk**
1	cup **flour**
3	tablespoons **granulated sugar**
1	teaspoon **vanilla**
½	teaspoon **salt**
¼	teaspoon ground **cinnamon**
½	cup (1 stick) **butter** or **margarine**
2	**apples**, pared and thinly sliced
3	tablespoons **brown sugar**

- In blender, mix eggs, milk, flour, sugar, vanilla, salt, and cinnamon until blended.
- Melt butter in 12-inch quiche or 9 x 13-inch pan in preheated 425° oven.
- Add apple slices to melted butter in pan and return to oven until butter sizzles. Do not brown butter.
- Remove dish from oven and immediately pour batter over apples. Sprinkle with brown sugar.
- Bake in middle of preheated 425° oven for 20 minutes or until puffed and brown.
- Serve immediately. Pancake will collapse soon after removal from oven.

LIGHTER-THAN-AIR WAFFLES

Yield: 10 to 12 waffles

2	cups sifted **flour** with dash of **salt**
3	**eggs**
3	cups **milk** (or less)
½	cup (1 stick) **butter**, melted
4	tablespoons **baking powder**

- Put flour and salt in bowl. Make hole in flour mound.
- In separate bowl, mix eggs and milk. Pour into hole in flour. Add melted butter. Mix well.
- Just before baking, add baking powder; mix barely. Batter will rise.
- Cook in waffle iron according to manufacturer's directions.
- Serve immediately.

63

NIGHT-BEFORE FRENCH TOAST CASSEROLE

Yield: 8 to 10 servings

1	10-ounce loaf of long thin **French bread**, 18 inches
8	**eggs**
3	cups **milk**
¼	cup **sugar**
¾	teaspoon **salt**
1	tablespoon **vanilla**
2	tablespoons **butter**, cut into 5 pats
½	teaspoon ground **cinnamon**
	Syrup

- Grease well a 13 x 9-inch baking dish.
- Cut bread into 18 1-inch wide slices.
- Arrange slices in 1 layer, in bottom of pan.
- Beat eggs, milk, sugar, salt, and vanilla in large bowl.
- When thoroughly mixed, pour over bread in pan. Bread will float on top of liquid.
- Cut each pat of butter into 4 pieces.
- Dot each piece of bread with a piece of butter. Sprinkle with cinnamon.
- Cover. Refrigerate overnight, or up to 36 hours.
- Place dish, uncovered, in cold oven.
- Turn oven temperature to 350° (325° if glass dish) and bake 45 to 50 minutes, or until bread is puffy and light brown.
- Remove from oven. Allow to set 5 minutes.
- Bread will rise to top with a layer of custard on the bottom, similar to a bread pudding.
- Serve with maple, raspberry, strawberry, or coconut syrups.

An excellent brunch dish, especially for holiday mornings, goes great with a fruit cup.

MAKE-AHEAD EGGS BENEDICT

Yield: 8 servings

4   **English muffins**, split and toasted

16 thin slices **Canadian bacon**

8   **eggs**

¼   cup (½ stick) **margarine** or **butter**

¼   cup all-purpose **flour**

1   teaspoon **paprika**

⅛   teaspoon ground **nutmeg**

⅛   teaspoon **pepper**

2   cups **milk**

2   cups shredded **Swiss cheese**

½   cup **dry white wine**

½   cup **cornflakes**, crushed (about 1 cup before crushing)

1   tablespoon **margarine** or **butter**, melted

- In a 13 x 9 x 2-inch baking dish, arrange muffins, cut side up.
- Place 2 bacon slices on each muffin half.
- Half-fill a 10-inch skillet with water; bring just to boiling.
- Break egg into a dish.
- Carefully slide egg into water.
- Repeat with 3 more eggs. Simmer, uncovered, 3 minutes or until just set.
- Remove eggs with slotted spoon.
- Repeat with remaining eggs.
- Place 1 egg on top of each muffin stack; set aside.
- For sauce, in a medium saucepan melt ¼ cup margarine or butter.
- Stir in flour, paprika, nutmeg, and pepper.
- Add milk all at once.
- Cook and stir until thickened and bubbly.
- Stir in cheese until melted.
- Stir in wine.
- Carefully spoon sauce over muffin stacks.
- Combine cornflakes and 1 tablespoon margarine or butter; sprinkle over muffin stacks.
- Cover, chill overnight.
- To serve, bake uncovered in 375° oven, 20 to 25 minutes or until heated through.

A delicious brunch dish that you can do ahead!

SCRUMPTIOUS EGGS

Yield: 10 servings

1½   pounds **Monterey Jack cheese**, shredded

¾   pound fresh **mushrooms**, sliced

½   large **onion**, chopped

¼   cup (½ stick) **butter**, melted

1   cup cubed **ham**

11   **eggs**, beaten

1¾   cups **milk**

¼   cup **flour**

1   tablespoon chopped **parsley**

1½   teaspoons **salt**

- Place half of cheese in buttered 9 x 13-inch dish.
- Sauté mushrooms and onions in butter until tender; place over cheese.
- Distribute ham.
- Beat eggs, milk, flour, parsley, and salt.
- Pour evenly over casserole and top with remaining cheese.
- Bake at 350° for 45 minutes.

From the Visiting Nurse Association in Kansas City.

BUSY DAY BREAKFAST

Yield: 12 servings

8   slices of **bread**, cubed

2   cups grated **Cheddar cheese**

1   pound hot or spicy **pork sausage**

4   **eggs**

3   cups **milk**

¾   teaspoon **dry mustard**

1   10¾-ounce can **cream of mushroom soup**

- Grease a 9 x 13-inch casserole.
- Cover bottom of dish with bread cubes.
- Sprinkle cheese over bread.
- Brown sausage; drain grease.
- Sprinkle sausage over cheese and bread.
- Beat eggs with 2½ cups milk and mustard; pour over top of casserole.
- Refrigerate overnight.
- Dilute soup with ½ cup milk and pour over casserole.
- Bake uncovered at 300° for 1½ hours.

This brunch recipe must be assembled a day in advance.

CRUSTLESS QUICHE

Yield: 8 servings

1   pound **small curd cottage cheese**

½   pound grated **Swiss cheese**

½   pound grated **mild Cheddar cheese**

4   **eggs**, beaten

½   cup **flour**

½   cup **milk**

½   cup (1 stick) **butter** or **margarine**, melted

1   10-ounce package **frozen spinach**, thawed and well drained

1   teaspoon **baking powder**

Dash of **salt**

- Put all ingredients in large bowl and mix well.
- Spread into a greased 9 x 13-inch pan.
- Bake at 350° for 1 hour.

This flavorful quiche is quick and easy! It freezes well, too (unbaked). Vary recipe by replacing spinach with a small can of crabmeat. Or use ham, bacon, frozen broccoli, sausage, or shrimp.

GARDEN QUICHE

Yield: 6 servings

1   9-inch unbaked **pie crust**

2   cups **mixed vegetables** (broccoli, carrots, green beans) cut into small pieces

1   cup grated **Monterey Jack cheese**

7   **eggs**

1   cup **cream**

1   teaspoon **sugar**

½   teaspoon **salt**

- Arrange crust in pie pan.
- Put vegetables and cheese into crust.
- In a mixing bowl, mix eggs, cream, sugar, and salt until smooth.
- Pour over vegetables and cheese.
- Bake at 350° for 1½ hours or until firm.

Great for leftover veggies! You can also use frozen vegetables.

DELICATE QUICHE

Yield: 6 servings

½ cup finely minced **shallots** or **green onions**

½ cup **dry white wine**

6 **eggs**

2 cups **heavy cream**

1 teaspoon **salt**

¼ teaspoon **pepper**

¼ teaspoon ground **nutmeg**

6 ounces grated **Gruyère** or **Swiss cheese**

1 10-inch, deep-dish **pie crust**, baked

- Combine shallots and wine in a small saucepan.
- Bring to a boil; turn heat to low and simmer for 2 minutes.
- Remove from heat and cool.
- Gently beat eggs and cream together.
- Stir in wine mixture, salt, pepper, and nutmeg.
- Sprinkle cheese over crust; pour egg mixture over top of cheese.
- Bake for 35 to 45 minutes at 350°, until quiche sets.
- Let stand 10 minutes before serving.

This quiche has a light and delicate texture and is very easy to make.

SOUPS and SALADS

S pend a morning enjoying Forest Park, then treat yourself to a light soup and salad lunch. The 1,300-acre park, host of the 1904 World's Fair, was established in the 1870s and is larger than New York's Central Park. Forest Park is home to the much-acclaimed St. Louis Art Museum, the St. Louis Zoo, the Jewel Box, the St. Louis Science Center, and the Missouri History Museum.

• • •

L'Auberge Bretonne

*Dubbed the "godfather of French cuisine in St. Louis" by local food critic
Joe Pollack, Jean-Claude Guillossou is due many thanks for bringing
excellent French cuisine to the Gateway City. A native of the province of
Breton, Chef Guillossou opened the first L'Auberge Bretonne (Inn of Breton)
in 1976 and has since led the way for a number of area French restaurants.
C'est magnifique!*

GRILLED TUNA CAESAR

Yield: 4 servings

2   heads **romaine lettuce**
     Croutons
     Grated **Parmesan cheese**
5   ounces grilled **tuna
     steak**, sliced

Dressing:

1   ounce **anchovies**
1   ounce **garlic** cloves
1   teaspoon **salt**
1   teaspoon **Dijon mustard**
½   teaspoon **Worcestershire
     sauce**
2   **egg yolks**
¼   cup **vinegar**
2   cups **olive oil**
3   tablespoons **water**

- Wash and tear 2 heads
  romaine lettuce.
- Add dressing and toss with
  croutons and Parmesan
  cheese.
- Serve with slices of fresh
  grilled tuna steak.

Dressing:

- In a food processor macerate
  anchovies and garlic.
- Add salt, mustard,
  Worcestershire sauce,
  egg yolks, and vinegar
  and combine.
- Add oil slowly until blended.
  Adjust consistency of dressing with water, if needed.

CAFE PROVENÇAL'S MUSSEL SOUP

Yield: 10 servings

1	gallon **water**
2	**celery** stalks, diced
1	**carrot**, diced
1	**onion**, diced
2	**bay leaves**
18	fresh **mussels**
1	pint **heavy cream**
	Salt and **pepper**, to taste
1	teaspoon **tarragon**
2	tablespoons chopped **garlic**
1	cup **white wine**
2	ounces **brandy**
	A few threads of **saffron**, crumbled

- In a large pot, bring the water to a rolling boil.
- Add celery, carrot, onion, and bay leaves. Simmer until vegetables are soft, about 30 minutes.
- Steam the mussels in this stock until mussels are firm, about 6 minutes. Shells will open up.
- Remove mussels from stock and cool. Discard shells. Chill mussels in refrigerator. (You may chop the mussels or leave them whole.)
- Strain stock; return to pot. Add cream slowly until soup reaches a nice thick consistency.
- Season to taste with salt, pepper, tarragon, garlic, white wine, brandy, and saffron. Heat thoroughly.
- Put mussels into soup bowls. Ladle the heated soup on top.

Chef Ed Neill shares this favorite from his restaurant, Cafe Provençal.

BERRY-PEACH SOUP

Yield: 4 servings

1   cup fresh **raspberries**

3   cups fresh or frozen sliced **peaches**

3   tablespoons **lemon juice**

1   cup **peach nectar**

1   8-ounce container **plain yogurt**

1   teaspoon **almond extract**

- Purée raspberries in a food processor; strain and chill.

- Purée peaches and lemon juice. Place in large bowl.

- Blend nectar and yogurt in food processor. Add almond extract.

- Mix well with puréed peaches and lemon juice.

- Cover and chill.

- Spoon peach mixture into individual bowls.

- Spoon raspberry purée on top. Swirl with toothpick.

GAZPACHO

Yield: 8 servings

1   clove **garlic**, minced

½   small **onion**, chopped

¼   cup **green pepper**, chopped

½   **cucumber**, peeled and chopped

4   large **tomatoes**, peeled and chopped

½   tablespoon **salt**

¼   teaspoon **pepper**
     Dash of **Tabasco® sauce**

1   tablespoon **olive oil**

3   tablespoons **red wine vinegar**

1   cup **V8® juice**
     Sour cream for garnish

- Put all ingredients except sour cream into blender; cover and blend for 5 seconds.

- Chill and serve with a teaspoon of sour cream in each bowl.

This is a wonderful summer soup when vegetables are at their best!

LOW-FAT GAZPACHO

Yield: 8 servings

2	cups finely chopped **tomatoes**
1	cup finely chopped **celery**
1	cup finely chopped **cucumber**
1	bunch **green onions**, thinly sliced
16	ounces **tomato sauce**
¾	cup **water**
¼	cup **vinegar**
1	tablespoon **olive oil**
	Pepper to taste
1	teaspoon **salt**
2	teaspoons **Worcestershire sauce**

- Combine the vegetables in large bowl.
- Combine remaining ingredients; pour over vegetables and stir.
- Cover and chill (at least overnight).

This popular summer soup improves with age.

TOMATO AND BASIL SOUP

Yield: 6 servings

⅓	cup **olive oil**
1	medium **onion**, chopped
1	teaspoon minced **garlic**
⅓	cup **flour**
1	14-ounce can chopped or diced **tomatoes**
2	14½-ounce cans **chicken broth**
2	teaspoons dried **basil**
½	teaspoon **salt**
½	teaspoon **pepper**

- In a large saucepan, heat olive oil. Sauté onion and garlic. Stir in flour.
- Add remaining ingredients.
- Blend well with a wire whisk.
- Simmer for 30 minutes, stirring frequently.
- Pour into food processor and purée until smooth.
- Pour back into pan until ready to serve.

This is even better made ahead and reheated.

Pumpkin Soup

Yield: 6 cups

¼	cup (½ stick) **butter**
1	cup chopped **onion**
1	clove **garlic**, crushed
1	teaspoon **curry powder**
⅛	teaspoon **salt**
⅛	teaspoon ground **coriander**
⅛	teaspoon **red pepper**
3	cups **chicken broth**
1	16-ounce can **pumpkin**
1	cup **half-and-half**
	Sour cream and **chives**

- In large saucepan, melt butter; sauté onion and garlic until soft.
- Add curry powder, salt, coriander, and red pepper; cook 1 minute.
- Add broth; boil gently, uncovered, for 15 to 20 minutes.
- Stir in pumpkin and half-and-half; cook 5 minutes.
- Pour into blender container. Cover; blend until creamy.
- Serve warm or reheat to desired temperature.
- Garnish with sour cream and chopped chives, if desired.

Zucchini Soup

Yield: 8 servings

1	pound **zucchini**
2	tablespoons **butter**
2	teaspoons chopped **shallots**
2	cloves **garlic**, minced
1	teaspoon **curry powder**
½	teaspoon **salt**
¼	teaspoon **pepper**
½	cup **water**
1	**chicken bouillon cube**
1	cup **heavy cream**
1	cup **milk**
	Chives

- Wash and slice zucchini.
- In a large saucepan, sauté the zucchini in butter with shallots, garlic, curry, salt, and pepper.
- Cook 5 minutes and stir.
- Add water with chicken bouillon cube. Simmer.
- Put all ingredients into food processor and chop fine.
- Return to pan.
- Stir in cream and milk.
- Top with chives.

SOUPE À L'OIGNON
(FRENCH ONION SOUP)

Yield: 4 servings

3	tablespoons **butter**
3	large **onions**, thinly sliced
1	tablespoon **flour**
½	teaspoon **salt**
	Freshly ground **pepper**
5	cups **beef broth**
4	thick slices **French** or **Italian bread**
	Grated **Parmesan cheese**
4	tablespoons grated **Swiss** or **Gruyère cheese**

- In a heavy pan, melt the butter, add the sliced onions, and cook, stirring occasionally, until golden.
- Sprinkle on the flour and stir for a few minutes to cook the flour.
- Season with salt and pepper.
- Add the broth, stirring constantly.
- Bring to a boil, lower the heat, and let the soup simmer, partially covered, for 30 minutes.
- Toast the slices of bread in the oven until brown.
- Place them in a large oven-proof soup tureen or individual bowls.
- Preheat the broiler. Sprinkle the bread with Parmesan cheese. Pour the soup over the bread and top with Swiss or Gruyère cheese.
- Brown the cheese under the broiler and serve immediately.

Instead of the broiler, the cheese can be melted in the microwave. (It will not brown.) Melt on medium or high for 1 minute at a time. Repeat if necessary, until melted.

CREAMY LEEK SOUP WITH BRIE

Yield: 6 servings

½   cup (1 stick) unsalted **butter**

8   large **leeks**, white part only, sliced and washed well

4   cups low-sodium **chicken broth**, homemade preferred

½   cup unbleached all-purpose **flour**

4   cups **half-and-half**

1½   pounds mild, creamy **Brie cheese**, trimmed of rind and cut in 1-inch cubes

½   cup dry **white wine**

Salt and ground **white pepper**, to taste

Chopped fresh **chives** for garnish

- Melt ¼ cup of the butter in a large, heavy sauté pan.
- Add leeks and sauté over medium-low heat until soft.
- Add chicken broth and increase heat to bring to a boil.
- Reduce heat, cover, and simmer 25 minutes.
- Cool slightly and purée leeks in food processor or blender.
- In a soup pot, melt remaining butter and add flour, stirring to incorporate well.
- Gradually add half-and-half; whisk until smooth. Add cheese, about a quarter at a time, and stir until melted and smooth.
- Add wine and chicken broth and puréed leeks.
- Add salt and pepper, to taste.
- Heat through.
- Serve garnished with fresh chives.

Fantastic first course! Or, a meal in itself with fresh bread or rolls.

BAKED POTATO SOUP

Yield: 6 to 8 servings

6   slices **bacon**, cut up

3   baking **potatoes**, chopped not peeled

1   cup chopped **onions**

½   cup chopped **carrots**

½   cup chopped **celery**

4   cups **milk**

2   teaspoons **salt**

¼   teaspoon **pepper**

1   cup dairy **sour cream**

2   tablespoons **flour**

2   teaspoons **paprika**

2   **green onions**, chopped

- Cook bacon in large saucepan until crisp. Set bacon aside.
- Drain, reserving 3 tablespoons drippings in pan.
- Add potatoes, onions, carrots, and celery to drippings. Cover and cook over low heat until potatoes are tender. Stir occasionally.
- Stir in milk, salt, and pepper. Bring mixture to a boil.
- In a bowl, mix sour cream, flour, and paprika.
- Slowly stir in 1 cup of the hot mixture into sour cream mixture. Stir until creamy.
- Add sour cream mixture into the hot mixture. Cook and stir until soup bubbles.
- Serve with bacon pieces and green onions sprinkled on top.

CHEESY VEGETABLE CHOWDER

Yield: 8 servings

½	cup chopped **onion**
1	clove **garlic**, minced
1	cup chopped **celery**
1	cup sliced **carrots**
1	cup cubed **potatoes**
3½	cups **chicken broth**
1	17-ounce can whole kernel **corn**, drained
¼	cup (½ stick) **butter**
¼	cup **flour**
2	cups **milk**
1	tablespoon **mustard**
¼	teaspoon **pepper**
¼	teaspoon **paprika**
2	tablespoons diced **pimiento**
8	ounces (2 cups) shredded **Cheddar cheese**

- Combine first 6 ingredients in large pot. Bring to boil.
- Reduce heat and simmer for 15 minutes.
- Add corn.
- Combine butter and flour in another saucepan; cook until roux is golden brown and flour is cooked.
- Add milk to flour mixture and stir until well blended.
- Add remaining ingredients; cook until cheese melts.
- Add 2 cups of vegetable mixture to milk mixture and blend.
- Gradually add milk mixture to vegetable mixture; blend and serve.

QUICK CLAM CHOWDER

Yield: 8 servings

6	slices **bacon**
3	medium **onions**, chopped
2	celery **stalks**, chopped
2	10¾-ounce cans **Campbell's®** **Cream of Potato soup**
4	cans **Reese® minced clams** in juice
1	large **potato**, cubed and boiled until tender
2	cups **half-and-half** **Salt** and **pepper**

- In large stockpot, fry bacon until crisp.
- Remove bacon and crumble.
- In the melted bacon fat, brown the onion and celery.
- Add remaining ingredients and simmer 30 minutes over medium heat to blend flavors.
- Serve hot with crumbled bacon bits as a garnish.

LOBSTER BISQUE

Yield: 4 servings

6	tablespoons **butter**, divided
4	tablespoons finely chopped **green pepper**
4	tablespoons finely chopped **onion**
1	finely chopped **scallion**
2	tablespoons finely chopped **parsley**
1½	cups sliced fresh **mushrooms**
2	tablespoons **flour**
1	cup **milk**
1	teaspoon **salt**
⅛	teaspoon **white pepper**
	Dash of **Tabasco® sauce**
1½	cups **half-and-half**
1½	cups cooked **lobster meat** (canned or frozen)
3	tablespoons dry **sherry**

- Heat 4 tablespoons of the butter in skillet.
- Add green peppers, onion, scallion, parsley, and mushrooms.
- Sauté until vegetables are soft (about 5 minutes).
- In saucepan, heat remaining 2 tablespoons of butter. Stir in flour.
- Add milk and cook over medium to medium-high heat, stirring constantly until thickened and smooth.
- Stir in salt, pepper, and Tabasco® to taste. Add sautéed vegetables and the half-and-half.
- Bring to a boil, stirring constantly, then reduce heat.
- Add the lobster meat. Simmer, uncovered, for 5 minutes.
- Just before serving, stir in the dry sherry.

An elegant first course for formal dining, or wonderful as a main course with a green salad of choice.

SHRIMP BISQUE

Yield: 4 to 6 servings

7	tablespoons **butter**
4	tablespoons **flour**
2	cups **milk**
1	pound cleaned, peeled, and chopped **shrimp**
4	**green onions** (white part only), chopped
1	teaspoon **dry mustard**
1	tablespoon **Worcestershire sauce**
1	tablespoon **A.1.® steak sauce**
1	teaspoon **salt**
1	teaspoon **white pepper**
½	teaspoon **paprika**
3	tablespoons **sherry**

- In a large saucepan over high heat, melt 4 tablespoons of the butter.
- Add flour and beat vigorously. Remove from heat.
- Add milk and whisk until smooth.
- Lower heat, and cook the sauce until creamy.
- In remaining butter, sauté shrimp with green onions.
- Combine shrimp with white sauce.
- Add mustard, Worcestershire sauce, A.1.® sauce, salt, white pepper, paprika, and sherry.
- Simmer to combine flavors. Serve warm.

SHRIMP AND CORN SOUP

Yield: 10 servings

10   tablespoons (1¼ stick) **butter** (no substitute)

1   large **yellow onion**, chopped coarsely

¼   small **bell pepper**, chopped coarsely

2½   stalks **celery**, chopped coarsely

2   16-ounce cans **whole kernel corn**

2   16-ounce cans **creamed corn**

1   10-ounce can **Rotel® tomatoes with green chilies**

2   10¾-ounce cans **cream of celery soup**

3   to 4 cups **water**
     McCormick Season All® seasoned salt, to taste
     Pinch of **sugar**

3   or 4 pounds peeled large **shrimp**

1   pound **crabmeat**, fresh or frozen, not canned (optional)

- In stockpot, melt butter over medium heat.
- Add onion, pepper, and celery to butter.
- Sauté until limp. Do not burn butter!
- Add cans of corn, tomatoes, and celery soup. Stir all ingredients together well.
- Add 3 or 4 cups water (depending on consistency, should be rather thick. Soup will thin out when shrimp are added. You can ease back on water until after shrimp have cooked).
- Add seasoned salt and pinch of sugar.
- Stir all together and simmer on low heat for 1 hour, stirring frequently to keep bottom from sticking.
- Add peeled shrimp and cook for 30 minutes more. Keep stirring!
- If you also add crabmeat, be sure to pick out shells. (Do not use canned crabmeat!)
- Soup should have a chowder consistency. After shrimp have cooked, add more water, if necessary.

Wonderful with French bread and fruity red wine. Freezes well. It is always better the day after!

HEART-WARMING VEGETABLE BEEF SOUP

Yield: 12 servings

2½ pounds **chuck roast** or **soup bone** with meat

7 cups boiling **water**

1 **onion**, sliced
Celery leaves from ½ bunch

1 tablespoon **salt**

1 teaspoon **pepper**

1 teaspoon **Lawry's®** **seasoned salt**

2 large **potatoes**, cubed

3 stalks **celery**, chopped

1 **onion**, chopped

2 16-ounce packages frozen **mixed vegetables**

1 46-ounce can **tomato juice**

1 16-ounce can chopped **tomatoes**

- In a large stockpot, brown the meat over high heat.
- Add water, onion, celery leaves, and seasonings.
- Simmer 2 to 3 hours until the meat is tender. Keep the pan covered.
- Remove meat and cut into small pieces.
- Add the remaining ingredients and the meat to the broth.
- Simmer for about 2 hours more. Taste and correct the seasonings.

This soup tastes better the second day after the flavors have blended even more.

STEAK SOUP

Yield: 6 cups

1	pound **ground beef**
1	tablespoon **vegetable oil**
1	cup thinly sliced **carrots**
½	cup chopped **onion**
½	cup thinly sliced **celery**
3	tablespoons **flour**
1	14-ounce can **beef broth**
1	14-ounce can **Italian tomatoes**, chopped with juice
⅓	cup **water**
1	teaspoon **Worcestershire sauce**
½	teaspoon **salt**
½	teaspoon freshly ground **pepper**
½	cup frozen **green peas**
2	tablespoons chopped fresh **parsley**

- Brown ground beef in large skillet over medium-high heat 5 minutes.
- With slotted spoon, transfer beef to plate; set aside.
- Drain grease from skillet.
- Add oil to skillet; add carrots, onion, and celery. Cover; cook until vegetables are softened, about 5 minutes.
- Stir in flour; cook 1 minute more. Gradually add beef broth, tomatoes with juice, water, Worcestershire sauce, salt, and pepper.
- Return browned beef to soup; bring to a boil.
- Reduce heat; simmer 25 minutes.
- Stir in peas and parsley; simmer 5 minutes more.

For a hearty meal, serve in hollowed-out large sourdough rolls with Burgundy wine.

MIXED GREENS, MUSHROOMS, AND HAZELNUT SALAD

Yield: 8 servings

¼   cup, plus 2 tablespoons **hazelnuts***

1   tablespoon, plus 1 teaspoon **lemon juice**

1   tablespoon, plus 1 teaspoon **coarse-grained mustard**

1   teaspoon **olive oil**

½   pound fresh **mushrooms**, sliced

2   cups torn **red leaf lettuce**

1   cup torn **romaine lettuce**

1   cup torn **arugula**

1   cup torn **radicchio**

1   cup torn curly **endive**

⅓   cup **chicken broth**

1   tablespoon, plus 1 teaspoon **raspberry vinegar**

1   teaspoon **hazelnut* oil**
    Salt and **pepper**, to taste

can substitute pistachio nuts for hazelnuts

hazelnut oil may be substituted with olive oil

- Toast hazelnuts on a baking sheet at 350° for 10 minutes.
- Rub briskly with a towel to remove skins. Coarsely chop and set aside.
- Combine lemon juice, mustard, and olive oil in a medium bowl. Stir well.
- Add mushrooms and toss gently to coat. Set aside.
- Combine salad greens in a large bowl. Toss.
- Combine remaining ingredients in a small bowl; stir with a wire whisk until blended.
- Pour liquids over greens. Toss well.
- Add mushroom mixture and hazelnuts; toss gently.
- Place salad mixture on individual salad plates.

Low-calorie, colorful, flavorful salad!

FRENCH GREEN SALAD WITH BACON

Yield: 4 servings

2 tablespoons **Dijon mustard**

½ teaspoon **salt**

2 tablespoons **red wine vinegar**

1 clove **garlic**, finely minced

½ cup **corn oil**

½ pound sliced **bacon**, cut into 1-inch pieces

2 slices **white bread**, cut into 1-inch pieces (Pepperidge Farm® Toasting White)

6 cups **mixed salad greens**, rinsed, dried, and torn into bite-sized pieces

- In a small bowl, whisk the mustard, salt, vinegar, and garlic; mix well.
- Slowly pour in the oil. Whisk until mixture is thick and smooth. Set aside.
- Cook bacon until crisp. Remove from pan and drain on paper towels.
- In bacon drippings, sauté the bread cubes, stirring until browned.
- Remove and drain on paper towels.
- Place greens in a large salad bowl; add the bacon, croutons, and dressing. Toss thoroughly.

A zesty first course, especially before a chicken entrée!

RED CABBAGE SALAD WITH BACON AND ROQUEFORT CHEESE

Yield: 6 servings

1	small head **red cabbage**
¼	cup **tarragon vinegar**
8	ounces **bacon**, cut in ¼-inch thick strips, fat reserved
½	cup **vegetable oil**
1	long loaf **French bread** or 3 to 4 **crusty white rolls**, sliced in ½-inch thick slices
16	to 20 **lettuce leaves**
3	ounces **Roquefort cheese**, frozen for easy grating

Vinaigrette Dressing:

1	tablespoon **mustard**
3	tablespoons **vinegar** **Salt** and **pepper**
¾	cup **oil**

- Quarter cabbage, remove core, and shred finely lengthwise, with a knife.
- Place cabbage strips in bowl.
- Bring ¼ cup vinegar to boil, pour over shredded cabbage; mix well and set aside.
- Blanch bacon pieces by placing them in pan of cold water. Bring to a boil; drain. Refresh under cold, running water; drain thoroughly.

- Heat 1 tablespoon oil in skillet. Add bacon and sauté until crisp.
- Drain on paper towels; reserve bacon fat.
- In frying pan in which bacon was fried, heat remaining oil and fry slices of bread until golden brown on both sides. Place slices on paper towels to absorb excess oil.
- Just before serving, toss cabbage with enough Vinaigrette Dressing to moisten cabbage well.
- To serve, arrange a bed of lettuce leaves on large plates.
- Mound cabbage salad in high domes in center.
- Place 4 to 5 fried bread rounds on the lettuce leaves at equal intervals.
- Sprinkle bacon on cabbage.
- With a fork, grate cheese over cabbage.

Vinaigrette Dressing:
- Whisk mustard with vinegar, salt, and pepper.
- Gradually whisk in oil and very small amount of reserved bacon fat until dressing emulsifies. Be careful not to add too much bacon fat because it will cause dressing to gel.

HEARTS OF PALM AND ORANGE SALAD

Yield: 6 servings

2 medium **oranges**
1 cup diagonally sliced **hearts of palm**
½ cup vegetable **oil**
¼ cup extra virgin **olive oil**
¼ cup **raspberry vinegar**
2 medium **shallots**, minced
Salt or **seasoned salt**, as desired
Freshly ground **pepper**
3 bunches **watercress**, stems trimmed

- With knife, peel and pith oranges; cut into sections.
- Combine oranges and hearts of palm in a bowl.
- In another bowl, whisk together oils, vinegar, and shallots. Season as desired.
- Combine with orange sections and hearts of palm.
- Cover and chill well.
- Before serving, arrange watercress on 6 salad plates.
- Spoon marinated orange and hearts of palm on top of watercress.

SPINACH SALAD WITH FETA CHEESE AND BASIL DRESSING

Yield: 6 servings

½ cup **olive oil**
¼ cup **red wine vinegar**
5 fresh **basil** leaves or 1 tablespoon dried
2 teaspoons **sugar**
1 clove **garlic**, minced
Salt and **pepper**, to taste
1 pound fresh **spinach**
1 **avocado**, peeled and sliced
½ cup crumbled **feta cheese**
½ cup toasted **walnuts**, chopped (optional)
Greek olives (optional)

- Combine first 6 ingredients in blender and chill for 1 to 2 hours. Reserve as dressing for spinach.
- Toss spinach with dressing, avocado, cheese, walnuts, and olives.

Toasted pine nuts are also great in this salad.

Spinach Salad with Prosciutto Dressing

Yield: 6 servings

1   10-ounce bag **spinach**
2½   cups sliced **mushrooms**
½   cup chopped **walnuts**, toasted
½   cup (2 ounces) grated **Parmesan cheese**

Dressing:

6   tablespoons **olive oil**
¼   cup (1½ ounces) chopped **prosciutto ham**
2   tablespoons minced **garlic**
6   tablespoons dry **white wine**
6   tablespoons **lemon juice**
2   tablespoons **sugar**
     Salt and **pepper**

- Combine salad ingredients.
- Toss with enough dressing to season to taste.

Dressing:

- Heat oil in heavy small skillet over medium heat.
- Add prosciutto and garlic and sauté 3 minutes.
- Add wine, lemon juice, and sugar and simmer 5 minutes.
- Transfer dressing to bowl and cool completely.
- Season to taste with salt and pepper.

Cucumber Vinaigrette

Yield: 4 servings

¼   cup **Dijon mustard**
2   teaspoons **tarragon vinegar**
¾   cup **corn oil**
¼   cup chopped **green onions**
4   **cucumbers**, peeled, seeded, and julienned
     Salt and **pepper**

- Mix together mustard and vinegar.
- Whisk in oil slowly until well blended.
- Add onions and cucumbers; stir.
- Season with salt and pepper, to taste.
- Chill until ready to serve.

This easy and refreshing dressing is great for a summer tossed salad.

MARINATED CUCUMBER SALAD

Yield: 6 servings

2   **cucumbers**
1   **onion**
⅔   cup **salad oil**
3   tablespoons **tarragon vinegar**
2   tablespoons **lemon juice**
½   teaspoon **dry mustard**
½   teaspoon **salt**
½   teaspoon **paprika**
¼   cup **sugar**

- Slice cucumbers and onion thin.
- Mix remaining ingredients and pour over cucumbers and onion.
- Refrigerate for at least 2 hours.
- Stir once or twice while in refrigerator.
- Serve cold.

Refreshing summer salad.

FRESH ASPARAGUS VINAIGRETTE

Yield: 6 servings

2   to 2½ pounds **fresh asparagus**
    Boiling water
3½ teaspoons **salt**
3   tablespoons **cider vinegar**
¼   cup **salad oil**
2   tablespoons **olive oil**
½   teaspoon **sugar**
    Dash of **pepper**
1   hard-cooked **egg**, chopped
2   **sweet gherkins**, chopped

- Cut off ends of asparagus stalks.
- Rinse asparagus well.
- Remove scales and skin from lower part of stalks.
- Tie stalks into a bunch with string.

- Stand upright in a deep saucepan. Add boiling water to a depth of 2 inches, and 1½ teaspoons of the salt.
- Bring to boil; cook covered, 15 to 20 minutes, or until tender. Drain well.
- Lay stalks in a shallow baking dish.
- In a jar with tight-fitting lid, combine 2 teaspoons salt, vinegar, oils, sugar, and pepper; shake well.
- Pour dressing over asparagus. Refrigerate 1 hour, turning stalks several times.
- Arrange asparagus on platter, sprinkle with egg and pickle.

Excellent dish for Easter lunch.

STUFFED ENDIVE LEAVES

Yield: 6 servings

1   3-ounce package **cream cheese,** softened

½   teaspoon **basil**

1   teaspoon **olive oil**

2   ounces **feta cheese**

4   pitted and finely chopped **Greek olives**

1   large **plum tomato**, chopped

18 **endive leaves**
    Pine nuts for garnish (approximately 54)

- In a blender, blend cream cheese, basil, olive oil, and feta cheese until smooth.
- Gently stir in chopped olives. Refrigerate overnight.
- The next day, stir tomatoes into the stuffing mixture.
- Divide stuffing equally and spread on endive leaves.
- Sprinkle 3 pine nuts over cheese spread for garnish.
- Arrange on platter and serve.

A wonderful salad for entertaining since you make the stuffing a day ahead.

DILLED POTATO SALAD

Yield: 8 to 10 servings

3   pounds small **red potatoes** (in skins)
    Salt

2   tablespoons **white wine vinegar**

½   cup chopped fresh **dill**

½   cup chopped **scallions**

1½ cups diced **celery**

1   cup **sour cream**

½   cup **mayonnaise**

8   thin slices **prosciutto ham**, cut into bits

½   cup crumbled **blue cheese**

- Boil potatoes whole in salted water until fork tender.
- Drain and slice or quarter potatoes, leaving skin on.
- Put drained potatoes into large bowl and sprinkle with vinegar immediately.
- In separate bowl, combine dill, scallions, celery, sour cream, mayonnaise, prosciutto, and blue cheese.
- Pour dressing over potatoes. Toss gently to coat thoroughly.
- Cover; refrigerate 3 to 4 hours.

Extremely popular at large gatherings.

BROCCOLI SALAD

Yield: 8 servings

1 bunch **broccoli**
1 cup light **mayonnaise**
¼ cup **sugar**
2 tablespoons **cider vinegar**
1 cup **raisins**
1 cup **sunflower seeds**
8 slices cooked **bacon**, cut into bite-sized pieces

- Cut off broccoli florets. Peel stems. Cut into bite-sized pieces.
- Mix mayonnaise, sugar, and vinegar. Pour over broccoli.
- Add raisins, sunflower seeds, and bacon. Toss.

Great salad, and so easy to prepare!

SUNSHINE SALAD

Yield: 8 servings

1 head **red leaf lettuce**
1 head **Boston lettuce**
1 **pineapple**, peeled, cored, and cut into cubes
1 quart **strawberries**, hulled and halved
½ pound **green grapes**, cleaned and halved
4 ounces sliced **almonds**

Poppy Seed Dressing:

⅔ cup **sugar**
1 teaspoon **dry mustard**
1 teaspoon **paprika**
¼ teaspoon **salt**
1 tablespoon **poppy seeds**
⅓ cup **light honey**
5 tablespoons **vinegar**
1 tablespoon **lemon juice**
1 cup **salad oil**

- Tear lettuce into bite-sized pieces.
- Add fruit and nuts.
- Drizzle with Poppy Seed Dressing.
- Toss and serve.

Poppy Seed Dressing:

- Mix all ingredients except salad oil in a blender.
- Turn on blender and slowly drizzle salad oil into blender. Dressing will thicken to consistency of honey.

91

POPPY SEED SALAD

Yield: 6 servings

6   cups **salad greens** (red leaf, Boston, spinach)

Nut-Cheese-Fruit:

1   cup **pecans,**

1   cup **Brie,** cubed

1   cup **raspberries**

or

1   cup **cashews**

1   cup **Swiss cheese**, cubed

1   cup **strawberries**

or

1   cup **walnuts**

1   cup **Havarti cheese**

1   cup **red apples**, cubed

Dressing:

1   cup **salad oil**

½   cup **sugar**

⅓   cup **white wine vinegar**

    Dash **salt**

1   teaspoon prepared **mustard**

1   teaspoon **onion powder**

2   tablespoons **poppy seeds**

- Wash and tear lettuces.
- Choose one nut-cheese-fruit combination. Add to salad greens.
- Mix dressing ingredients with whisk or blender.
- Toss salad ingredients with dressing.

RAINBOW FRUIT BOWL

Yield: 8 servings

6   medium **peaches** or **nectarines**, peeled, pitted, and sliced (1½ pounds)

3   tablespoons fresh **lemon juice**

½   cup **water**

3   tablespoons **sugar**

1   tablespoon **cornstarch**
Dash ground **cinnamon**
Dash ground **cloves**

1   **banana**, sliced

1   pound **plums**, pitted and quartered

1   cup seedless **green grapes**, halved

1½   cups **blueberries**

6   or 8 **strawberries**, halved

- In large mixing bowl, toss half of the peaches or nectarines with 1 tablespoon lemon juice; set aside.
- In medium saucepan, combine remaining sliced peaches, water, and 1 tablespoon lemon juice. Bring to a boil; reduce heat.
- Cover and simmer 5 minutes or until very tender. Do not drain.
- Pour peaches and liquid into blender or food processor; process until smooth. Return to pan.
- In small mixing bowl, combine sugar, cornstarch, cinnamon, and cloves. Add to saucepan.
- Cook and stir until thickened and bubbly; cook and stir 2 minutes more. Cool.
- Toss banana with remaining lemon juice.
- Layer fruits in a 2-quart straight-sided glass bowl, using half of reserved peaches or nectarines, all of the plums, and all of the grapes.
- Alternate bananas and strawberries around outside of bowl with the cut side of fruit toward glass.
- Continue layering remaining peaches and all of the blueberries.
- Spoon peach sauce over all. Cover and chill.

A beautiful, flavorful fruit salad!

93

STRAWBERRY AND ROMAINE SALAD

Yield: 8 servings

1 head **romaine lettuce**, washed and torn
1 pint **fresh strawberries**, sliced
1 **red onion**, sliced
¼ cup slivered **almonds**

Dressing:

2 cups **mayonnaise**
⅔ cup **sugar**
⅓ cup **light cream**
⅓ cup **raspberry vinegar**
2 tablespoons **poppy seeds**
2 to 3 tablespoons **raspberry jam**

- Combine dressing ingredients; set aside.
- Toss romaine, strawberries, and onion.
- Just before serving, drizzle dressing over salad.
- Garnish with almonds.

Quick and easy salad. Looks wonderful and tastes refreshing! Dressing will keep at least a week in refrigerator. Good on fruit, too.

FLAMINGO SURPRISE

Yield: 8 servings

2 3-ounce packages **raspberry gelatin**
2 cups boiling **water**
1 16-ounce can jellied **cranberry sauce**
1 16-ounce carton **sour cream**

- Dissolve gelatin in boiling water in a large bowl.
- Add cranberry sauce and beat with whisk until blended. (Small bits of cranberry sauce may not get blended. This is fine.)
- Stir in sour cream. Blend well.
- Pour mixture in 1½-quart mold or any other container of that size.
- Place in refrigerator to set overnight.
- Serve on lettuce leaves and garnish with fruit if desired.

The surprise of this recipe is the ingredients. No one will guess what went into this gelatin salad until you tell them! A simple, yet delicious accompaniment to any meal.

Reuben Salad

Yield: 6 servings

1 head **lettuce**, torn into small pieces
3 large **dill pickles**, diced
1 cup **sauerkraut**, drained
1 6-ounce package **Buddig corned beef**, cut into julienne strips
½ cup **sour cream**
½ cup **mayonnaise**
2 teaspoons **Worcestershire sauce**
12 ounces shredded **Swiss cheese**

- Tear lettuce into small pieces.
- Add diced dill pickles, sauerkraut, and corned beef in layers.
- Mix the sour cream, mayonnaise, and Worcestershire sauce; frost with this mixture.
- Top with the shredded Swiss cheese.
- Let stand in refrigerator 3 to 4 hours for flavor to develop. Before serving; toss.

Fabulous! It's just like a Reuben sandwich!

Chicken Salad Supreme

Yield: 8 servings

½ cup **whipping cream**, whipped
1 cup **mayonnaise**
2 tablespoons minced **parsley**
1 teaspoon **salt**
¼ teaspoon **curry powder**
2½ cups diced, cooked **chicken**
1 cup chopped **celery**
½ cup chopped **almonds**, toasted
1 cup sliced **seedless grapes**
Lettuce leaves, for garnish
Ripe olives (optional)

- In a large bowl, fold whipped cream into mayonnaise.
- Add parsley, salt, and curry powder to mayonnaise mixture; stir until well blended.
- Add chicken, celery, and almonds; stir until evenly mixed.
- Gently fold in grapes.
- Serve cold on lettuce leaves; garnish with stuffed or ripe olives.

GATEWAY CHICKEN SALAD

Yield: 4 servings

¾ cup **sun-dried tomatoes**

⅔ cup bottled or homemade **pesto sauce**

2 cups cooked **chicken breast meat**, in chunks

3 ounces whole **pine nuts**

½ cup **black olives**

½ cup **golden raisins**

- Prepare sun-dried tomatoes according to package directions, and then slice them (i.e., blanch them in boiling water; soak 5 minutes in olive oil or pesto).
- Mix all ingredients in bowl.

Serve alone or over linguine in pesto sauce, with a slice of melon and sourdough baguette.

ORIENTAL CHICKEN SALAD

Yield: 8 servings

2 to 3 **chicken breasts**, cooked

½ to ¾ head **cabbage** (purple, green, or both)

4 green **scallions**

2 tablespoons **sesame seeds**

½ cup slivered **almonds**

1 3-ounce package **Ramen noodle chicken soup mix** (not cooked)

2 tablespoons **sugar**

3 tablespoons **vinegar**

2 tablespoons **soy sauce**

½ tablespoon **sesame oil**

- Cut chicken breasts into cubes. Set aside.
- Shred cabbage. Chop scallions. Combine; set aside.
- Combine sesame seeds and slivered almonds and toast at 350° approximately 8 to 10 minutes, making sure they don't burn.
- To make dressing, combine seasoning packet from soup mix with sugar, vinegar, soy sauce, and sesame oil; whisk to blend.
- Mix all salad ingredients together, except dressing and Ramen noodles.
- At last minute, break up Ramen noodles and put on top of salad, along with the dressing.

CHINESE CHICKEN SALAD

Yield: 6 servings

4 whole, bone-in **chicken breasts**, or 8 halves

½ 12-ounce package **won ton skins**, fried in oil until lightly brown
Salt

2 heads **lettuce**, shredded

1 bunch **green onions**, sliced thin, including tops

1 2-ounce package sliced **almonds**, toasted in oven

½ cup **sesame seeds**, toasted in oven

Dressing:

4 tablespoons **sugar**

2 teaspoons **salt**

4 tablespoons **white vinegar**

½ teaspoon **pepper**

½ cup **salad oil**

1 tablespoon **sesame oil**

- Cook chicken breasts. Remove bone and skin; shred chicken.
- Lightly salt the fried won ton skins and break into small pieces.
- Place all salad ingredients except almonds and sesame seeds in a double-bag grocery sack.
- Add dressing and shake vigorously.
- Empty into salad bowl and add toasted almonds and sesame seeds.
- Serve within 10 to 15 minutes of adding dressing (chilled plates help keep the salad crisp).

Dressing:

- Mix first 4 ingredients in a small jar until dissolved.
- Add oils. Shake well in jar and refrigerate.

Dressing can be made a day ahead.

CHICKEN SALAD
WITH HONEY MUSTARD DRESSING

Yield: 4 servings

4   cups **spinach**, torn into bite-sized pieces

1   **hard-cooked egg**, peeled and chopped

½   cup grated **carrot**

½   cup diced, cooked skinless **chicken**

¼   cup diced **celery**

¼   **apple**, diced

2   tablespoons chopped **walnuts** or **pecans**

1½ tablespoons **raisins**

Honey Mustard Dressing:

2   cups **vegetable oil**

⅔   cup **vinegar**

½   cup **honey**

2   tablespoons **lemon juice**

2   tablespoons **sugar**

1   teaspoon **dry mustard**

1   teaspoon **paprika**

½   teaspoon **salt**

¼   cup, plus 2 tablespoons **prepared mustard**

½   teaspoon **dried tarragon**

- Make individual salads, or arrange spinach in a large 2-quart bowl.
- Place egg on top of spinach; sprinkle carrot around edges.
- Mix chicken, celery, apple, walnuts, and raisins; place in center.
- Serve with Honey Mustard Dressing on side.

Honey Mustard Dressing:

- Blend all dressing ingredients for 45 seconds.
- Stir well before using; refrigerate leftovers (makes 4 cups).

LUNCHEON SALAD
WITH WHIPPED CUMIN DRESSING

Yield: 4 servings

½   head **Bibb lettuce**

½   head **Boston lettuce**

1   **chicken breast**, cooked, skinned, and cut into strips

4   slices **Swiss cheese**, cut into strips

8   slices of **cotto salami** or **ham**, cut into strips

1½   cups **mandarin oranges**

1   large or 2 small **avocados**, sliced

½   cup pitted **black ripe olives**, sliced

Cumin Dressing:

1   cup **whipping cream**, whipped

¼   cup **mayonnaise**

2   tablespoons **chili sauce**

1   tablespoon **lemon juice**

½   teaspoon ground **cumin**

⅛   teaspoon **dry mustard**

⅛   teaspoon **garlic salt**

- Blend dressing ingredients; chill.
- Arrange lettuce on individual plates.
- Divide chicken, cheese, salami, oranges, avocados, and olives. Arrange on plates in a spoke pattern.
- Just before serving, spoon dressing over top.

Assemble this salad ahead of time and add the dressing just before serving. You can also put white corn tortilla chips around the edge.

SALAD PIZZA

Yield: 6 servings

1 sheet **frozen Pepperidge Farm® puff pastry**

3 cups **mixed greens** (spinach, romaine, Boston, and iceberg lettuce)

¾ cup **artichoke hearts**, quartered

6 **cherry tomatoes**, halved

½ cup sliced pitted **ripe olives**

4 ounces **herbed cream cheese**, softened

2 teaspoons **Dijon mustard**

2 teaspoons **milk**

2 cups shredded **mozzarella cheese**

1 medium **avocado**, peeled and sliced

- Thaw pastry according to package directions.
- On a lightly floured surface, roll pastry to a 12-inch square.
- Cut pastry into a circle and place in round pizza pan; prick bottom generously.
- Bake at 375° for 15 minutes or until golden; cool.
- Combine greens, artichoke hearts, tomatoes, and olives in a bowl.
- In another bowl stir together cream cheese, mustard, and milk.
- Combine cheese mixture to greens; toss well to coat. Set aside.
- Preheat broiler.
- Sprinkle 1½ cups mozzarella cheese over crust.
- Broil just until cheese melts, approximately 1 minute.
- Spoon salad mixture over cheese.
- Sprinkle pizza with remaining cheese.
- Arrange avocado on top.
- Cut into wedges and serve.

A very different type of salad entrée.

MEDITERRANEAN PASTA SALAD

Yield: 20 servings

2   pounds **wagon wheel pasta**
     Vinegar
1   pound **feta cheese**, crumbled
1   6-ounce can **black olives**, sliced
4   pints cherry **tomatoes**, cut in half
4   **green peppers**, cut into ¼-inch strips
4   **red peppers**, cut into ¼-inch strips
3   small **cucumbers**, sliced
2   14-ounce cans **artichoke hearts**, quartered
2   pounds **salami**, sliced
1   **red onion**, cut into slices
20 **Greek olives**, pitted
2   or 3 small **zucchini**, sliced

Dressing:

2   cups **olive oil**
⅔   cup **red wine vinegar**
5   cloves **garlic**, minced
1½ teaspoons **oregano**
1½ teaspoons **salt**

- Blend dressing ingredients; chill.
- Cook pasta according to package directions; drain and sprinkle with 5 to 6 shakes of vinegar.
- Mix all ingredients together with pasta and dressing.

An appealing salad with a wonderful combination of meat, cheese, and veggies.

TORTELLINI AND ARTICHOKE SALAD WITH RED PEPPER DRESSING

Yield: 6 servings

8   ounces **tortellini**

1   7-ounce jar **roasted red peppers**

1   6-ounce jar **marinated artichokes**

2   tablespoons **red wine vinegar**

1   tablespoon **sugar**

¼   teaspoon **salt**

¾   teaspoon **garlic powder**

⅓   cup diced **green pepper**

1   10¾-ounce can **garbanzo beans** (optional)

- Cook tortellini according to package directions.

- Place red peppers in blender. Add ¼ cup liquid from artichokes.
- Cut artichokes into halves and set aside.
- Add vinegar, sugar, salt, and garlic powder to blender. Blend until smooth, stopping blender to scrape down sides of container.
- Drain cooked tortellini, rinse well with cold water, and place in large bowl.
- Add other ingredients. Toss with dressing.
- Cover and refrigerate at least 2 hours before serving.

CHINESE NOODLE AND SHRIMP SALAD

Yield: 4 servings

1½   cups **bean sprouts**, rinsed and drained

2   cups cooked **shrimp**

1   8-ounce can **water chestnuts**, drained and minced

¼   cup minced **green onions**

¼   cup minced **celery**

5   ounces **chow mein noodles**

Soy Mayonnaise:

¾   cup **mayonnaise**

1   tablespoon **lemon juice**

1   tablespoon **soy sauce**

⅜   teaspoon powdered **ginger**

- Combine bean sprouts, shrimp, water chestnuts, green onions, and celery in a bowl.
- Combine Soy Mayonnaise ingredients in a separate bowl and mix well.
- Add Soy Mayonnaise to salad and stir together; refrigerate.
- Just before serving toss with chow mein noodles, or serve on top of chow mein noodles.

This is a simple recipe which can be made in advance.

ORIENTAL CHOPPED SALAD

Yield: 6 to 8 servings
(4 to 6 for entrée)

1	to 2 types of **lettuce**, washed and dried very well
3	**green onions**, chopped (green and white parts)
1	**red bell pepper**, cut julienne style
6	ounces fresh **snow peas**, stemmed and cut julienne style
1	pound of large **shrimp**, grilled and peeled (can also use chicken, turkey, or pork)
1	3-ounce package **Ramen oriental hot and spicy soup mix** (not cooked)
¼	cup **rice vinegar**
1	tablespoon **soy sauce**
6	tablespoons **peanut** or **vegetable oil**
2	tablespoons **sesame seeds**
1	tablespoon **sesame oil** **Salt** and **pepper**, to taste

- In a large bowl combine lettuce, onions, bell pepper, pea pods, and shrimp.
- Crumble dry noodles from soup mix over the mixture and refrigerate.
- In a small bowl combine seasoning packet from soup mix with vinegar and soy sauce; whisk to blend.
- Whisk in peanut oil, sesame seeds, and sesame oil. Season to taste with salt and pepper.
- Just before serving, pour dressing over salad and toss.

Great as a meal or as a first course.

Tasty Pasta Tuna Salad

Yield: 6 to 8 servings

½   pound **pasta**

1   12½-ounce can chunk light or solid white **tuna**, drained and flaked

2   cups thinly sliced **cucumbers**

1   large **tomato**, seeded and chopped

½   cup sliced **celery**

¼   cup chopped **green pepper**

¼   cup sliced **green onions**

1   cup bottled **Italian dressing**

¼   cup **mayonnaise**

1   tablespoon **prepared mustard**

1   tablespoon **dillweed**

1   teaspoon **salt**

⅛   teaspoon **pepper**

- Prepare pasta according to package directions.
- In a large bowl, combine pasta, tuna, cucumbers, tomato, celery, green pepper, and onions.
- In a small bowl, blend together Italian dressing, mayonnaise, mustard, and seasonings.
- Add dressing mixture to salad mixture; toss to coat.
- Cover and chill.
- Toss before serving.

This salad is great for luncheons. You can make it the evening before.

Roquefort Cheese Salad Dressing

Yield: 2 cups

1   cup **Hellmann's® mayonnaise**

½   cup **sour cream**

1   tablespoon **lemon juice**

1   clove **garlic**, crushed

3   tablespoons minced **chives**

1   cup **Roquefort cheese**

    Salt and **pepper**

    Tarragon vinegar (optional)

- Mix slightly all ingredients and serve over salad or as dip.
- If too thick, dressing can be thinned with tarragon vinegar.

HOT SPINACH SALAD DRESSING

Yield: 12 servings

¾ pound **bacon**, cut up
¼ large **onion**, chopped
1 cup **cider vinegar**
1½ cups **sugar**
1 cup **mayonnaise**

- Fry bacon; reserve ½ cup grease in pan, but remove bacon.

- Fry onion in bacon grease until transparent. Add vinegar and bring to a boil. Add bacon and sugar.
- Add mayonnaise, one spoonful at a time, and stir until smooth.
- Serve over spinach.

HONEY MUSTARD SESAME DRESSING

Yield: 8 servings

2 tablespoons **sesame seeds**
2 tablespoons **cider vinegar**
2 tablespoons **honey**
2 tablespoons **Dijon mustard**
1 clove **garlic**, minced
4 tablespoons **salad oil**
   Freshly ground **pepper**

- Toast sesame seeds by broiling in a pie pan. Watch carefully so they don't burn.
- Combine all ingredients in a glass jar and shake well.
- Toss with a large bowl of assorted salad greens.

Everybody loves this simple dressing.

WHITE HORSE SALAD DRESSING

Yield: 2¾ cups

4 cloves **garlic**, minced
6 teaspoons **Dijon mustard**
2 teaspoons dried **basil**
1 teaspoon dried **thyme**
½ teaspoon **dry mustard**
¾ cup **wine vinegar**
   Salt and freshly ground **pepper**
2 cups extra virgin **olive oil**

- Mix all ingredients together in blender, adding the oil gradually.

This recipe comes from the White Horse Inn, Newport R.I.

LEMON-VERMOUTH DRESSING

Yield: 12 servings

1	small **onion**, grated
¾	teaspoon **paprika**
1½	teaspoons **dry mustard**
1	teaspoon **salt**
¼	teaspoon freshly ground **pepper**
½	cup freshly squeezed **lemon juice** (3 lemons)
1½	teaspoons **Worcestershire sauce**
⅓	cup dry **vermouth**
⅔	cup **oil** (half salad and half olive oil)

- Put onion, paprika, dry mustard, salt, pepper, and lemon juice into blender container. Blend thoroughly.
- Add Worcestershire sauce, vermouth, and oil.
- Blend again; chill before using over green salad.

Especially good over Bibb lettuce. Can also blend by hand or with electric mixer.

FANTASTIC MAYFAIR DRESSING

Yield: 3 cups

1	clove **garlic**, minced
1	rib **celery**, sliced
½	medium **onion**
1	2-ounce can flat **anchovies**
2	tablespoons **prepared mustard**
1	tablespoon **lemon juice**
1	teaspoon **pepper**
1	teaspoon (heaping) **salt**
½	teaspoon **sugar**
2	cups **salad oil**
3	**eggs**

- Blend first 9 ingredients in blender.
- Add salad oil, ¼ cup at a time.
- Mix in 3 eggs.
- Store in refrigerator.

This dressing is wonderful on any kind of lettuce.

MEATS

St. Louis is a melting
pot of ethnic groups
and food, and hearty
main course dishes served
in St. Louis homes often
originated many miles away.
This ethnic influence is also
seen in the abundance of
popular community festivals
held each year including
the Strassenfest; the annual
Greek Festival; and Bastille
Day and Mardi Gras celebra-
tions. A stroll through the
dramatically restored Union
Station, a National historic
landmark, also reveals a wide
array of delicious international treats.

. . .

Dierdorf & Hart's® Steak House

Launched in 1983 by former St. Louis Cardinal football legends Dan Dierdorf and Jim Hart, Dierdorf & Hart's captures the spirit of the New York steak houses of the 1930s and 1940s. Employing the old-time method of broiling from above, the steak is almost instantly seared and retains all of its natural juices. The result is a tender, mouth-wateringly flavorful cut of beef...thoroughly reminiscent of the lavish post-depression era.

Beef Buying Tips

Buy your beef from a reputable grocery store or butcher shop. Get to know the butchers and speak with them any time you are making a beef selection. When selecting cut steaks, pay attention to how well-trimmed they are; there is no reason to pay for too much fat.

If you don't see a cut that suits your needs, ask the butcher to cut one for you. The grade, cut, and type of meat you're using will dictate how it should be prepared. For example, a prime tenderloin, closely trimmed, should not be marinated.

Whether you're cooking a roast or grilling a tenderloin, don't overcook the meat. Even a well-done piece of beef should have some of the natural juices left in it.

FRONTENAC HILTON'S POTOSI BISON STEW

Yield: 10 servings

2   tablespoons **peanut oil**
3   pounds cubed **bison stew meat**
¼   teaspoon chopped **garlic**
2   tablespoons diced **onion**
3   **apples**, cored and diced
3   **whole cloves**
1   **cinnamon stick**
2   **bay leaves**
½   teaspoon ground **allspice**
¼   teaspoon cracked **black pepper**
¼   teaspoon ground **nutmeg**
½   cup **Burgundy wine**
2   quarts **beef stock**
4   tablespoons **cornstarch**
    Water

- In a large stockpot, heat the peanut oil.
- Add bison stew meat and brown well on all sides.
- Add remaining ingredients, except cornstarch and water, and bring to a boil; reduce heat to simmer.
- Cover and simmer approximately 1½ hours or until meat is fork tender.
- Drain liquid into smaller pot.
- Bring liquid to a boil.
- Dissolve cornstarch in enough water to make a thick paste.
- Add the cornstarch mixture to the boiling liquid, whisking until thickened.
- Combine sauce and meat and serve.

This recipe was developed to highlight the fact that Missouri's Sayersbrook Farms raises apples for cider and also feeds apples to their bison.

Saint Louis Club Bison Fajitas

Yield: 6 servings

2 pounds **bison meat**, cut into finger-sized strips

2 cups **olive oil**

½ cup **red wine**

Dash of aged **vinegar**, such as balsamic or red wine vinegar

2 tablespoons ground **cumin**

2 handfuls coarsely chopped fresh **oregano**

2 large **onions**, diced

3 **bell peppers**, cut into strips

1 **Anaheim chili**, diced

2 **tomatoes**, diced

½ bunch **cilantro**, leaves only

Flour **tortillas**

Fresh **salsa**

- In a nonreactive bowl, combine olive oil, wine, vinegar, cumin, and oregano.
- Add meat to mixture; cover and marinate overnight in refrigerator.
- Drain meat well. Heat skillet until very hot; add more olive oil.
- Working quickly before oil can scorch, add drained meat to pan and brown well. The skillet must be quite hot so that the meat will sear, not boil.
- When meat is cooked to medium-rare, remove from pan and reserve.
- Into the same pan, add onions, peppers, and chili; cook until tender.
- Return meat to pan, along with tomatoes.
- Cook together 2 minutes. Add cilantro.
- Serve with warm tortillas and fresh salsa.

Bison adds an especially authentic Southwest touch to this fabulous fajita recipe from the Saint Louis Club's chef Bryan Carr.

DONOVAN'S VEAL GORGONZOLA

Yield: 1 serving

2 slices provimi **veal** or **veal leg** sliced thin
   Flour
2 teaspoons **olive oil**
¼ cup **cream** or **half-and-half**
2 tablespoons crumbled **Gorgonzola** or **blue cheese**
¼ teaspoon **butter**
1 teaspoon minced **garlic**
2 teaspoons **chicken stock**
1 pinch ground **red pepper**
   Salt and **pepper**, to taste

- Lightly pound veal under plastic wrap. Dust with flour.
- Heat the olive oil in a skillet. Add veal and cook 30 seconds on each side.
- Remove veal to serving dish; drain oil from skillet.
- Add to the skillet the cream, Gorgonzola, butter, garlic, chicken stock, red pepper, and salt and pepper.
- Heat sauce to a boil. Cover veal with sauce and serve.

Don Grahl of Donovan's Restaurant shares this long-time favorite.

SPIEDINI

Yield: 4 servings

8 2-ounce **veal scallops**, pounded about ⅛ inch thick
8 paper-thin slices **prosciutto ham**
8 slices **provolone cheese**, sliced ¼ inch thick and cut into 1 x 4-inch rectangles
⅓ cup **olive oil**
¾ cup Italian **bread crumbs**
2 **onions**, cut in wedges
4 **bay leaves**

- Top each piece of veal with 1 piece of prosciutto and 1 piece of cheese.
- Roll layers so that veal is on the outside.
- Dip each roll into olive oil and Italian bread crumbs.
- Thread veal roll, onion wedge, bay leaf, and another veal roll onto skewer. Repeat until all rolls are on skewers.
- Place skewers on a baking sheet, cover with foil, and bake at 350° for 15 to 18 minutes.
- Remove foil and place baking sheet under broiler for 1 minute or until golden.

VEGETABLE MEAT LOAF

Yield: 6 servings

2 teaspoons **olive oil**
½ cup chopped **onion**
1 cup shredded **carrots**
⅔ cup shredded **cabbage**
¾ cup mixed chopped **green and red sweet pepper**
1 teaspoon minced **garlic**
1 **egg**
1 **egg white**
½ teaspoon **salt**
1 teaspoon **basil**
¼ teaspoon **oregano**
½ teaspoon **pepper**
1 tablespoon **Worcestershire sauce**
⅓ cup **bread crumbs**
1 pound lean **ground sirloin**

- Sauté first 6 ingredients for 5 minutes on medium-high, then 10 to 15 minutes on medium-low.
- Remove from heat and cool.
- Combine remaining ingredients and then add vegetables.
- Place in loaf pan.
- Bake at 350° for 1 hour.
- Remove juices (drain) and bake 15 minutes more.

Don't let this humble dish fool you. It's fabulous and much healthier than the traditional recipe.

RACK OF LAMB

Yield: 8 servings

4 heaping teaspoons **Dijon mustard**
1 teaspoon **rosemary**
1 teaspoon **thyme**
1 teaspoon **oregano**
1 teaspoon **basil**
1 teaspoon **marjoram**
1 teaspoon **black pepper**
2 **racks of lamb**, 8 chops to a rack

- Combine mustard and spices; brush mixture on lamb.
- Wrap lamb in plastic wrap and marinate for 24 hours in refrigerator.
- Broil for 15 minutes. Outside will be medium while inside remains rare.

For added flavor try grilling the lamb.

AGNEAU À LA MOUTARDE

Yield: 8 servings

1	8-ounce jar **Dijon mustard**
½	cup **olive oil**
2	to 3 cloves **garlic**, minced
1	teaspoon crushed **rosemary**
1	teaspoon **thyme**
1	teaspoon crushed **bay leaves**
1	6-pound **leg of lamb**, boned and butterflied

- Mix first 6 ingredients to make marinade.
- Slash lamb and spread marinade generously on all sides.
- Cover and marinate for several hours, or overnight in refrigerator.
- Grill 25 to 30 minutes for medium.
- Reserve marinade for basting, or heat and serve as a sauce with the meat.

Note that weight of lamb (6 pounds) is before it is boned.

BARBECUED BEEF BRISKET

Yield: 10 servings

2	ounces **liquid smoke**
2	tablespoons **chili powder**
2	tablespoons **Lea & Perrins®️ steak sauce**
1	tablespoon **cayenne pepper**
1	tablespoon **sugar**
3	tablespoons **A.1.®️ steak sauce**
2	cups **apple cider vinegar**
1	2- to 4-pound **beef brisket Barbecue sauce**

- Combine first 7 ingredients in saucepan and bring to a boil. Remove from heat and cool.
- Put brisket in a baking pan and pour sauce over top.
- Cover with foil and refrigerate for 24 hours.
- Bake at 225° for 10 to 12 hours.
- Remove brisket from marinade and chill. Discard marinade.
- When cold, slice across the grain and layer in a baking dish.
- Baste with barbecue sauce and reheat.

This recipe must be made ahead. This method of marinating and slow cooking causes the beef to fall apart because it is so tender.

BARBECUED VEAL CHOPS

Yield: 4 servings

4	10-ounce **veal chops**
4	cloves **garlic**, finely minced
1	tablespoon finely minced fresh **ginger**
1	tablespoon grated or finely minced **lemon peel**
1	tablespoon grated or finely minced **orange peel**
4	to 6 tablespoons **chives**, minced
⅓	cup **lemon juice**
¼	cup **orange juice**
3	tablespoons **dry sherry**
3	tablespoons extra virgin **olive oil**
2	tablespoons **Dijon mustard**
2	tablespoons low-sodium **soy sauce**
½	teaspoon freshly ground **pepper**
2	ounces **macadamia nuts**, roasted

- Place chops in a single layer in a nonreactive dish.
- Combine all the remaining ingredients except the nuts.
- Pour the marinade over the chops and marinate 1 to 3 hours.
- Drain and reserve the marinade.
- Coarsely chop macadamia nuts with a knife (not a food processor).
- To grill meat, brush grilling rack with oil after coals are hot.
- Place chops on grill and cook 10 minutes on each side, basting with the reserved marinade.
- The veal is done when the internal temperature reaches 150° and the meat feels firm when pressed with your fingers.
- Place chops on dinner plates.
- Transfer marinade to small saucepan, bring to boil, and spoon over chops.
- Sprinkle with macadamia nuts.
- Serve at once.

VEAL SCALLOPINI
WITH ARTICHOKE CREAM SAUCE

Yield: 4 servings

8   large **shiitake mushrooms**, stems removed and discarded

3   tablespoons **olive oil**

1   **shallot**, minced

4   **artichoke hearts**, slivered

8   slices **veal scallopini**

¼   cup **flour**

½   cup **white wine**

½   cup **chicken broth**

1   tablespoon dried **basil** (or 3 tablespoons chopped fresh)

½   cup **heavy cream**

2   tablespoons grated **Parmesan cheese**

- Slice shiitake mushrooms. In a large skillet, sauté mushrooms in 2 tablespoons of the olive oil.
- Add shallot and sauté until soft. Add artichoke hearts, stir, and then set mushroom mixture aside in a bowl.
- Dip veal in flour to lightly coat both sides.
- Add remaining tablespoon olive oil to the skillet. Heat to medium-high.
- Sauté veal 2 minutes on first side, turn, then sauté 1 minute on other side. Remove from pan. (Veal scallopini is very thin and cooks quickly. If it is over-cooked, it will become tough.)
- Add the wine to sauté pan and cook for 3 minutes on medium-high. Be sure to scrape the pan drippings from the bottom, which will add flavor to the sauce.
- Add the chicken broth. Cook 3 minutes, and then add mushroom mixture.
- Add basil, heavy cream, and Parmesan cheese. Stir well and let sauce bubble slightly.
- Put veal into sauce just to heat, then remove.
- Serve veal with sauce on top.

The combination of flavors make this veal entrée unique and fabulous!

VEAL FORESTIES

Yield: 2 to 4 servings

1½ pounds **veal cutlet**, sliced thin and pounded
Garlic, to taste
Flour
¼ cup **butter** or **margarine**
½ pound sliced **mushrooms**
Salt and **pepper**, to taste
⅓ cup **dry vermouth**
2 teaspoons **lemon juice**
Chopped **parsley**

- Rub veal with garlic and coat with flour.
- Heat butter in large skillet; sauté veal until brown.
- Place mushrooms on top of veal and sprinkle with salt and pepper. Add vermouth.
- Cover and cook on low heat for 25 minutes until tender.
- Sprinkle with lemon juice and parsley just before serving.

FILET DU BOEUF AU POIVRE VERT

Yield: 4 servings

1 2-pound **beef tenderloin**
½ cup (1 stick) **butter**, softened
3 tablespoons **Dijon mustard**
½ cup **flour**
Sauce:
2 tablespoons **butter**
2 tablespoons **green peppercorns** (packed in brine, not vinegar)
½ cup **dry white wine**
½ cup **heavy cream**
1 tablespoon **Dijon mustard** (optional)

- Meat should be at room temperature; pat dry.
- Mix together next three ingredients and rub over beef.

- Bake tenderloin at 450° for 25 minutes for rare, 30 minutes for medium-rare, 35 minutes for well-done.
- Cool meat for 15 minutes before slicing.
- Pour sauce over beef or put sauce in a sauceboat.

Sauce:

- Melt butter.
- Add peppercorns to pan and mash slightly with wooden spoon; sauté for 1 minute.
- Pour in wine, cook 1 minute, then add cream.
- Reduce mixture over fairly high heat until slightly thickened.
- For stronger mustard flavor, add 1 tablespoon Dijon mustard.

ELEGANT BEEF TENDERLOIN

Yield: 8 servings

1	4-pound **beef tenderloin**
½	cup (1 stick) **butter**
2	tablespoons **tarragon**
1	clove **garlic**, minced
	Salt and **pepper**

- In a small pan, combine butter, tarragon, and minced garlic.
- Simmer together for 10 minutes over medium heat.
- Salt and pepper beef.
- Bake beef at 450° for 20 minutes.
- Pour butter mixture over the meat at this point.
- Continue to baste every few minutes while baking for 20 minutes more.

LIBERTY HALL
MARINATED BEEF TENDERLOIN

Yield: 4 to 6 servings

½	cup **ruby port**
¼	cup **olive oil**
¼	cup **soy sauce**
½	teaspoon **pepper**
½	teaspoon **thyme**, crushed
¼	teaspoon **hot pepper sauce**
1	**bay leaf**
1½	pounds boneless **beef tenderloin**, cut into 1½-inch slices

- Mix first 7 ingredients and pour over steaks.
- Cover and refrigerate 3 to 6 hours, turning occasionally.
- Remove steaks from marinade.
- Place steaks on a broiler pan and place in cold oven.
- Broil 3 inches from heat 7 minutes; turn and broil 7 minutes more.

This tenderloin recipe is from an historic bed and breakfast inn in South Carolina.

Peppercorn Beef Tenderloin

Yield: 6 to 8 servings

1	**beef tenderloin**, 3 to 4 pounds
3	tablespoons **Dijon mustard**
1½	tablespoons coarsely ground **green pepper-corn**
3	tablespoons coarsely ground **5-peppercorn blend**
8	**sage leaves**, large and fresh
2	tablespoons **butter**, unsalted and at room temperature
	Salt to taste, if desired.
4	**bay leaves**
	Béarnaise sauce (McCormick®)

- Cut tenderloin down middle, lengthwise, ½ to ⅔ way down.
- Spread mustard over split area.
- Spread green peppercorn and press into meat.
- Sprinkle half of 5-peppercorn blend over split area.
- Place sage leaves in row down middle.
- Close back to original shape and tie with string in several places.
- Rub outside with butter.
- Press remaining pepper blend to outside and sprinkle with salt (to taste).
- Place split side down in shallow baking dish.
- Place bay leaves under strings on unsplit side.
- Bake at 425°, 8 minutes per pound for medium rare.
- Let stand 5 minutes before carving.
- Pour juice over sliced meat.
- Serve with béarnaise sauce.

You can prepare ahead and refrigerate.

FILETS OF BEEF CHASSEUR

Yield: 8 servings

3	**garlic cloves**, crushed
1½	teaspoons **seasoned salt**
¼	teaspoon **pepper**
8	8-ounce **beef tenderloin** filets, sliced 1 inch thick
6	tablespoons **butter**
2	tablespoons **brandy**
3	tablespoons **flour**
2	teaspoons **tomato paste**
¾	cup **dry red wine**
1	cup **chicken broth**
½	cup **beef broth**
½	cup **water**
¼	teaspoon **Worcestershire sauce**
2	tablespoons **currant jelly**
½	pound fresh **mushrooms**, sliced

- Combine half of the garlic, the seasoned salt, and pepper; rub on steaks.
- Sauté steaks in 2 tablespoons of the butter until brown on outside with center raw.
- Arrange steaks in a 9 x 13-inch casserole dish.
- Cook brandy in same skillet over moderate heat, stirring constantly and scraping up the brown bits.
- Add remaining 4 tablespoons butter. Stir in flour.
- Reduce heat to low, stirring, until mixture is golden.
- Stir in tomato paste and remaining garlic; mixture will be thick and grainy.
- Remove from heat; whisk in wine, chicken broth, beef broth, and water.
- Bring to a boil over moderate heat, stirring constantly.
- Reduce heat and simmer 10 minutes; stir until liquid is reduced by a third.
- Add Worcestershire and currant jelly; when jelly is melted add mushrooms.
- Adjust seasonings to taste and thin sauce to coating consistency.
- Cool and pour over steaks.
- At this point steaks may be covered and refrigerated overnight. Allow steaks to warm to room temperature before cooking.
- Bake uncovered at 400° for 15 to 20 minutes for rare, 20 to 25 minutes for medium to medium-well.

This elegant beef entrée will get rave reviews at a dinner party and can be prepared ahead of time.

BOEUF BOURGUIGNONNE
(BEEF BURGUNDY)

Yield: 6 servings

2   pounds **round steak**, cut in 1½-inch cubes or strips

2   tablespoons **butter** or **bacon fat**

2   tablespoons **sherry**, heated
Salt

24 small white **onions**, canned or fresh

12 large **mushrooms**, quartered

1   teaspoon **tomato paste**

1   teaspoon **meat glaze** (optional)

3   tablespoons **flour**

1   cup beef **consommé**

1   cup **red wine**
Salt and **pepper**

½   teaspoon **Bouquet Garni**

2   tablespoons chopped **parsley**

- Brown meat quickly in hot fat then place in casserole dish.
- Pour heated sherry over meat. Sprinkle lightly with salt.
- Sauté onions and mushrooms in remaining fat; then place on top of beef.
- Stir tomato paste, meat glaze, and flour into skillet.
- Slowly add consommé and ¼ cup of wine. Bring to a boil stirring constantly.
- Season to taste with salt and pepper. Add Bouquet Garni and parsley.
- Pour mixture over meat.
- Cover and cook 3 hours at 250°.
- Add remaining wine at intervals during cooking.

This dish is a great entrée to serve for casual entertaining. It can be made ahead and frozen.

SUKIYAKI

Yield: 4 to 6 servings

1   pound **beef tenderloin**
     or **sirloin steak**
2   tablespoons **salad oil**
½   cup **beef broth**
2   tablespoons **sugar**
⅓   cup **soy sauce**
½   pound thinly sliced
     mushrooms
1   bunch **green onions**, cut
     into 1½-inch lengths
2   large **onions**, thinly sliced
1   8-ounce can **bamboo
     shoots**, drained
1   8-ounce can sliced **water
     chestnuts**, drained
3   **celery stalks**, sliced
     diagonally
3   cups fresh **spinach**
     Cooked **rice**

- Cut meat into strips about ¼ inch thick and 2 inches long.
- In large skillet or wok, heat oil; brown meat. Push meat to one side.
- Stir in broth, sugar, and soy sauce.
- Place mushrooms, onions, bamboo shoots, water chestnuts, and celery in a separate section of pan.
- Cover; simmer 10 minutes.
- Add spinach; simmer 5 minutes.
- Serve with rice.

A delicious and healthy entrée.

FRENCH BEEF STEW (BEEF CASSOULET)

Yield: 6 to 8 servings

3	pounds **stew beef**
3	large **carrots**, diced
1	16-ounce can small **onions**, drained
1	2-pound can **tomatoes** (2½ cups), do not drain
1	16-ounce can French-style **green beans**, drained
3	to 4 **potatoes**, cubed
½	10¾-ounce can beef **consommé**
½	cup **white wine**
4	tablespoons **Minute®** **tapioca**
1	tablespoon **brown sugar**
1½	tablespoons **salt**
½	cup **bread crumbs**
1	**bay leaf**

- Layer beef, carrots, onions, tomatoes, beans, and potatoes in order, in large stew or stockpot.
- Combine consommé, wine, tapioca, brown sugar, and salt; pour over meat and vegetables.
- Sprinkle bread crumbs on top. Lay bay leaf on top of bread crumbs.
- Cover pot and place in a 250° oven for 6 to 7 hours.
- Stir periodically to prevent sticking.
- Remove bay leaf before serving.

Great party stew—especially in sourdough "bowls"!

FIVE-HOUR BEEF STEW CASSEROLE

Yield: 8 servings

2   pounds lean **beef**, cut in small pieces
1   cup **celery**
6   medium **carrots**, sliced
3   sliced **onions**
1   20-ounce can **tomatoes**
1   tablespoon **sugar**
1   tablespoon **salt**
3   tablespoons **tapioca**
1   cup **bread crumbs**
     Other **seasonings**, by choice

- Mix ingredients together.
- Put in a covered deep Dutch oven or casserole.
- Bake at 250° for 5 hours, stirring occasionally.
- Serve over rice, pasta, or mashed potatoes.

This stew is ideal to serve in cold weather. The slow cooking time enhances the flavor and tenderness of the meat and vegetables.

CHINESE POT ROAST

Yield: 8 to 10 servings

4   pounds **chuck roast**
½   teaspoon **dry mustard**
1   clove **garlic**, crushed
¼   teaspoon **pepper**
1   tablespoon **cooking oil** or **shortening**
¾   cup **beer**
¼   cup **soy sauce**
1   tablespoon **honey**

- Blend mustard, garlic, and pepper. Rub into roast.
- Heat 1 tablespoon shortening or oil until smoking hot.
- Brown roast on both sides.
- Put roast into casserole.
- Pour remaining ingredients into skillet. Turn off heat and scrape the pan, pouring all the contents over the roast.
- Cover and cook at 325° to 350° for 2½ to 3 hours. You may thicken the gravy when the roast is done.

This roast is very tender and makes a good gravy.

HEAVENLY MEAT SAUCE

Yield: 4 to 6 servings

1	pound **ground chuck**
½	cup chopped **onion**
1	large clove **garlic**, crushed
1	cup minced **parsley**
3½	cups chopped **tomatoes**, canned or fresh
1½	cups **tomato paste**
2	cups **water**
1	large **bay leaf**
½	teaspoon **oregano**
½	teaspoon **basil**
1	teaspoon **salt**
¼	teaspoon **pepper**
2	teaspoons **sugar**

- In a large saucepan, brown chuck with onion.
- Add garlic and parsley. Sauté 1 minute.
- Mix in tomatoes, tomato paste, water, and seasonings. Stir to break up tomatoes and blend well.
- Simmer uncovered 1 hour, stirring occasionally.
- Remove bay leaf, and serve with cooked pasta of your choice.

This sauce freezes well. Mushrooms may be added if desired.

MOSTACCIOLI SAUCE

Yield: 6 to 8 servings

1⅓	cups chopped **onions**
1	clove **garlic**, chopped or crushed
½	cup chopped **green pepper**
½	cup sliced **mushrooms**
½	cup **cooking oil**
1½	pounds **ground beef**
2	6-ounce cans **tomato paste**
2½	cups chopped **tomatoes**
1	teaspoon **salt**

- In a Dutch oven or large pot, lightly brown onions, garlic, green pepper, mushrooms, and ground beef in oil. (Oil may be reduced or deleted, if desired.)
- Add tomato paste, tomatoes, and salt. Simmer 40 to 60 minutes.
- Add water if necessary.
- Serve with cooked mostaccioli.

Kids love this sauce!

CALYPSO ROAST PORK

Yield: 8 servings

1	tablespoon pressed **garlic**
1	tablespoon **ginger**
1	teaspoon **salt**
1	teaspoon **allspice**
¼	teaspoon freshly ground **pepper**
2	tablespoons **dark rum**, divided
3½	pounds boneless **pork loin roast**
⅔	cup firmly packed **brown sugar**
1	tablespoon **lime juice**

- In a small bowl, combine spices and 1 tablespoon of the rum; mix to a smooth paste.
- Score fat side of pork in a diamond pattern.
- Rub sides of pork well with spice mixture.
- Cover with plastic wrap and refrigerate overnight.
- Preheat oven to 450°.
- Place roast, fat side up, on a rack in a roasting pan.
- Place in oven and immediately reduce temperature to 325°. Cook 1 hour and 15 minutes.
- Meanwhile, in a small bowl combine brown sugar with remaining 1 tablespoon rum and lime juice. Spoon over top of roast.
- Continue roasting until surface is crusty and meat thermometer reaches 165°, about 30 minutes.

Prepare night before, and pop into oven. This recipe always receives rave reviews, and requires very little attention during cooking. Great for dinner parties!

JAKARTA CHOPS

Yield: 4 to 6 servings

6	or 8 loin **pork chops** (1 to 1½ inches thick)
	Salt and **pepper**
3	tablespoons **cooking oil**
¼	cup chopped **onion**
1	16-ounce can sliced **peaches** in syrup
2	tablespoons **brown sugar**
2	tablespoons **soy sauce**
1	teaspoon ground **ginger**
¼	teaspoon **dry mustard**
¼	teaspoon **garlic powder**
1	**bell pepper**
	Cooked **rice**

- Sprinkle chops with salt and pepper.
- Heat oil in large skillet; cook chops 15 minutes each side, then remove from heat.
- Drain oil from skillet, reserving about 2 to 3 tablespoons.
- Sauté onion in oil for 5 minutes or until clear.
- Return chops to skillet.
- Drain peaches, reserving syrup.
- Mix syrup, sugar, soy sauce, ginger, dry mustard, and garlic powder in bowl, then pour over chops.
- Cover and simmer for 30 minutes.
- Cut bell pepper into thin strips; add pepper strips and peaches to skillet.
- Simmer an additional 5 minutes.
- Serve over hot rice.

A new twist to sweet-and-sour pork.

PORK CHOPS WITH KIWI SAUCE

Yield: 4 servings

4	**pork chops** (about ½ inch thick)
1	tablespoon cooking **oil**
½	teaspoon **salt**
½	cup **apple juice**
2	tablespoons packed **brown sugar**
2	tablespoons **lime juice**
1	teaspoon **cornstarch**
¼	cup cold **water**
1	or 2 **kiwi fruit**, peeled and chopped

- Brown pork chops in oil, using a 10-inch skillet over medium heat; drain.
- Sprinkle with salt.
- Mix together apple juice, brown sugar, and lime juice; pour over pork chops.
- Heat to boiling; reduce heat.
- Cover and simmer until pork chops are tender, 20 to 25 minutes.
- Remove pork chops to a warm platter; keep warm.
- Mix cornstarch and water; gradually stir into skillet.
- Heat to boiling; stirring constantly.
- Boil and stir 1 minute.
- Stir in kiwi fruit.
- Pour over pork chops, placing slices of kiwi fruit on top of each pork chop.

A truly unique, attractive dish— easy to prepare!

PORK TENDERLOIN KOREAN

Yield: 8 to 10 servings

6   to 8 strips of **bacon**
3   to 4 **pork tenderloins**
½   cup **soy sauce**
1   tablespoon grated **onion**
1   clove **garlic**, crushed
1   tablespoon **vinegar**
¼   teaspoon **cayenne pepper**
½   cup **sugar**

- Wrap bacon around tenderloins; fasten with wooden picks.
- Place meat in a baking dish.
- Combine remaining ingredients; pour over meat.
- Let stand in refrigerator for 4 to 5 hours, turning meat at least once while marinating.
- Roast in a preheated 300° oven 1½ hours or until meat thermometer reaches 170°; baste occasionally, turning meat once. Serve pan juices separately to spoon over meat.

Wonderful and easy party dish!

PRIVATE-LABEL SEASONED SALT

Yield: 1¼ cups

1   cup **salt**
1½   teaspoons dried **oregano leaves**
1   teaspoon **garlic salt**
2½   teaspoons **paprika**
1   teaspoon **curry powder**
2   teaspoons **dry mustard**
½   teaspoon **onion powder**
¼   teaspoon dried **dillweed** (optional)

- Combine all ingredients and mix well.
- Pour into handsome jars with tight-fitting lids.

Nice, small gift. Wonderful on chicken or pork.

The rural-inspired fried chicken dinner has given way to a myriad of new and healthy ways to prepare chicken and other fowl. While St. Louis is a leading urban center, many St. Louisans regularly take time to enjoy the nearby countryside. Popular day trips include such scenic destinations as the Shaw Arboretum; the Daniel Boone Home; Purina Farms; the wineries in Augusta, MO; and historic Missouri towns including Ste. Genevieve, Hermann, and Kimmswick.

• • •

Cardwell's

Founded in 1987 by partners Chef Bill Cardwell and Rich Gorczyca, Cardwell's is a "seasonal cuisine restaurant and bar." The Cardwell's menu changes from season to season and is best described as Modern American. Located in the heart of Clayton, Missouri, Cardwell's was the front-runner in improving dining in Clayton and continues to be a leader among St. Louis restaurants.

PECAN WOOD GRILLED BREAST OF CHICKEN WITH JICAMA RELISH

Yield: 4 servings

4	whole, boneless, skinless **chicken breasts**
½	cup virgin **olive oil**
½	cup **dry vermouth**
½	cup **Dijon mustard** (regular or grain)
1	tablespoon minced fresh **tarragon**
1	tablespoon minced fresh **chives**
2	teaspoons cracked fresh **black pepper**
1	teaspoon **kosher salt**
1	teaspoon natural **lemon pepper**

- Lay chicken breasts flat in porcelain, ceramic, or nonmetal pan.
- Combine remaining ingredients; mix well and pour over chicken.
- Marinate 2 hours at room temperature or 8 hours in refrigerator.
- Remove chicken from marinade. Reserve marinade for basting.
- Grill chicken over hot coals approximately 5 minutes on each side, basting with marinade, until chicken is cooked.
- Serve topped with Jicama Relish.

JICAMA RELISH

⅓	cup extra virgin **olive oil**
⅔	cup **white wine vinegar**
	Salt, to taste
2	teaspoons minced fresh **oregano**
4	tablespoons minced fresh **cilantro**
1	tablespoon finely minced fresh **garlic**
1	large **jicama** (approximately 1 to 1½ pounds), peeled and diced into ¼-inch squares
2	to 3 **carrots**, peeled, diced, and blanched and cooled
1	medium **red onion**, peeled and diced into ¼-inch pieces
1	seedless **cucumber**, diced into ¼-inch squares
1	fresh **jalapeño pepper**, seeded and minced (approximately 2 teaspoons)
1	medium **red pepper**, seeded and diced into ¼-inch pieces

- In a bowl, combine the olive oil, vinegar, salt, oregano, cilantro, and garlic. Blend well.
- In a separate bowl, combine the vegetables.
- Add the dressing ingredients to the vegetables and coat well.
- Marinate 1 to 2 hours before serving. Serve well chilled.

Cardwell's grills its chicken over a wood grill. If you do not have pecan wood, use wood chips with charcoal.

FIO'S CHILLED SHIITAKE MUSHROOM AND PHEASANT SURPRISE

Yield: 1 serving

1   2-ounce boneless, skinless **pheasant breast**, all fat removed

3   fresh **shiitake mushrooms**, stems removed
     Pepper
     Low-sodium **soy sauce**

¼   cup **red wine**

3   **tomatoes**, peeled and seeded

1   cup plain nonfat **yogurt**

3   tablespoons **lemon juice**
     Curry powder, to taste

1   small clove **garlic**
     Cucumber slices and fresh **dill** for garnish

- Pound pheasant to form a thin, wide medallion; cut into 3 equal pieces.
- Season each mushroom with pepper and 1 or 2 drops of soy sauce.
- Wrap pheasant around each mushroom. Be sure to completely cover the top of each mushroom and not leave any part of it exposed.
- Place medallions in an oven-safe pan and season with pepper and red wine.
- Poach at 375° for 10 to 12 minutes. Pheasant should be cooked, but not dry.
- Remove pheasant from oven and chill in its own juices.
- Blend tomatoes, yogurt, lemon juice, curry powder, and garlic in a food processor. Chill.
- Spread sauce on a plate, top with pheasant, and garnish with cucumber slices and fresh dill.

This elegant entrée comes from Fio's LaFourchette restaurant.

SAVORY CRESCENT CHICKEN SQUARES

Yield: 4 servings

1	3-ounce package **cream cheese**, softened
2	tablespoons **margarine** or **butter**, softened
2	cups cooked **chicken breast**, cubed
¼	teaspoon **salt**
¼	teaspoon **pepper**
2	tablespoons **milk**
1	tablespoon **parsley**
1	tablespoon chopped **onion**
1	8-ounce package refrigerated **crescent rolls**
	Melted **butter**
	Bread crumbs or **crushed croutons**

- Blend cream cheese and margarine until smooth.
- Add chicken, salt, pepper, milk, parsley, and onion.
- Separate crescent rolls into 4 rectangles. Seal perforations.
- Spoon chicken mixture into center of rectangle. Pull up 4 corners.
- Brush with melted butter. Place squares on baking sheet.
- Sprinkle with bread crumbs or crushed croutons.
- Bake at 350° for 20 to 25 minutes or until golden brown.

MUSTARD TARRAGON CHICKEN WITH RED PEPPERS

Yield: 4 servings

1	tablespoon **vegetable oil**
4	**chicken breasts**, halved, skinned, and boned
1	clove **garlic**, pressed
⅔	cup **dry sherry**
⅓	cup **chicken broth**
2	teaspoons **Dijon mustard**
2	teaspoons **honey**
1½	teaspoons **Kitchen Bouquet**®
½	teaspoon **dried tarragon**, crushed
2	**red** or **green bell peppers**, cut into strips

- In large skillet, heat oil. Add chicken and brown both sides.
- Add garlic; cook 1 minute.
- In small bowl, combine sherry, broth, mustard, honey, Kitchen Bouquet®, and tarragon.
- Pour mixture over chicken in skillet. Bring to boil, reduce heat, and cook over medium-high heat about 10 minutes or until chicken is cooked through and sauce has a slight syrupy consistency.
- Add peppers and cook until tender.
- Remove from heat and serve.

A flavorful and attractive dish.

Cajun Roast Chicken

Yield: 8 to 10 servings

1 tablespoon plus 1 teaspoon **salt**
2 teaspoons **paprika**
¾ to 1 teaspoon **cayenne pepper**, or to taste
1 teaspoon **onion powder**
1 teaspoon dried **thyme**
¾ teaspoon **white pepper**
½ teaspoon **garlic powder**
½ teaspoon **black pepper**
1 5- to 6-pound **roasting chicken**
1 cup chopped **onions**

- In small bowl, combine dry ingredients.
- Rub into chicken inside and out.
- Cover and refrigerate overnight.
- Stuff chicken with onions.
- Roast uncovered in a slow oven (250°) 4 to 6 hours, basting occasionally.

This is a great recipe for a cold or rainy day. The aroma is delicious as the chicken roasts.

Chicken Diable

Yield: 4 servings

4 split **chicken breasts**
¼ cup (½ stick) **butter**
½ cup **honey**
¼ cup **Dijon mustard**
1 tablespoon **curry powder**
1 teaspoon **salt**

- Preheat oven to 350°.
- Arrange chicken in shallow baking pan.
- In small saucepan, melt butter. Stir in honey, mustard, curry powder, and salt.
- Pour mixture over chicken and turn pieces to coat.
- Cover and bake 45 minutes.
- Uncover and bake 15 minutes more, frequently basting with sauce, until chicken is tender and browned.

This chicken dish is great for "drop-in" company since all ingredients are usually on hand.

Chicken Enchiladas

Yield: 4 servings

2	boneless **chicken breasts**
1	cup chopped **onion**
1	clove **garlic**, minced
2	tablespoons **butter**
1	16-ounce can **tomatoes**, cut up
1	10- to 12-ounce can **enchilada sauce** (use less for milder flavor)
1	4-ounce can diced **green chili peppers**, drained (optional)
1	teaspoon **sugar**
1	teaspoon ground **cumin**
½	teaspoon **salt**
½	teaspoon dried **oregano**
½	teaspoon dried **basil**
2½	cups (10 ounces) shredded **Monterey Jack cheese**
¾	cup **sour cream**
8	small **flour tortillas**

- Cook chicken and cut in strips.
- Sauté onion and garlic in butter until tender.
- Add tomatoes with ½ of the juice, enchilada sauce, chilies, sugar, and seasonings.
- Bring to boil; reduce heat.
- Dip each tortilla in sauce, fill with some of the chicken and 2 tablespoons cheese.
- Roll up and place in baking pan, seam side down.
- Blend sour cream into remaining sauce mixture; pour over tortillas.
- Sprinkle with remaining cheese.
- Cover and bake at 350° for 40 minutes.

May be made and refrigerated overnight before baking.

BAKED CHICKEN TORTILLAS

Yield: 6 servings

2 tablespoons **vegetable oil**

6 **chicken breast halves**, boned, skinned, and cut into thin strips

½ cup thinly sliced **green onion**

1 clove **garlic**, minced

3 tablespoons **cornstarch**

4 cups **chicken broth**

2 cups grated **Monterey Jack cheese**, divided into 1-cup portions

½ cup **Miracle Whip® salad dressing**

½ cup **sour cream**

1 4-ounce can **green chili peppers**, chopped and drained

¼ cup chopped **cilantro** or **parsley**

½ cup sliced **ripe olives**

12 7-inch flour **tortillas**

2 **tomatoes**, chopped

- Heat oil in large skillet over medium-high heat.
- Add chicken, onions, and garlic.
- Sauté chicken until golden brown; remove from heat.
- In small bowl, mix cornstarch with ¼ cup of broth; whisk until blended.
- Pour remaining broth into large saucepan. Add cornstarch mixture; bring to boil.
- Boil broth for 2 to 3 minutes or until thickened.
- Reduce heat to low.
- Add 1 cup cheese, Miracle Whip®, and sour cream; whisk until smooth.
- Stir in chilies, cilantro or parsley, and ¼ cup olives.
- Remove 1 cup of sauce and stir into chicken.
- Recipe can be made to this point and refrigerated until ready to roll tortillas.
- Divide mixture evenly among tortillas and roll; place seam side down in a 9 x 13-inch baking dish.
- Spoon remaining sauce over tortillas.
- Sprinkle remaining cheese and olives on top.
- Bake at 350° for 25 minutes.

Top with fresh chopped tomatoes.

PHYLLO-WRAPPED CHICKEN
WITH CHEESE AND MUSHROOMS

Yield: 4 servings

4   tablespoons (½ stick) **butter**, melted

1   pound **phyllo dough**

⅓   cup dry **bread crumbs**

4   boneless, skinless **chicken breasts**

2   **lemons**

    Garlic salt

    Pepper

4   large **mushrooms**, sliced

    Provel cheese

1   cup **chicken gravy** or light **white sauce**

    Parsley

- Put a sheet of phyllo dough on work surface; brush with butter.
- Put a second sheet of phyllo across the bottom of the first to form an upside-down T; brush with butter.
- Put a third sheet on top of the first.
- Sprinkle ¼ of bread crumbs near bottom of T, about the size of a chicken breast.
- Put a chicken breast on top of crumbs; sprinkle with a few drops of lemon juice, garlic salt, and pepper, Provel cheese, and 1 sliced mushroom.
- Fold bottom of dough over chicken breast; then fold in 2 sides; brush with butter.
- Turn the chicken over and over, folding the dough around it to form a neat package.
- Put dough-wrapped chicken on baking sheet, seam side down; brush with butter.
- Repeat for remaining chicken breasts.
- Bake at 350°, or until golden brown, about 30 minutes.
- Serve with a spoonful of chicken gravy poured over the top of the chicken breasts. Sprinkle with parsley.

This recipe is from Tahiti.

CREAMED CHICKEN IN PUFF PASTRY

Yield: 6 servings

½	cup (1 stick) **butter**
½	cup **flour**
1	teaspoon **salt**
1	cup **chicken broth**
1	cup **half-and-half**
1	cup **whipping cream**
2	cups cooked **chicken**, in bite-sized chunks
1	4-ounce can **mushrooms**
1	teaspoon **curry powder**
¼	cup **dry sherry**
	Pepperidge Farm® frozen puff pastry shells, baked

- Melt butter in double boiler.
- Add flour, salt, broth, and both creams. Stir until thickened.
- Add chicken, mushrooms, curry, and sherry. Warm through.
- Serve over baked pastry shell.

An elegant entrée for a dinner party. Serve immediately after filling pastry shell.

CHICKEN BREASTS IN WINE

Yield: 6 servings

6	whole **chicken breasts**, skinned, boned, and cut in halves
2	beaten **eggs**
1	cup seasoned **bread crumbs**
	Vegetable oil
1½	cups shredded **Monterey Jack cheese**
1	cup **white wine**
½	cup sliced **mushrooms**

- Dip chicken in eggs, then bread crumbs.
- Place coated chicken in large skillet with oil and brown both sides lightly.
- Place chicken in a 9 x 13-inch glass baking pan.
- Top with cheese, wine, and mushrooms.
- Bake uncovered at 350° for 30 minutes.

CHICKEN WELLINGTON

Yield: 4 servings

2 whole **chicken breasts**, skinned and boned
1 tablespoon **butter**
1 tablespoon **vegetable oil**
½ pound fresh **mushrooms**, sliced (about 1½ cups)
1 cup thinly sliced **green onions**
1 tablespoon minced fresh **parsley**
1 clove **garlic**, minced
¼ cup **dry sherry**
1 sheet **Pepperidge Farm®** **frozen puff pastry**, thawed
1 **egg**, lightly beaten with 1 tablespoon water

- Cut chicken breasts in half.
- In large skillet over medium heat, melt butter with oil.
- Add chicken and brown on all sides, 4 to 5 minutes.
- Remove chicken from skillet; set aside.
- In drippings, cook mushrooms, green onions, parsley, and garlic.
- Stir in sherry; cook over medium-high heat, stirring frequently to reduce moisture, about 8 to 10 minutes.
- Cool completely.
- On lightly floured surface, roll thawed dough into 12 x 15-inch rectangle; brush with half of egg mixture.
- Spread mushroom mixture down center of dough.
- Place chicken end to end on top of mushrooms; wrap pastry around chicken, pinching edges to seal.
- Place seam side down in jellyroll pan.
- Make 3 crosswise slits in top of dough; brush with remaining egg mixture.
- Bake in 375° oven for 30 to 40 minutes, or until golden brown.
- Remove to platter; let stand 15 minutes before slicing with serrated knife.

This elegant dish is wonderful for a holiday brunch, served with a salad and hot fruit dish.

CHICKEN FLORENTINE

Yield: 6 servings

2 10-ounce packages chopped **frozen spinach**

4 tablespoons (½ stick) **butter**

4 tablespoons **flour**

1 clove **garlic**, crushed Dash **marjoram** and **basil**

1½ cups **medium cream** Meat from 5-pound **stewed chicken**

¾ cup **chicken stock** **Salt** and **pepper**

1 cup grated **Parmesan cheese**

- Cook spinach according to package directions; drain and set aside.
- In a large saucepan, melt 1 tablespoon butter.
- Blend in 1 tablespoon flour.
- Stir in crushed garlic clove.
- Add marjoram and basil.
- Add ⅔ cup of the cream and stir until thickened.
- Blend in spinach. Pour into bottom of casserole dish.
- Place meat from stewed chicken on top of spinach mixture.
- In saucepan melt 3 tablespoons butter; blend in 3 tablespoons flour.
- Add the remaining cream and chicken stock. Cook until thickened.
- Add salt and pepper, to taste. Pour over cooked chicken.
- Cover with grated Parmesan cheese.
- Bake uncovered in 400° oven for 20 minutes or until bubbly.

SPICY MARINADE FOR CHICKEN

Yield: 4 to 6 servings

¼ cup chopped **onion**

3 cloves **garlic**, minced

¼ cup **soy sauce**

2 tablespoons **peanut oil** (or **vegetable oil**)

¼ cup freshly squeezed **lemon juice**

1 teaspoon crushed **red pepper**

1 teaspoon ground **black pepper**

1½ teaspoons ground or minced fresh **ginger**

- Combine all ingredients in a 9 x 13-inch glass pan.
- Add 2½ to 3 pounds skinless chicken pieces.
- Cover with plastic wrap and refrigerate several hours.
- Grill over hot fire, bone side down first.

Chicken is good next day (cold) so it can be used for picnics. Also use this with boneless chicken breasts for grilled chicken sandwiches.

GRILLED CHICKEN WITH BALSAMIC VINEGAR

Yield: 6 to 8 servings

½ cup **white vinegar**

½ cup **balsamic vinegar**

½ cup **water**

1 teaspoon **chili powder**

½ teaspoon dried **oregano**

½ teaspoon freshly **ground pepper**

1 **bay leaf**, crushed

4 whole **chicken breasts** skinned, boned, and halved

- Combine vinegars, water, chili powder, oregano, pepper, and bay leaf in large zipper-seal plastic bag.
- Add chicken and marinate up to 2 hours.
- Prepare grill. Cook chicken over medium coals for 10 to 15 minutes.
- Baste with marinade.

SAUTÉED CHICKEN IN TOMATO VINEGAR SAUCE

Yield: 4 servings

3	tablespoons **olive oil,** divided
4	cloves **garlic**, minced
1	16-ounce can **Italian plum tomatoes**, diced
2	10½-ounce cans **chicken broth**
⅓	cup **red wine vinegar**
1	**bay leaf**
4	boneless **chicken breast halves**
	Salt and **pepper**
¼	teaspoon **rosemary**
2	tablespoons **butter**, cut into 8 pieces
2	tablespoons chopped **parsley**

- Heat 1 tablespoon of the olive oil in large saucepan.
- Add garlic and sauté 2 minutes.
- Add tomatoes with their juice, broth, vinegar, and bay leaf. Bring to a boil.
- Reduce heat and simmer about 25 minutes until slightly thickened.
- Season chicken breasts with salt, pepper, and rosemary.
- In a large skillet over medium heat, sauté chicken breasts in 2 tablespoons olive oil.
- Cook about 5 minutes per side until done.
- Transfer chicken to a platter and keep warm.
- Add sauce to the chicken skillet and simmer, scraping up browned bits.
- Mix in butter one piece at a time. Blend well; add parsley.
- Spoon sauce over chicken.

Great with oven-roasted potatoes or buttered noodles.

APRICOT CHICKEN DIVINE

Yield: 8 servings

2 tablespoons **margarine**

2 tablespoons **olive oil**

8 split, skinned **chicken breasts**

½ cup **unbleached white flour**

1 teaspoon **salt**

½ cup **apricot preserves**

1 tablespoon **Dijon mustard**

½ cup **nonfat yogurt** or **sour cream**

2 tablespoons **slivered almonds**

- Preheat oven to 375°.
- Melt margarine with oil in a shallow baking pan.
- Meanwhile, shake chicken in a plastic bag filled with flour and salt until chicken is coated.
- Place chicken in single layer, bone side down, in baking pan; bake for 25 minutes.
- Combine apricot preserves, mustard, and yogurt.
- Spread apricot mixture on chicken; bake for 30 minutes more or until done.
- Just before serving, brown almonds lightly in oven. Sprinkle over chicken.

Serve this chicken with rice.

CHICKEN TERIYAKI WITH PECAN PARMESAN RICE

Yield: 4 servings

½ cup **sherry**

½ cup **olive oil**

½ cup **soy sauce**

1 teaspoon **ginger**

1 teaspoon chopped **garlic**

4 **chicken breasts**

- In a shallow pan, mix sherry, olive oil, soy sauce, ginger, and garlic.
- Place chicken in marinade.
- Soak chicken for 2 hours.
- Grill chicken until done, about 6 to 7 minutes per side.

Pecan Parmesan Rice is the perfect accompaniment to this entrée.

PECAN PARMESAN RICE

Yield: 4 servings

2 cups **chicken broth**
1 teaspoon **olive oil**
1 cup uncooked **rice**
1 tablespoon minced **parsley**
¼ cup grated **Parmesan cheese**
1 teaspoon minced **garlic**
¼ cup **pecans**, chopped

- In a medium saucepan, mix chicken broth, olive oil, and rice.
- Cook rice according to package directions.
- Stir in remaining ingredients; serve.

CHICKEN BREASTS WITH RASPBERRY VINEGAR

Yield: 4 servings

2 whole **chicken breasts**
2 tablespoons **butter**
1 tablespoon **vegetable oil**
3 tablespoons minced **shallots**
⅓ cup **chicken stock**
¼ cup **raspberry vinegar**
⅓ cup **heavy cream**
Salt and **pepper**

- Halve, skin, and bone 2 whole chicken breasts.
- In large saucepan, heat the butter and oil over medium heat.

- Add chicken and lightly brown on each side.
- Remove chicken from pan and set aside.
- Add shallots and chicken stock to pan; simmer for 3 minutes.
- Add raspberry vinegar; bring to a boil and cook, stirring until mixture thickens.
- Stir in cream and return chicken to pan.
- Heat for 1 minute to warm chicken, turning pieces to coat with sauce.
- Season to taste with salt and pepper.

RASPBERRY CHICKEN

Yield: 4 servings

2   **chicken breasts**, skinned, boned, and halved
     Salt and freshly ground **black pepper**
1   tablespoon **butter**
1   tablespoon **vegetable oil**
¾   cup fresh **raspberries**
2   tablespoons dry **white wine**
1   tablespoon **raspberry vinegar**
2   tablespoons finely chopped **shallots**
⅓   cup **chicken stock**
⅓   cup **heavy cream** or **whipping cream**
     Lemon slices and **mint leaves** for garnish

- Flatten chicken breasts slightly with blunt edge of knife or mallet. Season with salt and pepper.
- Melt butter with oil in heavy 10- to 12-inch skillet.
- Sauté chicken over low heat until golden, about 5 to 6 minutes on each side.
- Transfer chicken to dish; keep warm.
- Purée ¼ cup raspberries through a sieve over a small bowl.
- In same skillet, bring wine, raspberry vinegar, and shallots to a boil.
- Reduce heat; simmer until liquid is reduced in half.
- Whisk in chicken stock, cream, and puréed raspberries.
- Simmer sauce until slightly thickened, about 5 minutes.
- Return chicken to pan; simmer 5 more minutes, basting often with sauce.
- Transfer chicken to serving platter.
- Add remaining raspberries to skillet; shake gently for 1 minute to warm berries.
- Spoon sauce over chicken and garnish with lemon slices and mint leaves.

SEVILLE-STYLE BRAISED CHICKEN

Yield: 4 servings

2   tablespoons **olive oil**
3   pounds **chicken parts**, cut up
    Salt and **pepper**
2   **onions**, chopped
¾   cup fresh **orange juice**
¾   cup **chicken broth**
2   tablespoons **medium-dry sherry**
¾   teaspoon ground **cinnamon**
⅛   teaspoon ground **cloves**
½   cup **raisins**
½   cup slivered **almonds**
2   **navel oranges** (remove peel, pith, and membranes)

- In a large skillet, heat oil and brown the chicken.
- Remove chicken, pat dry, season with salt and pepper, and transfer to plate.
- Add onions to skillet and cook over medium heat.
- Stir in orange juice, broth, sherry, cinnamon, cloves, and salt and pepper.
- Add the chicken, raisins, and almonds and simmer, covered, for 20 minutes.
- Add the orange sections and simmer 5 to 10 minutes.
- Remove chicken.
- Boil the sauce until thickened slightly.
- Spoon sauce over chicken.

MARINATED CORNISH HENS

Yield: 2 servings

2   **Cornish hens**, thawed
2   teaspoons **brown sugar**
1   teaspoon **mesquite flavoring**
⅓   cup **soy sauce**
1   teaspoon **white wine vinegar**
3   cloves **garlic**, minced

- Mix all ingredients but hens together.
- Pour marinade over hens and marinate in refrigerator overnight or for at least 3 hours.
- Roast hens at 350° for 1½ hours, basting periodically.
- Serve with wild rice.

Marinade can be used for other meats as well.

CORNISH HENS GLAZED WITH GRAND MARNIER APRICOT SAUCE

Yield: 8 servings

8   **Cornish hens**, patted dry with paper towels
     Soy sauce
     Extra virgin **olive oil**
     Salt and fresh cracked **pepper**
     Onion powder
     Garlic powder
     Thyme

Grand Marnier Apricot Sauce:

½   cup (1 stick) **unsalted butter**
8   ounces **apricot preserves**
¼   cup **Grand Marnier liqueur**
1½   tablespoons fresh **lemon juice**
¼   teaspoon **salt**

- Take the dry hens, rub with soy sauce, and arrange on a rack in a shallow roaster; let them dry for about 30 minutes at room temperature.

- Rub the hens with olive oil; sprinkle each hen lightly with the salt, cracked pepper, onion and garlic powders, and thyme. Let them air dry for another 30 minutes at room temperature.
- Place in preheated 350° oven, breast side down; roast for 30 minutes.
- Turn breast side up; roast another 30 minutes.
- Turn one more time and roast another 30 minutes.
- Baste with sauce; with breast side up, continue baking for 15 more minutes or until juices run clear.

Sauce:

- Melt butter in 4-cup microwave-safe bowl; whisk in preserves, then all other ingredients.
- Microwave on medium-high for 4 minutes; stir and continue to microwave for 12 more minutes, stirring every 4 minutes.

Sauce can be made day ahead and stored in refrigerator. Extra sauce should be heated and served on the side.

GRILLED TURKEY STEAKS WITH CHILI-LIME SAUCE

Yield: 4 servings

1 tablespoon **olive oil**

2 cloves **garlic**, minced

1 tablespoon **chili powder**

Grated peel of 1 **lime**

Juice of 2 **limes** (approximately ⅓ cup)

1 to 2 teaspoons **sugar**, to taste

Salt and **pepper**

1 to 1½ pounds **turkey steaks**, cut about ½ inch thick

4 tablespoons (½ stick) **butter**, cut in pieces

- Heat medium skillet over medium-high heat.
- When skillet is hot, add olive oil.
- When oil is hot, add garlic; sauté a few seconds or until soft.
- Stir in chili powder; cook over low heat, stirring constantly, 30 seconds.
- Stir in lime peel, lime juice, and sugar.
- Season to taste with additional sugar, salt, and pepper.
- Remove from heat; cool slightly.
- Pour mixture into shallow baking dish.
- Add turkey steaks. Turn to coat all over.
- Let stand 30 minutes at room temperature or refrigerate up to several hours.
- Remove turkey, reserving marinade in dish.
- Grill turkey steaks over hot coals about 4 minutes per side or until just cooked through.
- Meanwhile, in a small saucepan, bring reserved marinade to a boil.
- Cook until reduced to 1 to 2 tablespoons. Whisk in butter, piece by piece.
- Serve sauce over grilled steaks.

Fabulous summer turkey recipe!

FRENCH BREAD TURKEY PIZZA

Yield: 8 servings

½ pound **ground turkey**

1 tablespoon chopped **cilantro**

¼ teaspoon ground **red pepper**

1 loaf **French bread**

½ cup **salt-free tomato sauce**

2 tablespoons **pesto sauce** (commercial or olive oil, garlic, basil combined in food processor)

4 **plum tomatoes**, thinly sliced

1 cup shredded **part-skim mozzarella cheese**

- Cook turkey in medium nonstick skillet over medium heat until browned, stirring to crumble.
- Drain and pat dry with paper towels.
- In a bowl, combine turkey, cilantro, and red pepper; set aside.
- Slice bread lengthwise; place bread, cut side up, on a baking sheet.
- Broil 5½ inches from heat, 1 minute or until lightly browned. Remove from oven.
- Combine tomato sauce and pesto. Stir well and spread over bread halves.
- Top with tomato slices and turkey mixture. Sprinkle with cheese.
- Broil 5½ inches from heat 2 minutes or until cheese melts.

The pesto makes this pizza extra special!

Living in a river town, St. Louis cooks have always prepared an assortment of fish dishes and they enjoy shellfish as well. The St. Louis Riverfront offers many different sights and attractions including the Gateway Arch, which is the nation's tallest monument; Laclede's Landing, which has the only remaining streets laid out by Pierre Laclede in 1764 and features a huge entertainment and shopping district; and numerous riverboat cruise excursions for sightseeing and parties.

• • •

Tony's

One name says it all in St. Louis culinary circles: Tony's! Revered as one of the world's finest Italian restaurants, Tony's is St. Louis' only 5-Star-Award-winning restaurant and this country's most consistently praised dining room. The Bommarito family has been pleasing palates in unequalled fashion since 1946 and offers this seafood and pasta favorite to bring out the Italian artist in you.

PASTA CON PESCE

1	pound **pasta** of your choice
½	pound (2 sticks) **butter**
1	peeled and seeded fresh **tomato**, chopped
1	cup chopped fresh **mushrooms**
4	ounces **lobster meat**, cooked
4	ounces peeled and deveined **shrimp**, cooked
4	ounces **crabmeat**, cooked
2	tablespoons chopped fresh **parsley**
	Freshly ground **pepper**, to taste

- Cook pasta until almost done.
- Drain pasta but leave 2 ounces of the water. Return to heat.
- Add butter, tomatoes, and mushrooms. Stir well.
- Add seafood and parsley.
- Season well, using fresh pepper.
- Serve on preheated plates.

ZINNIA'S NUT-CRUSTED TROUT

Yield: 4 servings

¼ cup **pine nuts**

¼ cup **pecans**

1 tablespoon, plus 1 teaspoon **sesame seeds**

4 whole **trout** (about 10 ounces each), boned and heads discarded

4 teaspoons **unsalted butter**

1 clove **garlic**, minced

Salt and **pepper**

4 tablespoons **vegetable oil**

- In a food processor or by hand, chop fine the pine nuts and pecans.
- In a bowl, stir together nut mixture and sesame seeds.
- Open trout to reveal the flesh and arrange them, skin sides down, in 2 shallow dishes large enough to hold them in 1 layer.
- In a small saucepan, melt butter with garlic. Brush insides of trout with butter mixture.
- Sprinkle trout with nut mixture, and salt and pepper to taste. Pat mixture to help it adhere.
- Chill trout, uncovered, for 30 minutes.
- Preheat oven to 400°.
- In a heavy skillet, heat 1 tablespoon of the oil over moderately high heat until it is hot but not smoking.
- Sauté 1 trout, coated side down, for 2 minutes.
- Transfer the trout carefully to a plate, coated side down; keep it warm and covered.
- Sauté remaining trout in remaining oil in the same manner.
- Invert trout, coated sides up, onto a lightly oiled large baking sheet and bake them in the middle of the oven for 5 minutes, or until they just flake.

David Guempel shares his popular trout recipe from his restaurant, Zinnia. He uses wild-fed trout farmed in a pure natural cold spring in Southwest Missouri.

BLUE WATER GRILL SWORDFISH

Yield: 4 servings

4   8-ounce **swordfish steaks**

Wild Mushroom-Tomato Salsa:

1   pound wild **mushrooms**

2   large **tomatoes**

1   bunch green **onions**

½   cup **soy sauce**

¼   cup **rice wine vinegar**

2   tablespoons **sugar**

2   tablespoons **sesame oil**

Ginger Scallion Aioli:

1   **egg**

2   tablespoons **pickled ginger**

1   bunch **green onions**

2   tablespoons **rice wine vinegar**

1   pinch **salt**

1   pinch **pepper**

2   cups **vegetable oil**

Wild Mushroom-Tomato Salsa:

- Dice mushrooms, tomatoes, and green onions; set aside.
- Bring soy sauce, rice wine vinegar, sugar, and sesame oil to a boil.
- Remove from stove and add diced vegetables.
- Let steep until vegetables are tender, approximately 15 to 20 minutes.

Ginger Scallion Aioli:

- Put all ingredients, except the oil, into a blender.
- Slowly add oil while blending.
- Aioli should be consistency of a creamy mayonnaise.
- Chill until ready to use.

Swordfish:

- Grill swordfish 8 to 12 minutes, turning once.
- To serve, stripe the swordfish with the aioli and top with the salsa.

Chef Lisa Slay of the Blue Water Grill shares this specialty of her popular Southwestern restaurant. If you prefer not to use raw egg in the aioli, delete the egg and the oil from the recipe and substitute 2 cups of mayonnaise.

SALMON FILLETS

Yield: 2 servings

2 4-ounce **salmon fillets**, skin removed by vendor
Salt and **pepper**
Lemon
Fresh **dill sprigs**
1 medium **cucumber**, peeled, seeded, sliced into ¼-inch crescents
2 **scallions**, finely cut lengthwise

- Rinse salmon. Lightly salt and pepper both sides.
- Place salmon on a large piece of aluminum foil.
- Squeeze lemon over salmon. Cover with dill, cucumber, and scallions.
- Securely wrap foil.
- Place on ready coals 5 minutes; turn and grill another 5 minutes.

SALMON TARRAGON

Yield: 4 servings

4 **salmon steaks**
Butter
1 **lemon**, cut in slices
1 **red onion**, cut in rings
1 **green pepper**, cut into rings
Tarragon
1 cup **medium-dry white wine**
Cornstarch
Grapes for garnish

- Make 4 aluminum foil "boats" large enough to enclose salmon steaks and fold over.
- Place a little butter in each foil boat. Layer lemon, onion, and pepper.

- Place salmon over top with more lemon, onion, and pepper.
- Sprinkle with tarragon. Pour about 2 ounces wine over.
- Close foil and bake at 325° 20 minutes.
- Pour liquid from boats into saucepan. Add a little more wine.
- Add 1 to 2 teaspoons cornstarch to sauce. Bring to boil to thicken. Pour sauce into each boat and bake another 10 minutes.
- Remove salmon and sauce from boats.
- Garnish with grapes.

Serve with rice and steamed fresh vegetables.

BUNDLED FISH

Yield: 4 servings

1   16-ounce package frozen **fish fillets**

1   cup finely chopped **onions**

1   cup finely chopped **carrots**

1   cup thinly sliced fresh **mushrooms**

2   tablespoons **butter** or **margarine**

⅓   cup **plain yogurt**

½   teaspoon **salt**

¼   teaspoon **pepper**

½   teaspoon dried **dillweed**

1   8-ounce package refrigerated **crescent rolls**

1   beaten **egg**

1   tablespoon **water**

Lemon-Onion Sauce:

¼   cup chopped **green onions**

2   tablespoons **butter** or **margarine**

1   tablespoon **cornstarch**

1   cup **chicken broth**

¼   teaspoon grated **lemon peel**

2   teaspoons **lemon juice**

- Thaw fish fillets; drain well.
- In shallow baking dish, arrange fish pieces to make 4 portions.

- In saucepan, cook onions, carrots, and mushrooms in butter or margarine, covered, about 5 minutes.
- Uncover; simmer 2 minutes or until liquid has evaporated. Stir in yogurt, salt, pepper, and dill.
- Unroll crescent rolls. Press 2 triangles of dough together to form a 6 x 4-inch rectangle; repeat, making 4 rectangles.
- Spoon ¼ of the vegetable mixture (about ⅓ cup) over each fish portion.
- Top each with a rectangle of dough.
- Brush dough with mixture of egg and water; cut slits in top for escape of steam.
- Bake at 350° for 30 to 35 minutes.
- Serve with Lemon-Onion Sauce

Lemon-Onion Sauce:

- In saucepan, cook green onion in butter or margarine until tender but not brown.
- Stir in cornstarch. Add chicken broth all at once.
- Cook and stir until thickened and bubbly.
- Stir in lemon peel and lemon juice.

HICKORY TROUT FILLETS

Yield: 4 servings

4   to 5 boned **rainbow trout fillets**
1   cup **mayonnaise**
2   tablespoons **honey**
2   teaspoons **Colgin® hickory liquid smoke**
4   tablespoons **pine nuts**

- Open trout fillets on a foil-lined cookie sheet.
- Combine mayonnaise, honey, and liquid smoke.
- Spread evenly over trout fillets; save remaining sauce.
- Broil trout fillets, about 5 inches from heat, 5 minutes or until golden and bubbly.
- Remove from broiler. Spread remaining sauce over fillets.
- Sprinkle each fillet with 1 tablespoon of pine nuts.
- Serve immediately.

BROILED SHRIMP CREOLE

Yield: 4 to 6 servings

5   pounds **shrimp**, unpeeled
⅛   cup chopped **garlic**
4   ground **bay leaves**
½   teaspoon **thyme**
½   teaspoon **oregano**
½   cup **onions**, chopped
⅛   cup **bell pepper**, chopped
¼   cup **black pepper**, (for very hot), or to taste
⅛   cup **Tony Chachere's™ creole seasoning**
⅛   cup **sherry**
1   cup **olive oil**
    Butter

- Mix all ingredients except shrimp and butter in food processor or blender.
- Place shrimp in a large, flat jellyroll pan.
- Pour sauce over top of shrimp; top with slices of butter.
- Broil in oven about 5 inches from heat, until shrimp are pink; turn and broil other side.
- Serve with loaves of French bread and lots of napkins.

SHRIMP STEAMED IN BUDWEISER®

Yield: 4 servings

1	can **Budweiser® beer**
1½	pounds **shrimp** in their shells
½	teaspoon **thyme**
½	teaspoon **dry mustard**
1	**bay leaf**
1	clove **garlic**, chopped
½	tablespoon **salt**
1	tablespoon chopped **parsley**
¼	teaspoon **pepper**
½	teaspoon chopped **chives** or **onion**

Dunk Sauce:

4	tablespoons (½ stick) **unsalted butter**
2	tablespoons **lemon juice**
1	tablespoon chopped **parsley**
1	tablespoon chopped **chives** or **onion**
1	teaspoon **salt**

- In a large saucepan, for which you have a cover, combine the beer, unshelled shrimp, thyme, dry mustard, bay leaf, chopped garlic, salt, chopped parsley, pepper, and chopped chives or onion. Cover tightly, bring to boil (you'll hear it).
- Immediately reduce heat and start timing.
- Let shrimp simmer 3 minutes. They should get pink, no more.
- Serve at once with the Dunk Sauce.

Dunk Sauce:
- Melt the butter.
- Add all other ingredients and mix thoroughly.

GRILLED SHELLFISH IN SCOTCH, SOY, AND GINGER MARINADE

Yield: 4 to 6 servings

½   cup **soy sauce**

¼   cup **Scotch whiskey**

2   teaspoons grated fresh **ginger**

1   teaspoon finely minced **garlic**

2   tablespoons **honey**

2   pounds large **shrimp**, peeled and deveined

Mixed **salad greens**

Dressing:

½   **marinade** (first 5 ingredients above)

1   cup **olive oil**

2   tablespoons **sesame oil**

2   tablespoons **red wine vinegar**

- Combine first 5 ingredients to make a marinade.
- Reserve half of marinade for dressing. Add the other half of marinade to shrimp and marinate in the refrigerator 30 to 60 minutes.
- Skewer seafood and grill about 2 minutes per side. Do not overcook.
- Meanwhile, combine dressing ingredients; set aside.
- Serve on bed of mixed salad greens tossed with dressing.

Instead of shrimp, you may use sea scallops, or half shrimp and half sea scallops.

PEPPERY SHRIMP

Yield: 6 servings

5   pounds **shrimp**, unpeeled

1   pound **butter** or **margarine**

2   ounces ground **black pepper**

16 ounces **Italian salad dressing**

Juice of 4 **lemons**

- Put shrimp in roasting pan.
- In saucepan, melt butter and add remaining ingredients.
- Pour sauce over shrimp and bake, covered, at 350° for 30 to 45 minutes. Stir occasionally.
- Serve shrimp on large platters and pour some sauce over it.

Fun to eat. Spread newspaper on table and give guests bibs and large napkins.

SHRIMP CREOLE

Yield: 4 to 6 servings

1½ tablespoons **butter**

⅔ cup chopped **onion**

1 clove **garlic**, minced

½ cup chopped **celery**

½ cup chopped **green pepper**

1 16-ounce can **tomatoes**

1 8-ounce can **tomato sauce**

1 **bay leaf**

1½ teaspoons **salt**

1 tablespoon **sugar**

1½ tablespoons chopped **parsley**

2 **whole cloves**

4 dashes **Tabasco® sauce**

2 tablespoons **Worcestershire sauce**

¼ teaspoon **paprika**

½ teaspoon **rosemary**

1½ pounds **shrimp**, boiled and shelled

4 cups cooked **rice**

- In large stockpot, brown onions, garlic, celery, and green pepper in butter.
- Add tomatoes, tomato sauce, and all seasonings.
- Bring to boil, breaking up the tomatoes into very small pieces.
- Simmer, covered, for about 30 minutes.
- Add the cooked and shelled shrimp and warm through; do not cook more than 5 minutes.
- Serve immediately over hot cooked rice.

The cloves give this creole a nice, distinctive taste.

BROILED OR GRILLED SHRIMP

Yield: 4 servings

1½ pounds large **shrimp**, unpeeled

Salt and **pepper**

2 tablespoons **olive oil**

2 tablespoons **lemon juice**

2 tablespoons **dry white wine**

1 tablespoon chopped fresh **rosemary** (or 1 teaspoon dried)

1 tablespoon finely chopped **garlic**

6 tablespoons **butter**

2 tablespoons finely chopped **chives**

- Preheat grill or broiler.
- With a sharp knife, cut the shrimp at the back of the shell and open butterfly fashion.
- Place shrimp on a wire mesh grilling device and sprinkle with salt and pepper. Brush with olive oil.
- In a small saucepan, combine lemon juice, wine, rosemary, and garlic.
- Cut butter into small pieces.
- Bring liquid to boil and gradually add butter, stirring with whisk.
- When all butter is added and melted, remove sauce from heat.
- Broil or grill shrimp about 1½ minutes on each side.
- Add chives to butter mixture.
- Place shrimp, cut side up, on serving plate. Spoon sauce over.

You do not peel the shrimp ahead of time. Serve with warm crusty French bread, salad, and a dry white wine.

CAJUN BARBECUED SHRIMP

Yield: 4 servings

3   slices **bacon**

½   cup (1 stick) **butter** or **margarine**

2   tablespoons **Dijon mustard**

1½   teaspoons **chili powder**

¼   teaspoon **basil**

¼   teaspoon **thyme**

2   teaspoons **pepper**

2   tablespoons **chopped onion**

1   tablespoon **crab boil**

½   teaspoon **Tabasco® sauce**

1½   pounds fresh **shrimp**, peeled, or 12 ounces **frozen shrimp** and 8 ounces **sea tails** (imitation lobster)

- Thoroughly cook bacon, then crumble. Melt butter.
- Combine all ingredients in an oven-safe glass casserole.
- Bake at 375° for 35 to 40 minutes or until shrimp are completely done.
- Skim fat from the top.
- Serve with brown rice.

Fresh shrimp may need to cook a shorter amount of time, frozen a little longer. Check progress occasionally.

SHRIMP AND TORTELLINI

Yield: 4 servings

1   pound unpeeled medium **shrimp**

1   9-ounce package fresh **tortellini** with cheese, uncooked

⅓   cup **butter** or **margarine**

1   **shallot**, minced

2   tablespoons chopped fresh **basil** or 2 teaspoons dried whole basil

½   cup grated **Parmesan cheese**

- Peel and devein shrimp; set aside.
- Cook pasta according to package directions; drain and set aside.
- Melt butter in large skillet over medium-high heat; add shrimp, minced shallot, and basil. Cook about 5 minutes, stirring constantly.
- Add pasta and cheese. Toss gently and garnish with fresh basil, if desired.

Kids love this seafood pasta dish.

FETTUCINE WITH SHRIMP AND TOMATOES

Yield: 4 to 6 servings

½   cup extra virgin **olive oil**

1½   pounds uncooked medium **shrimp**, peeled and deveined

3   large **tomatoes**, seeded and coarsely chopped

1   teaspoon dried **basil**

3   cloves **garlic**, minced

2   tablespoons minced **shallots** or **green onions** **Salt** and **pepper**

1   pound **fettuccine**, cooked Grated **Romano** or **Parmesan cheese**

- Heat oil in heavy, large skillet over medium-high heat.
- Add shrimp, tomatoes, basil, garlic, and shallots.
- Season to taste with salt and pepper.
- Cook until shrimp turn pink, about 3 minutes, stirring constantly.
- Pour shrimp and sauce over pasta and toss.
- Sprinkle with cheese.
- Serve immediately.

Extra virgin olive oil makes a big difference in this dish.

CAJUN FETTUCINE

Yield: 6 to 8 servings

3   cups **Seafood Stock** (see next recipe)

3   cups **whipping cream**

½   cup (1 stick) **unsalted butter**

1   pound **andouille sausage**, diced

1   medium **onion**, chopped

1   medium **bell pepper**, chopped

3   cloves **garlic**, minced

1   tablespoon minced fresh **basil** (or 1 teaspoon dried basil)

1   pound peeled **crawfish tails**

1   pound peeled **shrimp**

3   tablespoons **unsalted butter**

3   tablespoons **flour**

6   **green onions**, chopped

1   pound **fettucine**, cooked
     Grated **Parmesan cheese**

- In heavy stockpot, reduce Seafood Stock by ½ over medium heat.
- Add whipping cream and simmer, reducing to ⅔ or ½.
- Meanwhile, in deep skillet, melt ½ cup unsalted butter.
- Add sausage, onion, bell pepper, garlic, and basil.
- Sauté until onion is slightly wilted and transparent (about 5 minutes).
- Add crawfish tails and shrimp. Cook for 3 to 5 minutes.
- Remove from heat and put mixture in bowl, set aside.
- In emptied skillet, melt 3 tablespoons unsalted butter. Add flour and cook for 5 minutes, stirring constantly.
- Slowly add cream-stock sauce and blend.
- Stir in crawfish-shrimp mixture. Add green onions and cooked fettucine and heat thoroughly.
- Serve with Parmesan cheese.

Instead of 1 pound shrimp and 1 pound crawfish, you could use all shrimp (2 pounds) or all crawfish (2 pounds).

SEAFOOD STOCK

1	pound **medium shrimp**, unpeeled
1	**onion**, unpeeled and quartered
1	teaspoon **whole cloves**
2	cloves **garlic**, unpeeled and quartered
1	large **lemon**, sliced
1	tablespoon **crab boil**
1	teaspoon **cayenne pepper**
1	teaspoon **salt**
10	cups **water**

- Peel shrimp, put shells in heavy stockpot, and refrigerate shrimp for use in fettucine.
- Put all other ingredients in stockpot.
- Bring to full rolling boil, skim foam, lower heat to medium, and cook 1 hour.
- Cool slightly and strain.
- Discard shells and vegetables.
- Pour stock in jars and cool to room temperature.
- Refrigerate until ready to use (within 2 days, can be frozen for up to 6 months).

SHRIMP NATURAL

Yield: 4 servings

½	cup (1 stick) **butter**, melted
1	cup chopped **onions**
2	cloves **garlic**, minced
1	teaspoon **Worcestershire sauce**
1	teaspoon **salt**
½	teaspoon **Tabasco® sauce**
2	pounds **shrimp**, peeled and deveined
2	tablespoons snipped **parsley**
2	tablespoons chopped **green onion tops**

- Melt butter in 2-quart casserole.
- Add onion and garlic. Microwave on high 5 minutes.
- In another casserole dish, mix Worcestershire sauce, salt, and Tabasco® with shrimp. Microwave on high 4 minutes, stirring once.
- Combine butter, onion, and garlic mixture with shrimp. Microwave on high for 3 more minutes, stirring once.
- Add parsley and onion tops.
- Toss before serving.
- Serve with rice.

SALSA SEAFOOD PASTA

Yield: 6 servings

1	tablespoon **butter**
2	**eggs**
1	cup **half-and-half**
1	cup **plain yogurt**
⅓	cup crumbled **feta cheese**
½	cup grated **Swiss cheese**
⅓	cup chopped **parsley**
1	teaspoon **basil**
1	teaspoon **oregano**
9	ounces fresh **angel hair pasta**
1	16-ounce jar thick and chunky **salsa**
½	pound medium **shrimp**, peeled and deveined
½	pound **imitation crab**
½	cup grated **Monterey Jack cheese**

- Preheat oven to 350°.
- Butter sides and bottom of 8 x 12-inch baking dish.
- Mix together eggs, half-and-half, yogurt, feta and Swiss cheese, parsley, basil, and oregano; set aside.
- Spread half of pasta over the bottom of dish and cover with salsa. Add half the shrimp and crab, and cover with remaining pasta. Pour and spread the egg mixture over pasta. Add remaining shrimp and crab, and top with Monterey Jack cheese.
- Bake for 30 minutes. Let stand 10 minutes.

Salsa adds a different swing to this colorful dish.

MATT'S FAMOUS LOUISIANA GUMBO

Yield: 10 to 12 servings

½ cup **flour**

½ cup **vegetable oil**

2 large **onions**, chopped

2 tablespoons chopped **garlic**

½ medium **bell pepper**, coarsely chopped

3 stalks **celery**, chopped

2 sprigs **parsley**, chopped

1 16-ounce can chopped **tomatoes**

3 to 4 cups **water**

   Salt and **pepper**

   Red pepper

   McCormick Season All®

   Tabasco® sauce, to taste

4 tablespoons **filé powder**

3 pounds large (or bigger) peeled **shrimp**

2 pounds fresh **crabmeat**

2 pounds **crawfish tails**, peeled (optional)

2 pounds good hearty **fish fillets** (such as red fish), cubed (optional)

   Shucked **raw oysters** (optional)

- In a large pot over medium heat, make a roux with flour and oil. Stir constantly, or flour will burn. (If this happens, throw away and start over.)
- Stir roux until walnut colored, about 30 minutes.
- Keeping heat at medium, add vegetables, except tomatoes, and sauté until limp.
- Add tomatoes and water, keeping heat at medium. Then add salt, pepper, red pepper, McCormick Season All®, and Tabasco®.
- Simmer over low to medium heat for 1 hour, stirring occasionally.
- Add filé, shrimp, crabmeat, any other seafood you choose (except oysters).
- Turn heat to low for 30 minutes, stirring frequently. If using oysters, drop in during last 5 minutes.
- Serve in a large bowl over steamed white rice with fresh French bread and a side dish of cold potato salad.

If you use oysters, discard before freezing leftovers—if you have any leftovers!

CIOPPINO

Yield: 6 to 8 servings

3	to 4 tablespoons **olive oil**
1	cup minced **yellow onion**
1	cup chopped **red pepper**
2	28-ounce cans whole peeled **tomatoes**
2	to 3 cloves **garlic**, crushed
	Basil, to taste
	Oregano, to taste
1	**bay leaf**
3	cups **dry red wine**
	Crushed **red pepper**, to taste
	Salt and **pepper**
¼	cup **sugar** (approximately)
4	tablespoons **tomato paste**
24	littleneck **clams**
1½	pounds **cod** or **halibut**
¾	pound **sea scallops**
24	**shrimp**, peeled and deveined, leaving tails intact

- In large, deep pot, heat olive oil. Add onions and red pepper.
- Sauté until onions are clear.
- Roughly chop tomatoes and add them with their juice to the pot.
- Season with mashed garlic, basil, oregano, and bay leaf.
- Simmer for 5 minutes at low boil, uncovered.
- Add wine and red pepper; season with salt and pepper, and sugar to taste.
- Add tomato paste to thicken mixture. Simmer, covered, at low boil for 1½ hours.
- Meanwhile, scrub outside of clams and clean rest of fish.
- Remove skin and bone from cod or halibut; cut into 2-inch pieces crosswise.
- Add clams and cook them until they open up.
- Remove open clams, add remaining seafood, and cook for 5 minutes on high heat.
- Put clams back in the pot to warm them up.
- Serve with French bread and pasta (with pesto, if desired).

This dish may include any combination of fish. It also reheats very well and is almost better the next day.

BOUILLABAISSE

Yield: 8 servings

¼	cup **olive oil**
1½	cups chopped **onions**
3	cloves **garlic**, minced
1	16-ounce can **stewed tomatoes**
2	6-ounce cans **tomato paste**
3	cups **water**
2	cups dry **white wine**
1	8-ounce bottle **clam juice**
2	tablespoons minced fresh **parsley**
2	teaspoons **basil**
1	teaspoon **thyme**
½	teaspoon **salt**
¼	teaspoon **pepper**
18	small **clams**
1	pound **white fish**, cubed
1	pound **crab legs**, cut in 2-inch pieces
1	pound **shrimp**, peeled and deveined, leaving tails intact

- In large stockpot, sauté onion and garlic in oil until crisp and tender, about 3 minutes.
- Add tomatoes, tomato paste, water, wine, clam juice, parsley, and seasonings; cover and simmer over medium heat 10 minutes.
- Add clams and fish; cover and simmer 5 minutes.
- Add crab and shrimp; cover and simmer 2 to 3 minutes, or until shrimp turn pink and clams open.
- Discard any unopened clams and serve.

Wonderful with crusty bread and salad, particularly in the winter.

NEW ORLEANS CRAB PIE

Yield: 6 servings

1½ cups herbed-seasoned packaged **bread stuffing**

¾ cup (1½ sticks) **butter**

3 tablespoons finely chopped **green onion**

¼ cup presifted **flour**

1½ cups **milk**

1½ cups flaked **crabmeat**

2 tablespoons chopped **pimientos**

¼ teaspoon **dry mustard**
Salt and **pepper**, to taste

½ cup **sour cream**

2 tablespoons chopped **parsley**

- Grease a 7- or 8-inch pie pan.
- Crush stuffing with a rolling pin and turn into a mixing bowl.
- Melt and stir in ½ cup of the butter.
- Press this mixture on the bottom and sides of pie pan to form a crust.
- Melt remaining butter in saucepan.
- Sauté onion, sprinkle with flour, gradually stir in milk.
- Cook over medium heat, stirring constantly until thickened and smooth.
- Stir in crabmeat, pimientos, and mustard. Season with salt and pepper.
- Remove from heat. Stir in sour cream.
- Turn into pie pan. Bake at 425° for 30 minutes.
- Sprinkle with parsley before serving.

Slices come out "cleaner" if you let this pie cool a few minutes before serving.

VEGETABLES and SIDE DISHES

A wide variety of traditional and exotic vegetables are always available to St. Louis cooks. Soulard's Open Air Farmers Market, started about 1779, still survives in St. Louis' oldest residential neighborhood. Produce stands pop up all across the area during the growing season and are a great source for fresh items.

• • •

Big Sky Cafe

A St. Louis favorite since opening its artfully dressed doors in 1991, Big Sky Cafe specializes in revitalized American favorites. Traditional American dishes that have been updated in terms of health, flavors, and presentation are served daily by Chef Mike Wilson and owner Tim Mallet. Taking a 1990s view of a home-grown American favorite, Roasted Garlic Mashed Potatoes is a popular accompaniment for Big Sky Cafe main courses.

ROASTED GARLIC MASHED POTATOES

Yield: 6 servings

Roasted Garlic:

5	to 6 **whole garlic heads**
	Oil
	Salt and **pepper**, to taste
2	tablespoons **chicken stock** or **water**

Mashed Potatoes:

5	pounds peeled **potatoes**, quartered
½	cup (1 stick) **butter**
1	pint **half-and-half**
½	cup puréed roasted **garlic**
	Salt and **pepper** to taste

Roasted Garlic:

- Place the garlic heads in a shallow dish with enough water to just cover the bottom.
- Rub tops of garlic heads with oil and sprinkle with salt and pepper.
- Bake in preheated oven at 325° to 350° for about 45 minutes to 1 hour until cloves are soft.
- Cool the garlic heads.
- When cool, remove the pulp from each clove by squeezing it. Place about ½ cup of the pulp into a blender.
- Purée, adding chicken stock or water to the pulp.

Mashed Potatoes:

- Boil the potatoes until very soft.
- Strain very well in a colander for at least 10 minutes.
- Place cooked potatoes in a large mixing bowl and add the remaining ingredients.
- Using a whip attachment, mash the potatoes to the desired consistency.
- Add more garlic purée or half-and-half to achieve the desired texture and flavor.

CHILLED ASPARAGUS IN MUSTARD SAUCE

Yield: 4 servings

1	pound fresh **asparagus**
½	cup plain **yogurt**
2½	tablespoons **Dijon mustard**
2	tablespoons **mayonnaise**
1	tablespoon fresh minced **dill**
1	tablespoon fresh minced **chives**
⅛	teaspoon freshly ground **pepper**
	Lettuce leaves for decoration

- Snap off tough ends of asparagus. Remove scales with vegetable peeler, if desired.
- Cook or steam asparagus until crisp tender.
- Rinse with cold water. Drain.
- Place asparagus in refrigerator to chill.
- Combine yogurt and remaining ingredients.
- Place chilled asparagus on lettuce-lined plate.
- Top with yogurt mixture.

Low-fat or nonfat yogurt and mayonnaise may be substituted.

THREE-BEAN BAKED BEANS

Yield: 8 servings

1	16-ounce can **green lima beans**, drained
1	16-ounce can **kidney beans**, drained
1	28-ounce can **baked beans with brown sugar**
6	slices **bacon**, diced
1	medium **onion**, diced
¾	cup **ketchup**
¾	cup **dark brown sugar**
1	tablespoon **Worcestershire sauce**
1	cup **sharp Cheddar cheese**, diced

- In a large bowl, combine drained lima and kidney beans with baked beans.
- Sauté bacon and onion. Drain excess grease. Add to beans.
- Stir in ketchup, brown sugar, Worcestershire sauce, and cheese.
- Bake in a 3-quart casserole, uncovered at 325°, about 2 hours.

A new twist to ordinary baked beans. Outstanding!

GREEN BEANS BALSAMIC

Yield: 6 servings

1½ pounds fresh **green beans**, ends trimmed
    Salt
½   cup **olive oil**
3   tablespoons **balsamic vinegar**
½   teaspoon **Dijon mustard**
1   **onion**, finely chopped
1   clove **garlic**, minced
    Salt and pepper, to taste
½   cup grated **Parmesan cheese**

- Rinse beans well.
- Bring a large pot of water to boil.
- Add a sprinkle of salt and the beans; cook for 6 minutes or until beans are crisp-tender.
- Drain well and pat dry on paper towels.
- Transfer beans to a serving plate or platter.
- In a bowl, blend the oil, vinegar, and mustard.
- Add the onion, garlic, salt, pepper, and cheese.
- Check the seasoning, adding more salt and pepper if needed.
- Pour dressing over the beans, tossing lightly but thoroughly.

Serve beans warm or at room temperature.

FRESH GREEN BEANS WITH HORSERADISH SAUCE

Yield: 4 to 6 servings

1   pound fresh **green beans**, trimmed
2   tablespoons **butter**
1   teaspoon **lemon juice**
    Salt and **pepper**
½   cup **sour cream**
1   tablespoon **horseradish**

- Steam green beans until crisp-tender; drain.
- Toss beans with butter, lemon juice, salt, and pepper.
- Mix sour cream and horseradish in a small bowl.
- Arrange beans on heated platter.
- Spoon horseradish sauce over beans and serve.

Delicious fresh green bean dish!

GREEN BEANS WITH PEPPERS

Yield: 4 servings

1	pound **green beans**
1	**red pepper**, cut into strips
1	**yellow pepper**, cut into strips
½	teaspoon minced **garlic**
1	teaspoon chopped **onion**
2	teaspoons chopped **parsley**
½	cup **olive oil**
3	teaspoons **red wine vinegar**

- Cut beans, remove strings, and wash.
- Place in boiling, salted water. When almost tender, add pepper strips.
- When tender, drain vegetables and put on a platter.
- Sprinkle the garlic, onion, and parsley on top, and then pour on the oil and vinegar. Toss.

This is a favorite side dish found in many Greek restaurants.

FRESH GREEN BEANS AND DILLY CARROTS

Yield: 6 servings

¾	cup **water**
1	teaspoon **sugar**
½	teaspoon **salt**
½	teaspoon dried **dillweed**
½	pound fresh **green beans**, trimmed
4	medium **carrots**, cut into thin strips 2 to 3 inches long
¼	cup **Italian salad dressing**

- In a small saucepan, combine water, sugar, salt, and dillweed. Heat to boiling.
- Add green beans; simmer, uncovered, 5 minutes.
- Add carrots; cover and cook 7 to 8 minutes, or until vegetables are crisp-tender.
- Drain any remaining liquid.
- Toss vegetables with salad dressing.
- Serve hot or cold.

Looks elegant served as "bundles" in a cooked squash ring.

BRUSSELS SPROUTS PARMESAN

Yield: 8 servings

32 ounces frozen **Brussels sprouts** ("baby" sprouts preferred)

¼ cup (½ stick) **butter**

⅔ cup **mayonnaise**

2 tablespoons **lemon juice**

½ teaspoon **celery salt**

2 tablespoons grated **Parmesan cheese**

½ cup sliced **almonds**, toasted in sauté pan over medium heat

- Cook Brussels sprouts, without salt, but according to package directions.
- Place in a buttered 1-quart casserole and keep warm.
- Melt butter in saucepan; add mayonnaise, lemon juice, celery salt, and cheese.
- Cook over medium heat until hot, stirring constantly; do not boil. Pour over sprouts and sprinkle with sliced almonds.

The flavor of the topping really complements the vegetables.

PECAN BROCCOLI CASSEROLE

Yield: 6 servings

2 12-ounce packages frozen chopped **broccoli**, or equivalent cooked fresh

1 10¾-ounce can **cream of mushroom soup**

1 cup **mayonnaise**

¾ cup chopped **pecans**

1½ teaspoons dry **minced onion**

2 well-beaten **eggs** Nonstick **cooking spray**

1 cup grated **Cheddar cheese** **Buttered bread** or **cracker crumbs**

- Cook broccoli until tender. Drain.
- Mix in soup, mayonnaise, and chopped pecans.
- Add beaten eggs and onions.
- Pour mix into 2-quart casserole sprayed with cooking spray.
- Sprinkle with grated Cheddar cheese and buttered crumbs.
- Bake at 350° for 30 minutes.

The pecans make this casserole different from other broccoli casseroles. Very tasty!

CARROT AND ZUCCHINI CASSEROLE

Yield: 6 servings

1	pound **carrots**, cut in ½-inch diagonal slices
3	to 4 small **zucchini,** sliced
½	cup **mayonnaise**
3	tablespoons grated **onions**
¾	teaspoon **prepared horseradish**
½	teaspoon **salt**
½	teaspoon **pepper**
½	cup **Italian bread crumbs**
½	cup grated **Parmesan cheese**
¼	cup (½ stick) **butter**, melted

- In a large saucepan, cook carrots and zucchini in boiling, salted water 5 minutes or until tender.
- Drain well, reserving ¼ cup cooking liquid.
- In a bowl, combine reserved cooking liquid, mayonnaise, onions, horseradish, salt, and pepper. Add to carrots and zucchini in saucepan. Stir well.
- Spoon mixture into greased 8-inch square baking dish.
- Combine bread crumbs, Parmesan cheese, and butter. Sprinkle over casserole.
- Bake at 375° for 15 to 20 minutes.

A wonderful combination of vegetables with an excellent sauce!

CELERY ALMONDINE

Yield: 4 servings

2 tablespoons **butter**
5 cups **celery,** chopped
1 **chicken bouillon cube**, crushed
1 tablespoon **instant onion**
1 tablespoon **Accent®**
½ teaspoon **sugar**
⅛ teaspoon **garlic powder**
⅛ teaspoon ground **ginger**
⅓ cup toasted slivered **almonds**

- Put all ingredients into heavy pot with tight-fitting lid.
- Cook on high, stirring gently until butter melts and all is mixed.
- Cover and lower heat. Cook 5 to 8 minutes until celery is barely tender.
- Do not overcook.

This side dish is delightfully different, easy to prepare, and not too high in calories.

CREAMED CORN

Yield: 8 servings

20 ounces **frozen corn**
1 cup **whipping cream**
1 cup **milk**
1 teaspoon **salt**
½ teaspoon **Accent®**
6 teaspoons **sugar**
   Pinch of **pepper**
2 tablespoons melted **butter**
2 tablespoons **flour**

- Combine all ingredients except the butter and flour; bring to a boil.
- Simmer for 5 minutes.
- Blend butter with flour and add to corn mixture. Mix well and remove from heat.

This recipe, from Orlando, Florida, is served in well-known St. Louis-area restaurants.

CAPONATA

Yield: 4 servings

2 medium **eggplants**

½ cup **olive oil**

2 **onions**, chopped

1 28-ounce can **Italian plum tomatoes**

1 cup sliced **celery**

2 ounces **capers**, washed

2 tablespoons **sugar**

4 tablespoons **wine vinegar**
   Salt and **pepper,** to taste

- Wash and peel the eggplants; cut into 1-inch cubes. Dry the pieces well.
- Add oil to a large skillet. Turn the heat on high and sauté the eggplant for about 10 minutes or until soft and slightly browned.
- Remove eggplant from the skillet with a slotted spoon; place in a large saucepan.
- Sauté the onions in the skillet in the same oil, adding a little oil if necessary.
- When the onions are golden, add the tomatoes and celery; simmer about 15 minutes or until the celery is tender.
- Add the capers to the skillet and put this vegetable mixture into the saucepan with the eggplant.
- In a small pan, dissolve the sugar into the vinegar; add the salt and pepper to taste, and heat the liquid slightly.
- Pour this sweet-and-sour mixture over the vegetables; cover and simmer about 20 minutes over very low heat, stirring occasionally to distribute the flavors evenly.

Serve warm as a side dish, cold as an appetizer.

BURGUNDY MUSHROOMS

Yield: 16 servings

1½	cups (3 sticks) **butter**
1	quart **Burgundy wine**
2	tablespoons **Worcestershire sauce**
1	teaspoon **dill seed** (or ¾ teaspoon **dillweed**)
1	teaspoon **black pepper**
1	teaspoon **garlic powder**
2	cups boiling **water**
3	**beef bouillon cubes**
4	pounds **mushrooms**

- Combine all ingredients except mushrooms in a large Dutch oven and bring to a boil.
- Add mushrooms to liquid and reduce heat to simmer.
- Cover and cook 5 hours.
- Remove lid and cook 4 more hours.
- When ready, liquid should just cover mushrooms.

Excellent party dish!

MUSHROOM CASSEROLE

Yield: 4 to 6 servings

1	pound small whole **mushrooms**
6	tablespoons **butter**
2	**beef bouillon cubes**
½	cup hot **water**
2	tablespoons **flour**
½	cup **half-and-half**
½	teaspoon **salt**
	Dash of **pepper**
½	to 1 cup grated **Parmesan cheese**
½	cup **bread crumbs**

- Sauté mushrooms in 2 tablespoons of the butter; transfer to greased 9 x 9-inch pan.
- Dissolve bouillon cubes in hot water.
- In a saucepan, melt remaining 4 tablespoons butter; blend in flour.
- Slowly add half-and-half, salt, pepper, and bouillon, cooking until smooth. Pour over mushrooms.
- Mix cheese and crumbs; spread over mushrooms.
- Bake at 350° for 30 minutes.

Very flavorful. Excellent with beef, game, or pork.

HERBED CHEESE ONIONS

Yield: 6 to 8 servings

6	cups thinly sliced **onions**
¼	cup (½ stick) **margarine**
¼	cup **flour**
1	12-ounce can **evaporated milk**
⅓	cup **water**
1	teaspoon dried **parsley flakes**
½	teaspoon **salt**
¾	teaspoon **marjoram**
1	cup shredded **Cheddar cheese**
	Paprika

- Preheat oven to 325°.
- Parboil onions in a small amount of water 2 to 3 minutes.
- Drain and place in 2-quart casserole.
- In a small saucepan, melt margarine. Blend in flour. Gradually, stir in evaporated milk, and then add water. Cook and stir until thick.
- Add remaining ingredients except paprika. Stir until cheese is melted.
- Pour sauce over onions.
- Bake at 325° for 1 hour.
- Sprinkle with paprika.

SNOW PEAS WITH ROQUEFORT SAUCE

Yield: 6 servings

1	pound **snow peas**, trimmed
½	cup **heavy cream**
2	tablespoons **Roquefort cheese** (or to taste)
2	tablespoons **butter**
	Salt, to taste
	Freshly ground **pepper**, to taste

- Cook snow peas in boiling water for 3 minutes, or steam until tender; don't overcook. (They should remain a bright green color.)
- Place cream in a saucepan and boil, stirring constantly, reducing by a third.
- Mash Roquefort and whisk into cream until smooth.
- Remove from heat and whisk in butter, salt, and pepper.
- Serve sauce over top of peas, or stir peas directly into sauce.

Simple, elegant, and delicious!

LOWER-FAT TWICE-BAKED POTATOES

Yield: 8 servings

4   large baking **potatoes**

3   **green onions**, chopped
     Salt and **pepper**

1   8-ounce container nonfat
     plain yogurt

⅓   cup grated **Cheddar
     cheese**
     Paprika

- Wash and scrub potatoes.
- Bake at 425° 50 to
  60 minutes. (Puncture skin
  with a fork halfway through
  cooking to allow steam to
  escape.)
- When potatoes are done,
  slice in half lengthwise and
  allow them to cool.
- When cool enough to
  handle, scoop out the pulp
  into a large mixing bowl,
  leaving the skin intact.
- Mash potatoes and add
  onions, salt and pepper,
  yogurt, and cheese. Mix well.
- Fill shells with potato
  mixture and sprinkle with
  paprika.
- Bake at 375° for 10 minutes.
  Then run under broiler until
  golden brown on top, about
  2 to 3 minutes.

*Nonfat yogurt reduces the fat
found in the traditional recipe.*

LOW-FAT ROASTED GARLIC
MASHED POTATOES

Yield: 6 servings

1   large **garlic head**

1   teaspoon **light olive oil**

2   pounds baking **potatoes**, peeled and cut in 1-inch cubes

2   tablespoons **unsalted butter**

¼   cup **2% low-fat milk**, warmed

1   cup **low-fat cottage cheese**, drained in a sieve for 1 hour

¼   teaspoon grated **nutmeg**

¼   teaspoon ground **white pepper**, or to taste

   Coarse salt, to taste

- Preheat oven to 350°.
- Cut the top off of the head of garlic with a sharp knife.
- Place the head of garlic on a piece of aluminum foil, drizzle with the olive oil, and enclose within the foil.
- Bake garlic for 1 hour. Cool.
- With a blunt knife, remove the garlic pulp from the cloves in the garlic head. (The pulp will separate very easily from the skin.) Set aside.
- Boil the potatoes until tender, about 12 minutes, and drain.
- Transfer potatoes to a large bowl and add butter.
- Add the milk, cottage cheese, and the roasted garlic pulp to the potatoes.
- Whip until smooth with a hand mixer or potato masher. Add seasonings and adjust to taste.

The roasted garlic gives these mashed potatoes a sweet, mellow flavor. A popular side dish for entertaining, you can make ahead and reheat.

MASHED POTATO CASSEROLE

Yield: 10 to 12 servings

10	medium **potatoes**
1	teaspoon **garlic salt**
1	teaspoon **onion salt**
1	8-ounce package **cream cheese,** softened
1	cup **sour cream**
	Melted **butter**
	Paprika
	Chives (optional)

- Peel potatoes; boil until tender.
- Combine potatoes, garlic salt, onion salt, softened cream cheese, and sour cream in a large bowl; using an electric mixer, blend until creamy.
- Spoon mixture into buttered 9 x 13-inch casserole.
- Generously brush the top with melted butter.
- Sprinkle lightly with paprika and garnish with chives.
- Bake for 30 minutes at 350° or until hot.

PARMESAN POTATOES

Yield: 6 servings

½	cup (1 stick) **butter**
6	large **potatoes**
½	cup grated **Parmesan cheese**
⅓	cup **flour**
½	teaspoon **salt**
¼	teaspoon **pepper**

- Cut butter into several pieces and place butter on jellyroll pan. Heat until melted. Set aside.
- Peel potatoes; quarter lengthwise.
- In a large plastic bag, combine cheese, flour, salt, and pepper.
- Add potatoes and shake to coat.
- Place potatoes in butter on pan.
- Bake at 375° for 1 hour or until tender, turning halfway through cooking.

POTATOES WITH SHIITAKE CREAM SAUCE

Yield: 6 servings

8   large **shiitake mushrooms**, stems removed and discarded

1   tablespoon **olive oil**

8   medium **red potatoes**, sliced ⅛ inch thick

3   tablespoons minced fresh **chives**

¼   cup (½ stick) **butter**, melted

    Salt and **pepper**, to taste

1¼   cups **heavy cream**

- Slice shiitake mushrooms in narrow ⅛-inch slices.

- Sauté in olive oil until softened and aromatic.
- Divide mushrooms, potatoes, and chives into thirds.
- Lightly butter 8 x 8-inch baking dish.
- Layer ⅓ of potatoes on the bottom. Drizzle ⅓ of butter over potatoes. Sprinkle with salt and pepper, to taste. Sprinkle ⅓ of mushrooms and ⅓ of chives.
- Repeat above step to get 3 layers.
- Gently pour cream over top.
- Bake at 350° for 1 hour.

Can be assembled early in the day and then baked that evening.

POTATOES BOURSIN

Yield: 8 servings

2   cups **whipping cream**

5   ounces **Boursin cheese with herbs**

3   pounds unpeeled, uncooked, thinly sliced **new potatoes**

1½   tablespoons **parsley**

- Preheat oven to 400°.
- Butter 9 x 13-inch baking dish.
- In a saucepan, stir whipping cream and cheese on medium heat until smooth.
- Layer the baking dish with half of the potatoes and half of the sauce, and then the other half of the potatoes and the sauce.
- Sprinkle with parsley.
- Bake at 400° for 1 hour, uncovered.

ROASTED NEW POTATOES WITH LEMON

Yield: 8 to 10 servings

3   pounds small new **red potatoes**, quartered
    Salt and freshly ground **pepper**

¼   cup (½ stick) **unsalted butter**

¼   cup **olive oil**

6   tablespoons **lemon juice**

2   teaspoons dried **thyme**

1   tablespoon grated **lemon peel**

3   tablespoons minced fresh **parsley**

- Preheat oven to 375°.
- Butter large, shallow oven-safe casserole.
- Add potatoes. Season generously with salt and pepper.
- Melt butter and oil in small saucepan over low heat. Add lemon juice.
- Pour butter mixture over potatoes. Sprinkle with thyme and toss.
- Bake 1 hour.
- Add lemon peel and toss, coating potatoes.
- Continue baking until potatoes are tender and browned, about 15 minutes.
- Sprinkle potatoes with parsley and serve.

Absolutely outstanding flavor!

Sweet Potato Soufflé
with Pineapple and Coconut

Yield: 10 to 12 servings

8	medium **sweet potatoes**
½	cup (1 stick) **margarine**
½	cup **granulated sugar**
¼	cup **brown sugar**
2	well-beaten **eggs**
2	teaspoons **baking powder**
1	cup drained, **crushed pineapple**
½	teaspoon **salt**
½	cup **coconut**

- Wash sweet potatoes and place in a jellyroll pan. Cover with foil.
- Bake at 400° for 45 to 60 minutes until fork completely penetrates potato.
- Cool, peel, and put potatoes in a large mixing bowl.
- Mash potatoes until smooth. Stir in margarine and sugars.
- Add the eggs, and baking powder, pineapple, and salt. Mix well.
- Transfer ingredients into well-greased 2-quart casserole dish.
- Bake at 350° for about 30 minutes.
- Remove from oven and cover the soufflé with coconut.
- Bake an additional 10 minutes (or until light brown).

Delicious and makes a nice presentation!

BUTTERNUT SQUASH CASSEROLE

Yield: 6 to 8 servings

2 pounds **butternut squash**, cubed (approximately 6 cups)

¼ cup chopped **onion**

1 10¾-ounce can condensed **cream of chicken soup**

1 cup **sour cream**

1 cup shredded **carrots**

1 8-ounce package **seasoned stuffing mix**

½ cup (1 stick) **margarine**, melted

- Cook squash and onion in boiling, salted water for 5 minutes. Drain; set aside.
- In a mixing bowl, combine cream of chicken soup and sour cream; then add shredded carrots.
- Mix stuffing mix and margarine. Place half of stuffing mix in bottom of baking dish.
  (Can make your own stuffing with cubed, toasted, or dried bread, browned in margarine.)
- Add half of squash and half of soup, cream, and carrot mixture.
- Then add rest of squash and soup mixture.
- Top with rest of stuffing mix. Bake at 350° for 25 to 30 minutes.

Can be made hours ahead and baked. Reheats extremely well in microwave.

PURÉED BUTTERNUT SQUASH

Yield: 4 to 6 servings

2	medium **butternut squash**
	Peanut or **vegetable oil**
1	**egg**, beaten
1	tablespoon **brown sugar**
¼	teaspoon ground **allspice**
¼	teaspoon **cardamom**
⅛	teaspoon **white pepper**
⅛	teaspoon **cayenne pepper**
⅛	teaspoon **salt**
2	to 3 tablespoons **cream**
2	**egg whites**, stiffly beaten
	Pecan halves, for garnish

- Cut the squash in half, scoop out the seeds, and brush the surface with oil.
- Bake, cut side down, on a foil-lined baking sheet in a 375° oven until tender.
- Let cool about 30 minutes.
- Scoop the baked squash into a bowl.
- Stir in the egg and seasonings, then the cream. Gently fold in the egg whites.
- Spoon into a buttered 1½-quart baking dish.
- Garnish with pecan halves.
- Bake at 350° for 30 to 35 minutes until top is golden.

A nice vegetable for Thanksgiving or autumn meals.

SUMMER SQUASH CASSEROLE

Yield: 6 to 8 servings

6 cups **yellow squash**, cubed

½ cup dairy **sour cream**

2 tablespoons **butter**, melted

½ cup shredded **Cheddar cheese**

1½ teaspoons **salt**

¼ teaspoon **paprika**

2 beaten **egg yolks**

2 tablespoons chopped **chives** or **sliced green onions**

½ cup grated **Parmesan cheese**

½ cup dry **bread crumbs**

2 tablespoons **butter**, softened

- Cook squash until tender; drain and set aside.
- In medium saucepan, combine sour cream, melted butter, cheese, salt, and paprika. Stir over low heat until cheese melts.
- Stir in egg yolks and chives. Stir in cooked squash.
- Place in buttered 2-quart casserole dish.
- Sprinkle with Parmesan cheese and bread crumbs; dot with butter.
- Bake at 350° 25 to 30 minutes or until bubbly and brown.

A wonderful way to use up all that summer squash.

FRESH AND SUN-DRIED TOMATOES WITH ZUCCHINI AND BALSAMIC VINEGAR

Yield: 4 servings

1 pound **tomatoes**, cut into thin wedges

½ pound **zucchini**, sliced in two lengthwise and then cut into ¼-inch slices

6 **sun-dried tomato halves** (in oil), cut into thin strips

2 tablespoons extra virgin **olive oil**

2 teaspoons **balsamic vinegar**

½ teaspoon **salt**

¼ teaspoon **pepper**

- Toss all ingredients together and let marinate at room temperature for 30 to 60 minutes.

This recipe has a Southwest touch. It's easy to make, yet refreshing and different. Especially good with summertime meals.

SPICY ZUCCHINI CASSEROLE

Yield: 6 servings

3 to 4 **zucchini**

1 medium **onion**

1 10-ounce can diced **tomatoes and green chilies**

½ teaspoon **salt**

¼ teaspoon **black pepper**

1½ tablespoons **butter**, softened

Freshly grated **Romano cheese**

- Scrub the zucchini. Slice ½ inch thick and put into 2-quart casserole.
- Slice onion and add to casserole. Stir in tomatoes and green chilies, salt, and pepper.
- Divide butter and dot on top of mixture.
- Sprinkle with Romano cheese until thickly covered.
- Cover and bake at 350° 50 minutes.

You can substitute Mexican stewed tomatoes for the diced tomatoes and green chilies.

SOULARD FARMERS MARKET
VEGETABLE PLATTER

Yield: 6 servings

1	pound **fresh broccoli**, cut into ½-inch pieces
½	head **cauliflower**, cut into florets
1	medium **zucchini**, cut into ¼-inch slices
2	tablespoons **water**
¼	cup (½ stick) **butter** or **margarine**
½	teaspoon **garlic salt**
2	medium **tomatoes**, cut into wedges
½	cup freshly grated **Parmesan cheese**

- On a microwave-safe platter, arrange broccoli and cauliflower around outer edge.
- Place zucchini in center of platter and sprinkle with water.
- Cover tightly with heavy-duty plastic wrap; fold back a small edge of wrap to allow steam to escape.
- Microwave on high 5 to 7 minutes or until vegetables are crisp-tender.
- Let stand, covered, 2 minutes.
- Combine butter and garlic salt in a 1-cup glass measure.
- Microwave on high 55 seconds; mix well.
- Lift plastic wrap from one side of platter and drain.
- Remove plastic wrap.
- Arrange tomato wedges around edge of platter; drizzle butter mixture over vegetables. Sprinkle with cheese and microwave on high 1 to 2 minutes.

CONNOISSEUR'S VEGETABLE CASSEROLE

Yield: 8 servings

1	12-ounce can **shoe-peg corn** (white), drained
1	16-ounce can **French-cut green beans**, drained
½	cup chopped **celery**
½	cup chopped **onion**
1	2-ounce jar **pimientos**, chopped
½	cup **sour cream**
½	cup grated **sharp Cheddar cheese**
1	10¾-ounce can **cream of celery soup**
½	teaspoon **salt**
½	teaspoon **pepper**

Topping:

1	cup **Ritz® cracker crumbs**
¼	cup (½ stick) **butter**, melted
½	cup **slivered almonds**

- Mix all ingredients except topping. Place in 1½-quart casserole.
- Combine topping ingredients.
- Sprinkle topping over casserole.
- Bake at 350° for 45 minutes.

This casserole has an excellent flavor and a good mix of textures

ITALIAN POLENTA WITH VEGETABLES

Yield: 6 to 8 servings

Polenta:

1	cup **yellow cornmeal**
4½	cups **water**
1½	teaspoons **salt**
½	cup shredded **Cheddar cheese**
	Salt, black pepper, and **cayenne pepper,** to taste
	Olive oil

Tomato Sauce:

2	tablespoons **olive oil**
1	small **onion**, chopped
3	cloves **garlic**, minced
1	6-ounce can **no-salt tomato paste**
1	8-ounce can **tomato sauce**
1	cup **water**
½	teaspoon **basil**
½	teaspoon **oregano**
½	teaspoon dried **parsley flakes**
½	teaspoon **Worcestershire sauce**
2	**bay leaves**
1	**chicken bouillon cube**
	Ground **black pepper**
	Splash of **red wine** (optional)

Vegetables:

1	tablespoon **olive oil**
1	clove **garlic**
1	**red pepper**, cut into strips
2	medium **zucchini**, julienned
½	pound **mushrooms**, sliced thin
	Salt and **pepper**

Topping:

½	cup grated **mozzarella cheese**
	Grated **Parmesan cheese**

Polenta:

- In a bowl, whisk together cornmeal and 2 cups of the water.
- Bring the other 2½ cups water and salt to a boil and add cornmeal mixture, whisking to remove any lumps.
- Whisk until mixture returns to a boil. Reduce heat to low and cook 25 to 30 minutes until very thick, whisking frequently.
- Remove from heat and stir in cheese. Season with salt and peppers.

ITALIAN POLENTA WITH VEGETABLES *(continued)*

- Brush a 9 x 13-inch baking pan lightly with olive oil.
- Spread mixture in pan, smoothing top.
- Cover and refrigerate for at least 3 hours or overnight.

Tomato Sauce:
- Sauté onion and garlic in olive oil about 2 to 3 minutes (until onion is softened).
- Add tomato paste, tomato sauce, and water; mix well.
- Add seasonings and wine, and simmer 10 to 15 minutes, stirring occasionally.
- Adjust seasonings if necessary.

Vegetables:
- Sauté garlic and pepper strips in olive oil 2 minutes.
- Add zucchini and mushrooms; cook, stirring 4 to 5 minutes until zucchini is crisp-tender.
- Season with salt and pepper.

To Assemble:
- Cut polenta into 3-inch squares, then cut diagonally into triangles.
- Remove from baking dish.
- Remove bay leaves from sauce and ladle enough sauce into baking dish to generously cover the bottom of the dish.
- Arrange the polenta triangles over sauce in slightly overlapping rows.
- Spoon vegetables over polenta and sprinkle with grated mozzarella and Parmesan cheese.
- Bake at 375° for 25 to 30 minutes, or until cheese bubbles and polenta is heated.

Polenta is a traditional Italian dish. It's a wonderful vegetarian entrée or is an excellent side dish for grilled meats.

MEDITERRANEAN SAUTÉ

Yield: 4 servings

1	cup **green pepper** strips
1	cup **zucchini** slices
½	cup **onion** rings
½	teaspoon dried **oregano** leaves, crushed
1	tablespoon **margarine**
½	cup **cherry tomato** halves
¾	cup crumbled **feta cheese**

- Combine peppers, zucchini, onions, oregano, and margarine in 1½-quart casserole.
- Cover and microwave on high 4 minutes, stirring after 2 minutes.
- Add tomatoes; continue to microwave 1 minute.
- Top with cheese and serve.

Great in the summer when fresh vegetables are bountiful. You can make conventionally too, by sautéing vegetables together until tender; then top with cheese.

VEGETABLE PAELLA

Yield: 8 servings

1	tablespoon **olive oil**
1	tablespoon chopped **jalepeño pepper**
1	large **red onion**, quartered and thick sliced
1	large **red pepper**, chopped
1	large **green pepper**, chopped
2	cloves **garlic**, minced
1½	teaspoons **paprika**
1	teaspoon **thyme**
4	large fresh chopped **tomatoes**
	Salt and **pepper**, to taste
1¼	cups **brown rice**
2	cups **chicken stock** or **bouillon**
1	**zucchini**, halved and sliced in ½-inch thick pieces

- In a large skillet, heat oil and add next 4 ingredients.
- Cook 20 minutes on medium-low heat until vegetables are tender.
- Add next 4 ingredients, and salt and pepper. Cover and simmer 15 minutes.
- Add rice and chicken stock and bring to a boil. Reduce heat to medium-low, cover, and simmer until rice is almost tender, about 45 minutes.
- Add zucchini and continue to cook 15 minutes.

An iron skillet works best for this recipe. Here is a foolproof way to "season" yours: Place a thick layer of salt in skillet. Cover with ¼ inch of vegetable oil. Heat on medium heat until skillet smokes. Pour out salt and oil and wipe with paper towel. Avoid soaps on skillet to preserve seasoning.

MIXED GRILL OF SEASONAL VEGETABLES

Yield: 4 to 6 servings

Spring:

> Baked **artichokes**, trimmed, cut in half lengthwise, and blanched
>
> **Asparagus**, quickly blanched
>
> **Garlic heads**, cut in half lengthwise
>
> **Green onions** or **baking leeks**
>
> Sliced **yellow** and/or **green squash**

Summer:

> **Tomato** halves
>
> **Green** and/or **golden zucchini**, cut into lengthwise slices
>
> **Red, yellow,** and **green bell peppers**, cut into quarters
>
> **Eggplant**, sliced or halved
>
> **Red onion** slices

Fall:

> Whole large cultivated **white** or **brown mushrooms**
>
> Whole **shiitake mushrooms**

> **Onion** slices
>
> Blanched **turnip** slices
>
> **Potato** slices
>
> **Banana** or **butternut squash**

Winter:

> **Belgian endive**, cut in half lengthwise
>
> **Radicchio**, cut in half or quarters lengthwise
>
> Blanched **fennel** slices
>
> Blanched sliced **beets**

For grilling vegetables:

> Extra virgin **olive oil**
>
> **Salt**, to taste
>
> **Fresh seasonal herbs**
>
> **Lemon** wedges

- Heat gas or charcoal grill, or a ridged stove-top griddle until medium-hot.
- Lightly brush vegetables with olive oil.
- Cook until grill marks are apparent, being careful not to overcook.
- Transfer to large platter. Drizzle with olive oil, herbs of your choice scattered over the vegetables, or with lemon wedges.

Pasta and rice dishes have always been popular in St. Louis, and their ingredients and preparation have been greatly influenced by the Italian Hill neighborhood in the south part of the city. The Hill, with its tidy streets, yards, and small brick homes, offers a wide variety of fine Italian restaurants, bakeries, and grocery stores which feature hard to find ingredients and specialties.

• • •

Kemoll's

*In 1927, Dora Kemoll (Camuglia) opened a confectionary in North
St. Louis, which grew into the oldest family-owned and operated restaurant
in St. Louis. Neighbors to the St. Louis Cardinals when they called
Sportsman's Park their home, Kemoll's Restaurant was a North St. Louis
landmark for over 60 years. The Kemoll and Cusamano families relocated
their famous restaurant to downtown in 1990 and continue to be a leader in
fine Italian-style dining and outstanding made-on-the-premises pastas.*

PAGLIA E FIENO (STRAW AND HAY)

Yield: 4 servings

2   ounces **prosciutto ham**,
      sliced thin and diced
      Olive oil

1½   cups **heavy cream** (40%)

¼   cup (½ stick) **unsalted
      butter**

1   cup sliced **mushrooms**
      Salt and **pepper**

8   ounces fresh or dried
      yellow fettucine, cooked
      and drained

4   ounces **spinach
      fettucine**, cooked and
      drained

¼   cup **peas**

1   cup grated **Asiago** or
      Parmesan cheese

- In a large skillet, sauté
  prosciutto with 2 to 3 drops
  olive oil until very crispy.
- Add cream, butter, mushrooms, and salt and pepper,
  to taste. Boil until reduced
  by a third.
- Add pasta and peas. Continue to reduce sauce until
  thick and creamy.
- Serve tossed with cheese.

*To "lighten" this recipe, substitute
chicken stock or wine for ½ cup
of the cream and omit the butter.*

BENEDETTO'S PENNETTI CON PORCINI

Yield: 6 servings

1   ounce dried wild **Italian (porcini) mushrooms**, or ¼ pound fresh **morel mushrooms**

1   cup warm **water**

2   tablespoons **butter**, if using morel mushrooms

6   to 8 cups **chicken broth**

5   tablespoons **butter**

1   medium **onion**, finely chopped

2½   cups **pennetti pasta**

¾   cup **dry white wine**

½   cup freshly grated **Parmesan cheese**
     Salt

- Soak porcini mushrooms in warm water for 20 minutes.
- Drain mushrooms, reserving liquid; strain liquid.
- Rinse mushrooms under cold running water. Squeeze to remove as much moisture as possible.
- If using morel mushrooms, sauté in 2 tablespoons butter until golden brown; set aside.
- Heat broth in medium saucepan.

- In large saucepan, melt 4 tablespoons butter. When butter foams, add onion. Sauté over medium heat until pale yellow.
- Add pennetti pasta to onion and mix well.
- When pasta is coated with butter, add wine. Cook, stirring constantly, until wine has evaporated.
- Add drained porcini mushrooms and reserved mushroom liquid. (If using morel mushrooms, skip this step.)
- Stir in 1 or 2 ladles of broth, or enough to cover the pasta. Stir over medium heat until broth is absorbed.
- Continue cooking and stirring pasta, adding broth a little at a time until pasta is done, 15 to 20 minutes. Pasta should be tender, but firm to the bite.
- Stir in Parmesan cheese, the remaining 1 tablespoon of the butter, and sautéed morel mushrooms, if using them.
- Season with salt.
- Place in a warm dish. Serve immediately.

Benedetto Buzzetta of Benedetto's Ristorante shares his popular pasta dish.

PUTANESCA SAUCE
(FOR USE ON PASTA OR FISH)

Yield: 4 servings

2	tablespoons **olive oil**
1	to 2 teaspoons minced fresh **garlic**
1	16-ounce can recipe-ready diced **tomatoes**
1	teaspoon **sugar**
1	teaspoon **salt**
⅛	teaspoon **red pepper flakes**
¼	cup sliced **black olives**
1	to 2 tablespoons **capers**
1	teaspoon chopped **fresh parsley**

- In a skillet or saucepan, heat oil over medium heat.
- Add garlic and toss to lightly sauté, but do not brown.
- Add tomatoes (undrained), sugar, salt, red pepper, olives, capers, and parsley.
- Sauté over medium heat for 10 to 12 minutes.
- Toss with pasta or spoon over grilled fresh fish fillets, such as tuna, halibut, or swordfish.

A quick, easy, and versatile sauce.

HERBED COUSCOUS AND VEGETABLES

Yield: 4 servings

1	cup sliced fresh **mushrooms**
1	tablespoon **butter** or **margarine**
1	cup **water**
1	tablespoon minced fresh **parsley**
1	tablespoon fresh chopped **basil**
¼	teaspoon **salt**
⅛	teaspoon dried **oregano**
	Dash **pepper**
⅔	cup uncooked **couscous**
1	medium **tomato**, chopped

- In a medium saucepan, cook mushrooms in hot butter until tender.
- Stir in water, parsley, basil, salt, oregano, and pepper. Bring to a boil; remove from heat.
- Stir in couscous and tomato. Cover and let sit for 5 minutes.

Delicious, quick, and low-fat side dish.

VEGETABLE RICE CASSEROLE

Yield: 4 servings (8 as a side dish)

3   cups cooked long-grain **white rice** (or brown)

1½   cups chopped **broccoli**

½   cup chopped **cauliflower**

2   medium **carrots**, sliced ¼ inch thick

1   small **zucchini**, sliced ¼ inch thick

¼   cup **olive oil**

1   small yellow **onion**, chopped

3   cloves **garlic**, minced (or 1 teaspoon garlic powder)

2   medium **tomatoes**, cut into eighths

6   ounces fresh **spinach**, washed and stemmed

1   teaspoon **salt**

½   teaspoon **pepper**

⅓   cup grated **Parmesan cheese**

¼   cup (generous) **bread crumbs**

1½   cups grated **Cheddar cheese**, divided

- Preheat oven to 350°.
- While rice is cooking, partially steam broccoli, cauliflower, carrots, and zucchini. (If using microwave, add 3 tablespoons water to vegetables. Cook on high 5 minutes and 50 seconds in microwave-safe dish covered with plastic wrap.)
- Heat oil in a 12-inch frying pan. Add onion and garlic, stir in tomatoes, and sauté for 10 minutes.
- Add well-rinsed spinach (a handful at a time, covering frying pan and allowing spinach to shrink). Continue to sauté 5 minutes longer.
- In large bowl, combine rice and vegetables. (If using microwave, drain water.)
- Mix in salt, pepper, and remaining ingredients, except ½ cup grated Cheddar cheese. Do not overmix.
- Transfer to greased 3-quart casserole dish and top with remaining ½ cup cheese. Sprinkle salt and pepper on top, if desired.
- Cover and bake 10 minutes. Remove lid and bake 10 minutes longer.

Wonderful when served with warm French bread and a fresh fruit salad.

BROWN RICE WITH SPINACH AND CHEESE

Yield: 4 servings

1   teaspoon **butter**
1   teaspoon **vegetable oil**
1   **onion**, finely chopped
1   cup brown **rice**
1   cup hot **water**
1   cup **chicken broth**
4   ounces **white Cheddar cheese**, grated
2   large **eggs**, beaten
2   tablespoons chopped fresh **parsley**
1   pound fresh **spinach**, stems removed, chopped or 10-ounce package frozen spinach, thawed and squeezed dry of liquid
¼   cup minced **sun-dried tomatoes** *(see note)*
⅛   teaspoon grated **nutmeg**

Topping:

2   tablespoons **whole wheat bread crumbs**
1   tablespoon **butter**, melted
2   teaspoons minced fresh **parsley**
⅛   teaspoon **salt** or **seasoned salt**
⅛   teaspoon **cayenne pepper**

- Melt butter with oil in saucepan; sauté onion until soft. Add rice and stir to incorporate.
- Add hot water and broth; stir.
- Cover and simmer 40 minutes or until rice is tender and liquid is absorbed.
- Remove rice into a bowl and allow to cool about 10 minutes.
- Stir cheese into the rice. Add the eggs, parsley, spinach, tomatoes, and nutmeg.
- Spoon rice mixture into a buttered 1-quart soufflé dish.
- Mix the topping ingredients together and sprinkle over the top.
- Bake in a preheated 350° oven for about 35 minutes or until top is golden.

If preparing ahead, cover spinach and rice mixture and refrigerate up to 1 day in advance. When ready to serve, bring spinach and rice to room temperature, mix and add topping, and bake as directed.

*If using tomatoes in oil, drain well before mincing; if using dehydrated tomatoes, allow to soak 10 minutes in hot water, then drain and mince.

ARTICHOKE PROSCIUTTO LINGUINE

Yield: 2 servings

½ tablespoon **olive oil**

½ tablespoon **butter**

2 teaspoons **flour**

¾ cup **chicken stock** or **bouillon**

2 cloves **garlic**, minced

1 tablespoon fresh **lemon juice**

½ cup chopped fresh **parsley**

8 cooked **artichoke hearts** (canned works well), sliced in quarters or eighths

2 tablespoons freshly grated **Parmesan cheese**

⅛ to ¼ pound **prosciutto ham**, trimmed of fat and sliced thin

¼ pound **mushrooms**, sliced and sautéed

¾ pound **linguine**
   Salt and **pepper**

- In a skillet, heat olive oil and butter until moderately hot. Add flour, stirring constantly and gently simmering for 1 minute.
- Add chicken stock, garlic, lemon juice, and parsley. Stir over medium heat 5 minutes.
- Add artichoke hearts, Parmesan, prosciutto, and mushrooms. Cover and cook over low heat 5 to 7 minutes.
- Serve over linguine prepared according to package directions.
- Salt and pepper to taste.

RIGATONI ALLA GIOVANNI

Yield: 2 servings

1   to 2 tablespoons **olive oil**
1   medium **onion**, chopped
2   cloves **garlic**, minced
½   pound **ground veal**
½   pound **ground pork**
1   14½-ounce can **tomatoes**
1   cup **dry red wine**
2   teaspoons dried **oregano**
2   teaspoons dried **basil**
¼   teaspoon **fennel seed**, crushed
    Salt and **pepper**
6   tablespoons **whipping cream**
8   ounces **rigatoni** or **other pasta**, cooked

- Heat olive oil in saucepan over medium heat.
- Sauté onion and garlic until translucent.
- Add veal and pork and brown thoroughly. Drain and discard fat.
- Stir in tomatoes (chopped slightly), wine, oregano, basil, and fennel.
- Simmer over low heat 30 to 45 minutes.
- Season to taste with salt and pepper.
- Just before serving, stir in cream and heat through.
- Serve sauce over pasta (rigatoni, penne, ziti, or other tubular noodle), along with crusty bread and a dry red wine.

Sauce can be made in advance and reheated.

PENNE WITH VODKA-TOMATO CREAM SAUCE

Yield: 4 servings

1   tablespoon **butter**

1   tablespoon **olive oil**

1   small **onion**, finely chopped

1   28-ounce can **Italian plum tomatoes**, drained, seeded, and chopped

1   cup **whipping cream**

¼   cup **vodka**

¼   teaspoon dried crushed **red pepper**
      Salt and **pepper**

1   pound **penne pasta**, cooked and drained

2   tablespoons fresh **basil leaves**, finely chopped

¼   cup freshly grated **Parmesan cheese**

- Melt butter with oil in heavy sauté pan over medium heat.
- Add onion and sauté until tender, about 8 minutes.
- Add tomatoes and cook until juice has almost evaporated, stirring frequently, about 25 minutes.
- Add cream, vodka, and red pepper. Bring to a boil and allow to thicken, about 2 minutes. Season to taste with salt and pepper.
- Add pasta and toss to cover. Add the basil and about 1 tablespoon of the Parmesan.
- Divide among plates. Sprinkle with additional cheese.

Sauce can be made ahead and refrigerated. Reheat when pasta is cooked just prior to serving.

FETTUCINE VISTAFJORD

Yield: 4 to 5 servings

3   tablespoons **butter**

1   cup **onions**, chopped

¼   pound **ham**, cut into strips

1½   cups **heavy cream**

1   pound **fettucine**
     (½ green and ½ white if possible)

¾   cup (about 3 ounces) grated **Gruyère cheese**
     Salt and freshly ground **pepper** to taste

½   cup (about 2 ounces) freshly grated **Parmesan cheese**

- Bring salted water for pasta to a boil.
- Meanwhile, in a large skillet, heat butter and sauté onions and ham until onions are limp, but not brown.
- Stir in heavy cream and keep warm over low heat.
- Add fettucine to boiling water and cook until just done.
- Rinse pasta under hot water and drain.
- Place pasta in a warm serving bowl; add cream mixture and Gruyère. Toss to mix.
- Add salt and pepper to taste.
- Sprinkle with Parmesan cheese and serve.
- Pass additional Parmesan if desired.

Adapted from the chef of the cruise ship Vistafjord.

SPAGHETTI CARBONARA

Yield: 4 to 6 servings

¼ pound **bacon**, cut into 1-inch lengths

3 tablespoons **olive oil**

1½ cups chopped **onion**

½ cup finely chopped **parsley**

1 cup finely diced **fontina cheese**

⅔ cup finely shredded **prosciutto** or **Virginia ham**

2 **egg yolks**, lightly beaten
  Red hot pepper flakes

1 pound **spaghetti**
  Freshly ground **pepper**

1 cup freshly grated **Parmesan cheese**

- Heat bacon pieces in a heavy skillet and cook, stirring frequently, until crisp.
- Using a slotted spoon, transfer the bacon to a paper towel to drain.
- Pour off almost all the fat from the skillet, but do not wash the skillet. Add olive oil and onion. Cook until onion is tender.
- Prepare (chopping, beating, and so on) the parsley, cheese, prosciutto, and egg yolks. Keep these ingredients, plus the bacon bits and pepper flakes, close at hand.
- Have a hot dish ready for tossing the spaghetti, and hot bowls ready to receive the portions.
- Cook the spaghetti in boiling salted water to the desired degree of doneness.
- Drain quickly, then pour the spaghetti into the hot dish.
- Add the bacon bits, onion, parsley, fontina cheese, prosciutto, beaten egg yolks, and red pepper flakes to taste. Toss quickly and thoroughly with a fork and spoon.
- Serve in hot bowls and pass the pepper and Parmesan cheese.

Careful adding pepper flakes - very hot!

209

LEMON LINGUINE PARMESAN

Yield: 4 servings (2 as main dish)

2   tablespoons **olive oil**
2   cloves **garlic**, minced
½   cup **milk**
1   9-ounce package **linguine**
⅓   cup fresh **lemon juice**
½   cup grated fresh
    Parmesan cheese
¼   cup minced **parsley**
    Pepper

- Heat the olive oil in a skillet and sauté the garlic for 1 minute.
- Add milk and heat gently. Keep warm.
- Meanwhile, cook linguine.
- Drain linguine and toss with lemon juice.
- Pour garlic mixture over pasta and toss.
- Add Parmesan, parsley, and pepper. Mix well and serve immediately.

PEPPERONI PASTA

Yield: 4 servings

3   tablespoons **olive oil**
2   cloves **garlic**, crushed
1   small yellow **onion**, peeled
    and diced
2   ripe **tomatoes**, chopped
½   pound **pepperoni**, thinly
    sliced
¼   cup **whipping cream**
1   teaspoon **salt**
    Pepper to taste
½   pound **pasta**, cooked
    al dente
    Grated **Parmesan cheese**

- Heat oil in large frying pan and sauté garlic and onion until transparent.
- Add tomatoes and pepperoni. Sauté until the tomatoes cook down a bit, about 3 minutes.
- Stir in cream, salt, and pepper.
- Toss with pasta and Parmesan cheese.

Spinach Manicotti

Yield: 3 to 4 servings

Sauce:

1	**onion**, small to medium, chopped
⅛	cup **olive oil** **Salt** and **pepper**
1	16-ounce can peeled **tomatoes**
2	cloves **garlic**, sliced
⅛	teaspoon crushed **red pepper**
8	fresh **basil** leaves, torn (or ¾ teaspoon dried)
1	6-ounce can **tomato paste** (optional)

Filling:

6	**manicotti shells**
2	cups part-skim **ricotta cheese**
1	10-ounce package **frozen chopped spinach**, thawed and drained
3	ounces grated **Parmesan cheese**
½	teaspoon **garlic powder**
½	teaspoon **salt**
½	teaspoon **pepper** Dash of **nutmeg**
3	ounces shredded **mozzarella cheese**

Sauce:

- Sauté chopped onion in olive oil in large, deep frying pan until onion is transparent. Add salt and pepper.
- Stir in canned tomatoes. Crush tomatoes with spoon, if desired.
- Add garlic, red pepper, and basil.
- Simmer until sauce reaches desired consistency. To thicken the sauce more quickly, add small can tomato paste. Take care not to make the sauce too thick.

Filling:

- Cook manicotti shells according to package directions. Cool.
- In a large bowl, combine ricotta cheese, spinach, Parmesan cheese, garlic powder, salt, pepper, and nutmeg. Mix well.
- Spread ⅓ cup sauce over bottom of 13 x 9-inch baking dish.
- Stuff some spinach mixture into each shell and place in dish with sauce.
- Top with remaining sauce and sprinkle with mozzarella cheese.
- Cover with foil and bake at 350° for 20 to 25 minutes.

Lots of flavor and simple to prepare!

FLORENTINE PASTA SHELLS

Yield: 10 to 12 servings

1 small **onion**, chopped

2 cloves **garlic**, minced

1 tablespoon **olive oil**

2 10-ounce packages **frozen spinach**, thawed and drained (do not cook).

½ pound **imitation crab**, shredded

8 ounces each shredded **provolone** and **mozzarella cheeses**, blended

1 cup **bread crumbs**

½ cup **Romano cheese**

1 teaspoon **thyme**, crushed
Salt and **pepper**

1 12-ounce package **jumbo pasta shells**, cooked

3½ cups **spaghetti sauce**

- Cook onion and garlic in oil over medium-high heat 5 to 7 minutes.

- In a large bowl, combine onion mixture, spinach, crab, 1 cup of the provolone-mozzarella cheese mixture, bread crumbs, Romano cheese, thyme, salt, and pepper.

- Spoon mixture into cooked pasta shells and arrange in a 9 x 13-inch baking pan.

- Pour spaghetti sauce over stuffed shells and cover with aluminum foil.

- Bake, covered, at 350° for 20 minutes.

- Remove cover. Sprinkle remaining provolone-mozzarella cheese mixture over shells.

- Bake an additional 10 minutes or until cheese is melted and sauce is bubbly.

QUICK PASTA PRIMAVERA

Yield: 6 servings

8	ounces **pasta**
½	cup (1 stick) **butter**
8	ounces **whipping cream**
8	ounces grated **Parmesan cheese**
	Salt and **pepper**
2	cups **mixed fresh vegetables**, broccoli, carrots, zucchini, snow peas, etc.

- Cook pasta; drain and keep warm.
- Melt butter; pour over pasta.
- Toss pasta with cream and Parmesan cheese.
- Season with salt and pepper.
- Steam vegetables until just tender.
- Toss pasta and vegetables together.
- Microwave 1 minute on high to warm.

SPICY PASTA PRIMAVERA

Yield: 4 to 6 servings

1	pound **linguine**
½	cup **olive oil,** divided
1	cup **broccoli**
½	cup chopped **shallots** or **onions**
1	cup chopped **tomatoes**
4	cloves **garlic,** pressed
3	tablespoons chopped fresh **basil**
	Red pepper flakes, to taste
	Salt, to taste
	Goat cheese (or grated **Romano** or **Parmesan cheese**)

- Bring large pot of water to boil.
- Add linguine and 2 tablespoons olive oil.
- Meanwhile, steam broccoli and chop; set aside.
- In saucepan, sauté the onions, tomatoes, garlic, and crushed red pepper in the remaining olive oil until onion is tender.
- Drain pasta; return to pot.
- Add onion, tomato, and olive oil mixture, along with chopped broccoli, to pasta.
- Toss pasta with vegetables. Add basil and salt to taste.
- Sprinkle each serving with cheese.

The goat cheese makes this a truly different and tasty pasta dish.

213

RAVIOLI ROLLS WITH FRESH TOMATO-BASIL SAUCE

Yield: 12 rolls

Ravioli Filling:

1	pound ground **veal**
½	pound ground **Italian sausage** or **pork**
	Salt and **pepper**
1	pound fresh **spinach**
¼	cup fresh **parsley**, chopped
4	ounces grated **Swiss cheese**
4	**eggs** or 1 cup **egg substitute**
¼	cup grated **Parmesan cheese**
½	teaspoon crushed **garlic**
1	teaspoon **lemon juice**
1	teaspoon ground **black pepper**
1	teaspoon **salt**
6	**saltine crackers**, finely ground
½	teaspoon **oregano**
2	tablespoons **olive oil**
½	pound **lasagne pasta strips**

Fresh Tomato-Basil Sauce:

¾	cup (1½ sticks) **margarine**
6	tablespoons **olive oil**
1	large **onion**, chopped
2	teaspoons crushed **garlic**
1	⅔-ounce package fresh **basil leaves**, chopped
6	tablespoons chopped fresh **parsley**
3	tablespoons **sugar**
¾	teaspoon ground **black pepper**
1	teaspoon **salt**
¼	sweet **red** or **yellow pepper**, chopped
8	cups fresh Roma **tomatoes** (about 20 tomatoes), chopped
1	6-ounce can **tomato paste**
	Grated **Romano cheese**, to taste

Ravioli Filling:

- Mix veal and Italian sausage and brown in skillet. Lightly salt and pepper.
- With slotted spoon, transfer meat mixture from pan to food processor.
- Pulse 2 to 3 seconds to finely chop meats, but do not purée.
- Remove and cool slightly.
- Meanwhile, rinse fresh spinach in a colander, but do not squeeze excess water.
- Cook spinach and parsley over medium heat until wilted.

RAVIOLI ROLLS WITH
FRESH TOMATO-BASIL SAUCE *(continued)*

- Drain spinach, discarding the spinach water. Put into food processor.
- Chop the cooked spinach and parsley.
- Combine the meat and vegetable mixtures with remaining filling ingredients and mix well.
- Keep filling mixture chilled until pasta and sauce are ready.
- Cook pasta according to package directions al dente.
- Keep moist with cold water to prevent sticking.

Fresh Tomato-Basil Sauce:
- In a large saucepan, melt margarine and olive oil. Add all ingredients except tomatoes, tomato paste, and cheese.
- Cook approximately 3 minutes until onions are transparent but not brown.
- Add Roma tomatoes and simmer 5 minutes.
- Add tomato paste to thicken the sauce.

Assembly:
- Preheat oven to 350°.
- Place lasagne pasta strip on cutting board.
- Spread ravioli filling the length of the strip.
- Starting with narrow end, roll up pasta strip.
- Repeat above 3 steps, making about 12 rolls.
- Place seam side down in a 9 x 13-inch pan.
- At this point, ravioli rolls may be frozen as casserole or individually on a cookie sheet.
- Spoon tomato-basil sauce over rolls to cover.
- Bake at 350° for 45 minutes. Let cool 5 minutes.
- Serve with extra sauce and sprinkle of Romano cheese.
- Ravioli rolls can also be placed upright, closely positioned in 8 x 11 x 2-inch pan for a beautiful presentation.

This outstanding ravioli recipe has been enjoyed by a St. Louis Italian family for three generations!

Linguine with Sautéed Vegetables and Basil

Yield: 6 servings

8	ounces **haricots verts** (or other green beans, julienned)
6	tablespoons **olive oil**
1	large **garlic** clove, flattened
1	**yellow bell pepper**, julienned
½	pound **zucchini**, julienned
8	ounces **tomatoes**, peeled and seeded, or canned plum tomatoes, drained, cut into thin strips.
12	ounces **linguine**
1	cup grated **Parmesan cheese** (about 3 ounces), preferably Parmigiano Reggiano
½	cup fresh **basil** leaves, sliced
	Salt and **pepper**
	Additional grated **Parmesan cheese**

- Bring small pot of water to boil. Add green beans and cook until just tender, about 4 minutes.
- Drain and refresh beans under cold water. Drain well.

- Heat oil in heavy, large saucepan over medium heat.
- Add garlic and cook until pale golden, about 2 minutes.
- Discard garlic. Increase heat to medium-high and add bell pepper and zucchini.
- Sauté until vegetables are lightly colored, about 3 minutes.
- Increase heat to high; add tomatoes.
- Sauté tomatoes until juices evaporate, about 3 minutes.
- Add beans; cook until heated through, about 30 seconds.
- Meanwhile, cook pasta in large pot of boiling, salted water, stirring occasionally, until just tender but still firm to the bite.
- Drain pasta thoroughly.
- Add pasta to sauce and toss. Add cheese and basil.
- Season with salt and pepper.
- Serve with additional Parmesan cheese.

This recipe originates from Giuseppe Palermino, chef of La Braja in Italy.

Champagne and sweets top off the annual New Year's Eve Gala at Powell Hall where the world-renowned St. Louis Symphony Orchestra performs. But one of St. Louis' most beloved dessert treats is Ted Drewes frozen custard. St. Louis is also home to many outstanding small bakeries that feature a tantalizing assortment of American and European pastries.

• • •

Ted Drewes Frozen Custard

A St. Louis tradition since 1930, Ted Drewes Frozen Custard serves up a long list of unique and popular frozen treats. Family-owned and operated since day one, Ted Drewes Frozen Custard is known far and wide for the custard creations that pop through its front windows at a steady rate and for the sidewalk camaraderie shared by patrons.

FOX TREAT

A 1990s creation recognizing the fabulous Fox Theatre and its long-standing tradition of bringing outstanding theatrical productions to St. Louis.

Act I: Start with a fabulous mound of Ted Drewes Frozen Custard.

Act II: A lavish topping of fresh raspberries.

Act III: Dress and drizzle with hot fudge.

Act IV: The final act—sprinkle with dry-roasted, unsalted macadamia nuts.

Encores a must!

HAWAIIAN DELIGHT

In need of a tropical getaway? Don your most colorful Hawaiian print shirt, follow the Hawaiian Delight instructions, and you'll feel yourself getting closer to paradise with every spoonful.

- Begin with Ted Drewes Frozen Custard.
- Top with sliced bananas.
- Top that with fresh pineapple.
- Top that with dry-roasted, unsalted macadamia nuts.
- Then add flaked, unsweetened coconut.

Bon voyage!

APPLE CRANBERRY TART

Yield: 6 to 8 servings

1   9-inch unbaked **pie crust**
1¼   cups **apple cider**
1⅓   cups **granulated sugar**
4   Jonathan **apples**, chunked
12   ounces **cranberries**, washed and sorted
½   cup **pecans**, chopped
½   cup **flour**
⅓   cup **dark brown sugar**
6   tablespoons **butter**, melted
     Whipped cream (optional)

- Bake pie crust and cool.
- Heat cider and sugar over low heat until dissolved.
- Bring to a boil, simmer 2 minutes, and add all fruit. Boil again.
- Reduce heat and simmer until berries burst and apples are tender (8 to 10 minutes).
- Cool and refrigerate several hours.
- Meanwhile, make the streusel topping, mixing pecans, flour, brown sugar, and butter until crumbly; set aside.
- Put filling in crust.
- Sprinkle streusel over top.
- Put tart on a baking sheet (to catch drips).
- Bake at 375° for 30 minutes. Cool.
- Serve with whipped cream, if desired.

A new twist on an old favorite, the streusel really complements the cranberries.

HAZELNUT DACQUOISE WITH CAPPUCCINO CREAM AND CHOCOLATE TRUFFLE ICING

Chocolate Truffle Icing:

2 cups **heavy whipping cream**

4 tablespoons **butter**

¼ cup **sugar**

1 pound **Bissinger's® semisweet chocolate**

Dacquoise:

Parchment paper

Nonstick **cooking spray**

4 ounces **hazelnuts**

¾ cup plus 2 tablespoons **sugar**

1 tablespoon **flour**

4 **egg whites**

¼ teaspoon **lemon juice**

1 tablespoon **sugar**

Cappuccino Cream:

2 cups **heavy whipping cream**

2 tablespoons **instant coffee**, dissolved in 1 tablespoon **brewed coffee**

1 tablespoon **kahlua liqueur**

½ cup **powdered sugar**

Whipped Cream:

2 cups **heavy whipping cream**

¼ cup **honey**

Fresh **strawberries** for garnish

Chocolate Truffle Icing:

- Place cream, butter, and sugar in heavy 2-quart saucepan.
- Bring to a rolling boil. Make sure it does not boil over.
- Remove from heat and add chocolate.
- Process until smooth. Chill overnight.

Dacquoise:

- Line a 12 x 18-inch cookie sheet with parchment paper and thoroughly spray paper with nonstick cooking spray.
- Process hazelnuts and sugar with flour until finely ground.
- Meanwhile, whip egg whites until very frothy; add lemon juice and sugar and increase speed until stiff peaks form.
- Fold egg white mixture into ground hazelnut mixture; spread in a rectangular, smooth layer on prepared cookie sheet.
- Bake at 400° until lightly browned.
- Invert immediately onto a flat surface to cool.

HAZELNUT DACQUOISE WITH CAPPUCCINO CREAM AND CHOCOLATE TRUFFLE ICING *(continued)*

Cappuccino Cream:
- Chill mixing bowl and beater.
- Whip cream until soft peaks form.
- Add dissolved coffee, kahlua, and powdered sugar.
- Whip until firm peaks form and use immediately.

Whipped Cream:
- In another chilled bowl, whip cream and honey until soft peaks form.
- Use immediately.

Assembly:
- Soften Chocolate Truffle Icing to room temperature so that it is consistency of mayonnaise.
- Cut cooled Dacquoise into 4 equal rectangles.
- Place first piece on a serving dish. Spread carefully with 4 ounces of the Chocolate Truffle Icing.
- Reserve the rest of the Chocolate Truffle Icing for icing the rest of the entire dessert.
- Place second layer of Dacquoise on top of icing.
- Cover with all of the Cappuccino Cream.

- Place another layer of Dacquoise on top and cover with the Whipped Cream.
- Cover with final layer of Dacquoise and gently level top and sides.
- Place dessert in the freezer for 1 hour.
- When firm, ice the entire dessert with the rest of the softened Chocolate Truffle Icing.
- Garnish with fresh strawberries.
- Chill until 30 minutes before serving.

This elegant dessert masterpiece comes from chef Tim Brennan of Cravings, LTD., a dessert restaurant in Webster Groves.

Pavlova

Yield: 8 to 10 servings

4	**egg whites**
1¼	cups **sugar**
1	tablespoon **cornstarch**
1	teaspoon **white vinegar**
1	teaspoon **vanilla**
	Parchment paper
2	cups 40% **gourmet whipping cream**
2	tablespoons **sugar**, for whipping cream
	Fresh sliced **fruit** (strawberries, raspberries, kiwi, blueberries, mandarin oranges)

- Beat egg whites until stiff.
- Beat in sugar.
- Fold in cornstarch, vinegar, and vanilla.
- Spread mixture on pizza pan covered with parchment paper.
- Bake 1½ hours at 275°.
- Turn off oven. Let cool 10 minutes in oven; remove parchment paper carefully.
- Put on cake plate.
- Whip cream until peaked.
- Add 2 tablespoons of sugar to whipped cream. Spread whipped cream on top of baked meringue.
- Decorate with fresh sliced fruit.

Meringue is very delicate. Whipping cream will cover any cracks. Have fun decorating with different fruits.

HEAVENLY RED RASPBERRY MERINGUE

Yield: 8 servings

Meringue:

4	**egg whites**, room temperature
¼	teaspoon **cream of tartar**
1	cup **sugar**

Filling:

4	cups fresh **raspberries**
¾	cup **sugar**
2½	tablespoons **cornstarch**
¼	teaspoon **salt**
⅓	cup cold **water**
2½	tablespoons fresh **lemon juice**
2	tablespoons **lemon gelatin**
1	tablespoon **unsalted butter**
	Whipped cream

- Lightly oil 9-inch pie pan.
- Beat egg whites until foamy.
- Add cream of tartar and beat until just stiff.
- Add sugar, 1 tablespoon at a time, and beat until meringue is very stiff and glossy.
- Place meringue in pie plate, piling it up the sides and depressing it in the center.
- Bake for 1 hour and 15 minutes at 275° without opening oven door.
- Cool in oven with door slightly ajar.
- Prepare filling while meringue is baking. Combine ¼ cup of the raspberries and ¼ cup of the sugar with the cornstarch, salt, water, and lemon juice, in a food processor.
- Mix until smooth.
- Scrape the mixture into a heavy saucepan and cook until thick, stirring constantly.
- Remove from stove; add gelatin, butter, and the remaining ½ cup sugar.
- Stir until gelatin is dissolved.
- Set aside to cool.
- Spread a thin layer of this glaze over the bottom of the meringue shell.
- Stir carefully 2¾ cups raspberries into the remaining glaze.
- Pour over first layer.
- Top with remaining 1 cup of raspberries.
- Top with sweetened whipped cream.

Recipe does take a bit of time, but it is truly divine!

LEMON MERINGUE DELIGHT

Yield: 10 servings

Meringue Shell:

Parchment paper

3	**egg whites**
¼	teaspoon **cream of tartar**
¾	cup **sugar**

Lemon Curd:

3	whole **eggs**
3	**egg yolks**
1½	cups **sugar**
⅛	teaspoon **salt**
½	cup **lemon juice**
½	cup (1 stick) **butter**
	Grated rind of 2 **lemons**

Meringue Shell:

- Cut out an 8-inch circle of brown paper or parchment paper. Place on a cookie sheet.
- Beat egg whites until foamy.
- Add cream of tartar and beat until stiff.

- Slowly beat in sugar and continue beating until glossy peaks form.
- Spread ⅓ of the meringue over the paper circle to make a ½-inch thick bottom.
- Fill a pastry tube with the remaining meringue.
- Make peaks close together around the circle's rim.
- Bake shell at 275° until light brown (55 minutes).
- Turn off heat and keep meringue shell in oven for 2 hours.
- Carefully remove paper and place meringue shell on a flat attractive serving dish.

Lemon Curd:

- In top of a double boiler, lightly beat eggs.
- Stir in remaining ingredients.
- Cook, stirring often, until thickened and smooth (30 minutes).
- Cool.
- Fill meringue shell and refrigerate 8 hours before serving.

This meringue is beautiful! Lovely for springtime, Mother's Day, or a shower.

LEMON DAINTY

Yield: 4 servings

3 tablespoons **butter**, softened

⅛ teaspoon **salt**

¾ cup **sugar**

2 tablespoons **flour**

2 **egg yolks**, slightly beaten

1 cup **milk**

Juice of 1 **lemon** and grated rind

2 **egg whites**, beaten stiff

- Combine butter, salt, sugar, and flour. Mix well.
- Add egg yolks, milk, lemon juice, and rind. Beat with egg beater until smooth.
- Fold in stiffly beaten egg whites.
- Pour into buttered baking dish, set in pan of hot water.
- Bake in 350° oven for 45 minutes or until golden brown.
- Serve warm, or at room temperature.

This light dessert sets up as cake on top, pudding on the bottom. For an extra-elegant touch, serve in individual soufflé dishes.

CHOCOLATE MOUSSE

Yield: 6 servings

1 8-ounce package **semi-sweet chocolate**

2 **eggs**

2 to 3 tablespoons hot strong black **coffee**

¾ cup boiling **milk**

1 teaspoon **rum** or **orange liqueur**

1 cup **whipping cream**

Whipped cream and **shredded chocolate** for garnish

- Put all ingredients in blender for 1 to 2 minutes at high speed until mixed.
- Pour mixture into a 9-inch ring mold.
- Chill for 8 hours.
- Top with whipped cream and shredded chocolate.

A rich, chocolatey dessert that's simple to prepare!

FROZEN CHOCOLATE CREPES WITH HAZELNUT HOT FUDGE SAUCE

Yield: 6 servings

Crepes:

2	**eggs**
½	cup **flour**
¼	cup **sugar**
2	tablespoons **unsweetened cocoa**
1	cup **milk**
1	tablespoon **butter**, melted
1	teaspoon **vanilla**
	Nonstick **cooking spray**

Quick Chocolate Mousse:

2	cups (12 ounces) **semi-sweet chocolate chips**
1½	teaspoons **vanilla**
	Pinch **salt**
1½	cups **whipping cream**, heated to boiling point
6	**egg yolks**

Hazelnut Hot Fudge Sauce:

1	cup **hazelnuts**, toasted and chopped
4	tablespoons **butter**
4	ounces **unsweetened chocolate**, broken into small pieces
1	cup **sugar**
¾	cup **light corn syrup**
1½	cups **whipping cream**
1	teaspoon **vanilla**

- With electric mixer, combine eggs and flour. Add sugar and cocoa. Pour in milk gradually, beating continuously and scraping sides of bowl to blend. Add butter and vanilla and beat until well mixed.
- Allow batter to stand covered 1 hour before making crepes.
- Place 8-inch skillet over high heat and spray with nonstick cooking spray.
- Pour about ¼ cup batter into pan. Quickly lift pan off heat and swirl to coat bottom and sides. Return to heat and cook about 1 minute, or until bottom darkens slightly and looks dry. Turn crepe onto waxed paper.
- Continue until all batter is used, spraying pan with the nonstick cooking spray each time.
- When crepes are cooled, place about 1 heaping tablespoon of Quick Chocolate Mousse on each and roll cigar-fashion.
- Place crepes seam side down on baking sheet and freeze.

FROZEN CHOCOLATE CREPES WITH HAZELNUT HOT FUDGE SAUCE *(continued)*

- When firm, wrap crepes carefully and keep in freezer until ready to serve.
- To serve, place 1 or 2 crepes on each plate and spoon warmed Hazelnut Hot Fudge Sauce over them.

Quick Chocolate Mousse:

- Combine chocolate, vanilla, and salt in food processor and mix 30 seconds.
- Add boiling cream and continue mixing 30 seconds more or until chocolate is completely melted.
- Add egg yolks and mix 5 seconds.
- Transfer to bowl and allow to cool.

Hazelnut Hot Fudge Sauce:

- To toast hazelnuts, preheat oven to 350°. Spread nuts on baking sheet and bake on center rack 10 minutes. While nuts are still hot, roll in clean kitchen towel and rub to remove skins.
- Place butter, chocolate, sugar, and corn syrup in saucepan over low heat. Stir constantly until the butter and chocolate have melted.

- Pour in the cream and continue to stir.
- Cook the chocolate sauce over low heat, stirring often, until the mixture is thickened and smooth, about 15 to 20 minutes.
- Remove the pan from heat and stir in vanilla and hazelnuts.
- Can make 5 to 7 days ahead and reheat over very low heat, stirring constantly.

These crepes are quite impressive and can be made well in advance.

POTS DE CRÈME MOCHA

Yield: 10 servings

2	cups **semisweet chocolate chips**
2	**eggs**
¼	cup **honey**
2	teaspoons **instant coffee**
2	teaspoons **vanilla**
¼	teaspoon **salt**
1½	cups **milk**, heated to boiling
	Confectioners sugar

- Place chocolate chips, eggs, honey, instant coffee, vanilla, and salt in blender.
- Blend 1 minute, gradually adding hot milk.
- Pour into 10 Pots de Crème pots or demitasse cups.
- Chill 2 hours.
- Sift confectioners sugar on top before serving, or top with dollop of whipped cream.

CHOCOLATE BAVAROISE

Yield: 6 servings

1	tablespoon (1 envelope) **unflavored gelatin**
¼	cup cold **water**
2	squares **baking chocolate**
1	cup **sugar**
	Few grains **salt**
½	cup hot **milk**
1	teaspoon **vanilla**
2	cups **heavy cream**, whipped
24	**ladyfingers**
2	tablespoons **rum**
1	cup **heavy cream**, whipped and sweetened

- Soak gelatin in cold water.
- Melt the baking chocolate in double boiler; add sugar, salt, and hot milk; blend.
- Add the gelatin to the hot mixture. Cool.
- Beat mixture until light and spongy (about 2 minutes), and add the vanilla.
- Fold in the whipped cream.
- Line the bottom and sides of a fancy mold with lady-fingers.
- Spoon rum lightly over ladyfingers.
- Pour in cream mixture.
- Mold and chill.
- Garnish with sweetened whipped cream.

This elegant dessert is very easy to make. Use a fancy mold with scalloped edges, and ladyfingers will fit very well. The ladyfingers can be cut in half, if too thick.

SWEET POTATO SOUFFLÉ

Yield: 8 to 10 servings

2 cups mashed **sweet potatoes** (29-ounce can)
¼ cup (½ stick) **margarine**
½ cup **milk**
2 **eggs**
½ cup **raisins**
1 teaspoon **lemon flavoring**
½ teaspoon ground **nutmeg**
1 cup **sugar**
½ cup **coconut**

Topping:
⅓ stick (8 teaspoons) **margarine**
½ cup **light brown sugar**
½ cup **pecans**
3 cups **miniature marshmallows**

- Mash potatoes; mix with the next 8 ingredients.
- Pour into a 2-quart casserole or soufflé dish.
- Bake at 350° for 30 minutes.

Topping:
- Melt margarine. Add sugar and nuts and mix well.
- Sprinkle over the top of potatoes and bake an additional 15 minutes.
- Top with marshmallows and bake until puffy.

A special holiday dish. Even better the next day.

GOODY BANANAS

Yield: 5 servings

5 **bananas**
½ cup **brown sugar**
¾ teaspoon ground **cinnamon**
½ cup **white wine**

- Peel and slice bananas lengthwise in half.
- Arrange halves in a greased shallow baking dish.
- Sprinkle with a mixture of brown sugar and cinnamon.
- Pour wine over fruit.
- Bake at 350° 15 to 20 minutes until brown.

Fast, fun dessert. Serve over white cake or ice cream.

CRANBERRY KUCHEN
WITH WARM BUTTER SAUCE

Yield: 8 to 10 servings

1   cup **granulated sugar**
2   tablespoons **butter**, room temperature
2   cups **flour**
1   tablespoon **baking powder**
     Dash **salt**
1   cup **milk**, room temperature
1   teaspoon **vanilla**
3   cups whole fresh **cranberries**
     Powdered sugar

Butter Sauce:

½   cup (1 stick) **butter**
1   cup **granulated sugar**
¾   cup **heavy cream**

- Grease and flour an 8- to 9-inch square pan.
- In large mixing bowl, cream together sugar and butter.
- In a separate bowl, sift together the flour, baking powder, and salt.
- Combine milk and vanilla in a 1-cup measure.
- Add dry ingredients, milk, and cranberries to the creamed sugar-butter mixture, alternately folding over using spatula. Do not overmix. Batter can be lumpy.
- Pour batter into prepared pan.
- Bake in preheated 350° oven 25 to 30 minutes.
- Cool the cake in the pan; sprinkle with powdered sugar.
- To serve, ladle sauce over individual pieces of kuchen on dessert plates.

Butter Sauce:

- In small saucepan, brown butter slightly (when it stops "singing"); remove just before golden brown.
- Add sugar and cream.
- Bring to a boil and remove from heat.
- Cool to room temperature.
- Warm in microwave when serving (not too hot).

This is a very simple dessert with outstanding flavor! Great contrast with tart berries and sweet sauce!

LINZERTORTE

Yield: 6 to 8 servings

1½	cups (3 sticks) **butter**, softened
1	cup **confectioners sugar**
1	**egg**
2¾	cups sifted **flour**
1½	cups ground **hazelnuts** (filberts)
	Pinch of **salt**
½	teaspoon ground **cinnamon**
2	cups **raspberry jam**
2	teaspoons **lemon juice**

- Cream butter and sugar until light and fluffy. Beat in egg.
- Stir flour into creamed mixture, alternating with hazelnuts, salt, and cinnamon.
- Chill dough.
- Line 9-inch springform pan with dough making a 1-inch rim up the side.
- Reserve a little dough for lattice strips.
- Spread 1½ cups of the raspberry jam and the lemon juice onto the dough.
- Cut strips of reserved dough and form a lattice over jam.
- Bake at 375° for 40 minutes.
- When cool, fill squares with the extra jam.
- Sprinkle with confectioners sugar before serving.

For a cocktail party pick-up dessert, use 24 small torte pans. Bake the tortes for 20 minutes, or until golden.

APPLE CRISP

Yield: 4 servings

4	cups peeled and thinly sliced **apples**
¼	cup **water**
1	teaspoon ground **cinnamon**
½	teaspoon **salt**

Topping:

¾	cup **flour**
1	cup **sugar**
⅓	cup **butter** or **margarine**, softened

- Mix together apples, water, cinnamon, and salt. Place in 8 x 8-inch baking pan.
- Mix together topping until crumbly (can use hands).
- Spread topping over apples.
- Bake uncovered at 400° for 40 to 50 minutes. Serve warm with vanilla ice cream.

Easy! Can substitute sliced and peeled peaches for the apples.

Butterscotch Nut Torte

Yield: 12 servings

6   **eggs**, separated
1½   cups **sugar**
1   teaspoon **baking powder**
2   teaspoons **vanilla**
1   teaspoon **almond extract**
2   cups **graham cracker crumbs**
1   cup chopped **pecans**
½   pint **whipping cream**, whipped, or 8 ounces **Cool Whip® nondairy topping**

Sauce:

1   cup **brown sugar**
¼   cup **orange juice**
1   tablespoon **flour**
½   teaspoon **vanilla**
¼   cup (½ stick) **butter**
¼   cup **water**
1   **egg**, well beaten

- Line two 9-inch cake pans with waxed paper.
- Beat egg whites enough to hold a peak.

- In a separate bowl, beat egg yolks well; add sugar, baking powder, and flavorings.
- Add graham cracker crumbs and pecans. Fold in egg whites.
- Pour batter into prepared pans. Bake at 325° for 30 to 35 minutes. Cool.
- Put 1 layer on cake plate and spread about ⅓ of the whipped cream on top.
- Put second layer on top; spread the remaining whipped cream on top and sides.
- Refrigerate until ready to serve.

Sauce:

- In a small saucepan, mix all ingredients together (can put in refrigerator until ready to serve).
- Heat until well blended and just about to boil.
- To serve, pour sauce into a nonglass serving dish. Slice torte and ladle sauce on the side of each slice.

The blend of cool torte and warm sauce is delightful!

AMARETTO SABAYON TOPPING

Yield: 6 servings

4	large **egg yolks**
¾	cup **amaretto liqueur**
⅓	cup **sugar**
1	cup **whipping cream**
2	tablespoons **sugar**

- In the top of a double boiler, combine yolks, liqueur, and sugar.
- Whisk until well blended.
- Place over simmering water and whisk constantly until the mixture thickens and coats a metal spoon, about 20 minutes. Do not boil or mixture will curdle.
- Transfer to bowl and cool.
- Whip cream with sugar until stiff peaks form.
- Fold into thoroughly cooled egg mixture.
- Serve as a topping on fresh seasonal fruits, such as strawberries, sliced peaches, or raspberries.

This is also good by the spoonful in coffee.

HOT FUDGE SAUCE

Yield: 12 servings

5	squares (5 ounces) **unsweetened chocolate**
½	cup (1 stick) **butter**
3	cups **powdered sugar**
1	12-ounce can **Pet®** **evaporated milk**
1¼	teaspoons **vanilla**

- Melt chocolate and butter. Remove from heat.
- Mix in powdered sugar, alternating with Pet® milk.
- Return to heat and bring to boil over medium heat, stirring constantly for 8 minutes until thick.
- Add vanilla.
- Serve over ice cream.

This reheats well in the microwave.

233

AMARETTO MOCHA PIE

Yield: 6 to 8 servings

3   1.65-ounce **chocolate bars**
3   teaspoons **instant coffee**
1½ cups **miniature marshmallows**
⅓   cup **milk**
¼   cup **amaretto** (almond) liqueur
1   cup **whipping cream**
1   baked **pie crust**
    Whipped cream, **chocolate shavings**, and fresh **strawberries** for garnish.

- Break candy bars in pieces.
- Combine chocolate, instant coffee, marshmallows, and milk in 1-quart glass bowl.
- Microwave on 70 percent power 3 to 4 minutes.
- Mix until smooth.
- Cool completely. Stir in liqueur.
- Whip cream until stiff.
- Fold into marshmallow mixture.
- Pour into baked pie crust. Chill until set.
- Garnish with whipped cream, chocolate shavings, and fresh strawberries.

FUDGE SUNDAE PIE

Yield: 8 to 10 servings

1   cup **Pet® evaporated milk**
6   ounces **chocolate chips**
¼   teaspoon **salt**
1   cup **miniature marshmallows**
1   **graham cracker** or **chocolate cookie pie crust**
½   gallon **ice cream**

- Cook milk, chocolate chips, and salt in a double boiler. Stir constantly until chips melt.
- Remove from heat. Mix in marshmallows until melted. Cool.
- Pack ice cream loosely in graham cracker crust.
- Pour chocolate all over the top. Freeze.

Great for those hot and humid St. Louis nights.

FUDGE PIE

Yield: 8 servings

¼ cup **cocoa**

¼ cup **flour**

1 cup **sugar**

2 **eggs**

½ cup (1 stick) **butter** or **margarine**, melted

1 teaspoon **vanilla**

1 9-inch unbaked **pie crust** (not deep-dish)

- Beat all ingredients (except pie crust)until smooth.
- Pour into unbaked pie crust.
- Bake at 350° for 30 to 40 minutes, or until a knife inserted comes out clean. Do not overbake.

Top with whipped cream or ice cream.

HALLOWEEN PIE

Yield: 8 servings

1 pint **orange sherbet**, softened

1 8-ounce container **Cool Whip® nondairy whipped topping**, thawed

1 9-inch **Oreo® pie crust**

9 **Oreo® chocolate sandwich cookies**, chopped

Candy corn (optional)

- Place sherbet in bowl; stir until smooth.
- Stir in half of Cool Whip® until well blended. Spoon into crust.
- Sprinkle with chopped Oreo® cookies, pressing firmly into sherbet. Cover with remaining Cool Whip.
- Freeze 4 hours or until firm.
- Garnish with finely chopped Oreo® cookies (dust-like) and candy corn, if desired.

Festive and quite tasty! Perfect for Halloween!

RASPBERRY MOUSSE PIE
WITH BROWNIE CRUST

Yield: 8 servings

Brownie Crust:

½	cup (1 stick) **butter**
2	ounces **unsweetened chocolate**
½	teaspoon **instant coffee powder**
1	cup **sugar**
2	large **eggs**
½	teaspoon **vanilla**
½	cup **flour**
¼	teaspoon **salt**
½	cup chopped **walnuts**

Filling:

1	10-ounce package **frozen raspberries**, in heavy syrup, thawed
2	large **egg whites**, room temperature
2	tablespoons **granulated sugar**
1¼	cups **whipping cream**
3	tablespoons **confectioners sugar**
2	teaspoons **kirsch liqueur**
1	cup **fresh raspberries** **Chocolate shavings**

Brownie Crust:

- Preheat oven to 350°.
- Butter a 9-inch metal pie pan. Line bottom and sides of pan with a sheet of aluminum foil. Butter foil.
- In top of a double boiler placed over lightly boiling water, combine 4 table-spoons butter, chocolate, and coffee powder.
- Stir constantly until mixture is smooth and shiny, 4 to 5 minutes. Set mixture aside to cool.
- With electric mixer, cream together remaining 4 table-spoons butter and sugar until light and fluffy. Add eggs and continue to beat until well incorporated.
- On slow speed, add vanilla and chocolate mixture.
- In a small bowl, combine flour and salt. Slowly add to batter.
- Fold nuts into batter. Pour batter into prepared pie plate.
- Bake crust until a toothpick inserted in center comes out clean, 30 to 35 minutes.

RASPBERRY MOUSSE PIE
WITH BROWNIE CRUST *(continued)*

- Remove brownie crust from oven. While crust is still hot, protecting your fingers with a clean kitchen towel, gently press down against the center of crust and then push out toward the edges to form a pie shell.

- Repeat process several times, always pressing gently, until the shell is about 1 inch deep.

- Cool pie crust completely, 40 minutes to 1 hour. Then using foil as an aid, lift pie crust from plate and peel off foil. (Pie crust can be made 1 day in advance, covered with plastic wrap, and refrigerated until needed.)

Filling:

- Purée raspberries and their syrup in a food processor. Then strain purée through a fine mesh sieve into a saucepan to remove seeds.

- Reduce purée over medium heat to ½ cup. This will take about 10 minutes. Watch carefully so purée does not burn.

- Cool reduced purée to room temperature, about 20 minutes.

- Beat egg whites until they begin to mound. Gradually add granulated sugar. Continue to beat until whites are just firm but still moist. Set aside.

- In another bowl, whip cream until it starts to mound. Slowly add confectioners sugar and kirsch. Beat until cream is quite firm.

- Fold in cooled raspberry purée, then fold in egg whites and fresh raspberries.

- Mound raspberry mousse into the prepared crust. (The pie may be prepared to this point several hours before serving; keep refrigerated.)

- To garnish, shave some chocolate over the top of the pie.

Soft, light mousse with chewy brownie is a great combination!

PRALINE CHOCOLATE PECAN PIE

Yield: 8 servings

2	**eggs**
1	cup **sugar**
1	tablespoon **cornstarch**
¼	cup (½ stick) melted **butter**
2	ounces **praline liqueur**
1	cup finely chopped **pecans**
1	6-ounce package **chocolate chips**
1	9-inch unbaked **pie crust** **Whipped cream** or **vanilla ice cream** and **additional liqueur** (optional)

- Beat eggs slightly.
- In another bowl, combine sugar and cornstarch. Gradually add to eggs, mixing well.
- Stir in melted butter. Add praline liqueur, pecans, and chocolate chips; stir to blend.
- Pour mixture into unbaked pie crust.
- Bake in a preheated 350° oven 35 to 45 minutes. Cool before serving.
- If desired, garnish with whipped cream or vanilla ice cream, then drizzle 1 tablespoon of praline liqueur over all.

A rich dessert with incredible flavor!

THE BEST PECAN PIE

Yield: 6 servings

½	cup (1 stick) **butter**
1	cup **Karo® light corn syrup**
1	cup **sugar**
3	large **eggs**, beaten
½	teaspoon **lemon juice**
1	teaspoon **vanilla** Dash of **salt**
1	cup chopped **pecans**
1	9-inch unbaked **pie crust**

- Brown butter in saucepan until golden brown; do not burn. Cool.
- In separate bowl, add the next 7 ingredients in order listed; stir.
- Add browned butter; blend.
- Pour filling into unbaked pie crust.
- Bake at 425° for 10 minutes, then lower to 325° for 40 minutes.

CHOCOLATE PECAN AND CARAMEL PIE

Yield: 8 servings

½   cup (1 stick) **butter**, melted

1   8½-ounce package **chocolate wafers**, rolled into crumbs

¾   cup finely chopped **pecans**

1   envelope **unflavored gelatin**

¼   cup cold **water**

2   cups **whipping cream**

6   ounces **semisweet chocolate chips**

2   **eggs**

1   teaspoon **vanilla extract**

1   cup **caramels** (about 22)

2   tablespoons **butter**

Pecans for garnish (optional)

- In a microwave-safe bowl, melt butter in microwave.
- Add cookie crumbs and pecans.
- Press into pie pan and press up sides to form a high rim.
- Bake at 350° for 10 minutes. Cool.
- In a small saucepan, sprinkle gelatin over cold water. Let stand 1 minute.
- Stir over low heat until gelatin is completely dissolved, about 3 minutes.
- Stir in 1 cup of the cream. Bring just to the boiling point, then immediately pour into blender with chocolate.
- Process until chocolate is completely melted, about 1 minute.
- While processing, through feed cap, add ½ cup cream, eggs, and vanilla. Process until blended.
- Pour into large bowl and chill until thickened, about 15 minutes.
- Meanwhile, in a small saucepan, combine caramels, ¼ cup cream, and butter.
- Simmer over low heat, stirring occasionally, until caramels are completely melted and mixture is smooth.
- Pour onto chocolate-pecan crust to cover bottom.
- Cool at room temperature, about 10 minutes.
- With wire whisk or spoon, beat gelatin mixture until smooth.
- Pour into prepared crust. Chill until firm, about 3 hours.
- Garnish with remaining ¼ cup cream, whipped, and, if desired, pecans.

239

APPLE CRUMB PIE

Yield: 8 servings

5　to 7 **apples**, peeled, cored, and sliced
1　9-inch unbaked **pie crust**
¾　cup **sugar**
1½　teaspoons ground **cinnamon**
　　Dash of **salt**
　　Dash of **nutmeg**
3　tablespoons **butter**
Crumb Top:
½　cup **sugar**
¾　cup **flour**
5　tablespoons **butter**
¾　teaspoon ground **cinnamon**

- Put apples in pie crust.
- Mix together sugar, cinnamon, salt, and nutmeg.
- Pour sugar mixture over apples and dot with 3 tablespoons butter.
- Mix crumb ingredients in a food processor and pour on top of pie.
- Bake at 400° for 40 minutes, or until apples are soft and top is golden.

BLUEBERRY-BANANA CREAM PIE

Yield: 6 to 8 servings

1　9-inch baked **pie crust**
2　**bananas**, sliced
1　8-ounce package **cream cheese**, softened
1　cup **sugar**
1　teaspoon **vanilla**
1　cup **whipping cream**, whipped, or one 8-ounce container **Cool Whip®** **nondairy topping**, thawed
1　20-ounce can **blueberry pie filling**

- Slice bananas and place in bottom of baked pie crust.
- Mix cream cheese, sugar, and vanilla. Add whipped cream or Cool Whip® and mix well. Pour mixture on top of bananas.
- Top with blueberry pie filling. Refrigerate until ready to serve.

Scrumptious, unusual, and simple to prepare!

BLUE-RIBBON LEMON MERINGUE PIE

Yield: 6 servings

1   3.9-ounce package **lemon pudding and pie filling**

1   teaspoon **lemon juice**

¼   teaspoon **lemon extract**

¼   cup (½ stick) **butter** or **margarine**

1   9-inch **pie crust**, baked and cooled

4   **egg whites**

1   7½-ounce jar **marshmallow cream**

- Prepare pie filling according to package directions, adding lemon juice, lemon extract, and butter to mixture.
- Cook as directed on package, stirring constantly until mixture is thickened and smooth.
- Remove from heat; cool.
- Pour into cooled pie crust.
- For meringue, beat egg whites with electric mixer on high speed until foamy.
- Reduce speed to medium. Beat in marshmallow cream. Continue beating about 5 minutes.
- Spread meringue over top of cooled filling, sealing edges well. (Meringue will cover one pie, piled high, but can also cover two 9-inch pies.)
- Bake in a preheated 425° oven 8 minutes, until meringue is set and peaks are golden. Cool.

Extra lemon makes pie extra tangy, and marshmallow cream gives the meringue a unique flavor and texture.

CRANBERRY PIE

Yield: 8 to 10 servings

2 cups fresh **cranberries**
1½ cups **sugar**
½ cup chopped **walnuts**
2 **eggs**
1 cup **flour**
½ cup (1 stick) **margarine**, melted
¼ cup **vegetable oil**
Whipped cream

- Grease large 10-inch pie plate.
- Spread berries evenly.
- Sprinkle ½ cup sugar and nuts.
- Beat eggs in bowl; gradually add the remaining cup of sugar. Beat.
- Add flour, melted margarine, and oil to egg and sugar mixture. Beat 1 minute.
- Pour batter over cranberries.
- Bake at 325° for 1 hour.
- Serve with whipped cream. May be served slightly warm.

There is no crust to the pie, but when it is baked, the topping turns into a texture resembling cake.

FRESH STRAWBERRY PIE

Yield: 6 to 8 servings

1 9-inch unbaked deep-dish **pie crust**
1 cup **sugar**
3 tablespoons **cornstarch**
1 cup **water**
1 cup crushed fresh **strawberries**
1 quart fresh **strawberries**, hulled and halved, or smaller
2 cups **heavy whipping cream**
½ cup **sugar**
Additional **strawberries** for garnish

- Bake pie crust; let cool.
- In saucepan, combine sugar, cornstarch, water, and crushed berries. Boil about 5 minutes until thick and sauce-like.
- Add halved berries and let cool.
- Pour the cooled strawberry filling into pie shell. Refrigerate for several hours.
- Before serving, whip the cream with the ½ cup sugar.
- Immediately before serving, top with the whipped cream.
- Garnish with fresh berries.

PRALINE CHEESECAKE

Yield: 12 servings

1	cup **graham cracker crumbs**
3	tablespoons **sugar**
3	tablespoons **butter**, melted
3	8-ounce packages **cream cheese**, softened
1½	cups firmly packed **dark brown sugar**
3	**eggs**
2	tablespoons **flour**
½	cup coarsely chopped **pecans**
1½	teaspoons **vanilla** **Maple syrup** Finely chopped **pecans**

- Preheat oven to 350°.
- In a bowl, combine graham cracker crumbs, sugar, and melted butter.
- With the back of a large spoon, press the mixture into the bottom of an 8-inch springform pan.
- Bake the crust for 10 minutes and let it cool in the pan.
- In a large bowl, beat the cream cheese with the brown sugar until the mixture is fluffy.
- Beat in the eggs, one at a time, and sift in the flour. Add the coarsely chopped pecans and vanilla.
- Pour the mixture into the cooled crust and bake 55 minutes or until set.
- Let the cake cool in the pan.
- Brush the top with maple syrup and garnish with finely chopped pecans.
- Chill for at least 3 hours.

A very easy dessert that looks and tastes delicious!

German Chocolate Cheesecake

Yield: 15 to 18 servings

1   18½-ounce **German chocolate cake mix**

⅓   cup **margarine**, softened

3   **eggs**

2   8-ounce packages **cream cheese**, softened

¾   cup **sugar**

2   teaspoons **vanilla**

Topping:

2   cups **sour cream**

¼   cup **sugar**

1   teaspoon **vanilla**

- Mix cake mix, margarine, and 1 egg on slow speed of electric mixer until crumbly.
- Press mixture gently into ungreased 9 x 13-inch pan.
- Beat until fluffy the cream cheese, sugar, the remaining eggs, and vanilla.
- Spread over chocolate mixture.
- Bake in 350° oven 20 to 25 minutes.
- Meanwhile, mix together the sour cream, sugar, and vanilla.
- Remove cake from oven. Spread the sour cream topping onto the hot cake.
- Cool and then refrigerate 8 hours or longer.
- Remove from refrigerator 30 minutes before cutting or serving.

Everyone raves about this cake!

CHOCOLATE MOUSSE CHEESECAKE

Yield: 8 to 10 servings

Crust:

¾	cup **graham cracker crumbs**
¼	cup (½ stick) **unsalted butter**, softened
2	tablespoons **sugar**

Filling:

3	8-ounce packages **cream cheese**, softened
2	large **eggs**
1	cup **sugar**
1	8-ounce package **semisweet chocolate**, melted
2	tablespoons **heavy cream**
7	tablespoons very strong **coffee** (espresso)
¾	cup **sour cream**
1	teaspoon **dark rum**

- Preheat oven to 350°.
- To make the crust, place cracker crumbs, butter, and sugar in a food processor and pulse to mix.
- Press into the bottom of an 8-inch springform mold. Set aside.

- To make the filling, put the cream cheese, eggs, and sugar into the processor bowl and mix until smooth.
- Add the remaining ingredients and blend thoroughly.
- Pour batter on top of the crust.
- Bake for 45 minutes without opening the oven door (make sure the oven temperature is accurate).
- Cake will be slightly soft in the middle, but will firm up as it cools.
- At the end of the baking time, turn off the heat and prop oven door open slightly with a pot holder or knife.
- Allow cake to cool in the oven for 1 hour before removing.
- Refrigerate.
- Remove cake from the refrigerator at least 15 minutes before serving.

Excellent party dessert! Garnish with fresh strawberries or raspberries (depending on season), chocolate shavings or chips.

CHOCOLATE CHIP CHEESECAKE

Yield: 16 servings

24 **Oreo® cookies**, crushed

2 tablespoons **butter**, melted

3 8-ounce packages **cream cheese**, softened

3 **eggs**

1 14-ounce can **sweetened condensed milk**

1 teaspoon **vanilla**

6 ounces **mini chocolate chips**

- Mix cookie crumbs and butter.
- Press evenly on bottom of ungreased springform pan.
- In a large bowl, beat remaining ingredients (except chocolate chips) until smooth. Mix in chocolate chips.
- Pour cheese mixture over crumb mixture.
- Bake at 300° for 1 hour.
- Cover and refrigerate for at least 3 hours.

PUMPKIN CAKE

Yield: 12 to 15 servings

4 **eggs**

2 cups **granulated sugar**

1 cup **vegetable oil**

2 cups **flour**

2 teaspoons **baking soda**

1 teaspoon **salt**

1 teaspoon **baking powder**

2 teaspoons ground **cinnamon**

2 cups **pumpkin** (16-ounce can)

Icing:

1 3-ounce package **cream cheese**, softened

1 teaspoon **vanilla**

½ cup (1 stick) **butter**, softened

2 cups **confectioners sugar**

- Preheat oven to 350°.
- Grease 9 x 13-inch pan.
- Beat eggs, sugar, and vegetable oil until dissolved.
- Add remaining cake ingredients and beat 4 minutes.
- Pour into pan.
- Bake 40 to 45 minutes.
- Cake is done when edges come away from pan.
- Combine icing ingredients and beat until light and fluffy.
- Frost when cake has cooled.

This is better made day before serving—if you can wait!

PUMPKIN PIE CAKE

Yield: 8 servings

4	**eggs**, beaten well
1	16-ounce can (2 cups) **pumpkin**
1	14-ounce can **Milnot®** (if using Eagle® Brand, cut out sugar)
1½	cups **sugar**
2	teaspoons **pumpkin pie spice** (or to taste)
	Nonstick **cooking spray**
1	18½-ounce **yellow cake mix**
1	cup (2 sticks) **margarine**, melted
	Chopped **walnuts**

- Mix first 5 ingredients with electric mixer.
- Pour into 9 x 13-inch glass pan sprayed with nonstick cooking spray.
- Sprinkle dry cake mix over top.
- Pour 1 cup melted margarine over top.
- Sprinkle with walnuts, to taste.
- Bake at 350° for 1 hour or until top is brown.

Serve with whipped cream.

PUMPKIN BUNDT® CAKE

Yield: 10 servings

½	cup chopped **pecans**
1	18½-ounce **spice cake mix**
1	cup canned **pumpkin**
1	3.9-ounce package instant **vanilla pudding mix**
3	**eggs**
½	cup **salad oil**
1	teaspoon ground **cinnamon**
½	cup **water**
12	**pecans halves**

- Preheat oven to 350°.
- Grease and flour a Bundt® cake pan.
- Place larger nut pieces in bottom of pan, securing in place with dots of butter.
- In a large bowl, combine spice cake mix with all other ingredients except nuts.
- Beat at medium speed of electric mixer for 5 minutes; add remaining nuts.
- Pour batter into pan and bake about 50 minutes.
- Cool in pan for 10 minutes.
- Loosen center and sides with plastic spatula. Invert cake on wire rack to cool.
- Dust with powdered sugar.

Bake in pumpkin-shaped muffin tins. Decorate like jack-o-lanterns.

GERMAN APPLE CAKE

Yield: 10 to 12 servings

Nonstick **cooking spray**

2   cups sifted **flour**

2   teaspoons ground **cinnamon**

½   teaspoon **salt**

1   teaspoon **baking soda**

2   cups **sugar**

2   **eggs**

¾   cup **vegetable oil**

4   cups thinly sliced **apples**, peeled and cored

Icing:

1½   cups **powdered sugar**

1   3-ounce package **cream cheese**, softened

3   tablespoons melted **butter**

1   teaspoon **vanilla**

- Prepare a Bundt® cake pan with nonstick cooking spray.
- Preheat oven to 350°.
- Place all cake ingredients in large bowl.
- Mix all together with wooden spoon (batter is too stiff to mix with mixer).
- Spread into the Bundt® cake pan.
- Bake 45 to 50 minutes.
- Meanwhile, mix together the icing ingredients.
- Cool cake in pan at least 20 minutes.
- Loosen center and sides of cake with plastic spatula.
- Invert cake on a wire rack to cool further.
- When cake is completely cool, spread the icing.

Whenever this is served, it's always a big hit.

WHITE TEXAS SHEET CAKE

Yield: 16 to 20 servings

1   cup (2 sticks) **butter** or **margarine**
1   cup **water**
2   cups **flour**
2   cups **sugar**
2   **eggs**, beaten
½   cup **sour cream**
1   teaspoon **almond extract**
1   teaspoon **salt**
1   teaspoon **baking soda**

Frosting:
½   cup (1 stick) **butter** or **margarine**
¼   cup **milk**
4½   cups **confectioners sugar**
½   teaspoon **almond extract**
1   cup chopped **walnuts**

- In a large saucepan, bring butter and water to a boil.
- Remove from heat; stir in flour, sugar, eggs, sour cream, almond extract, salt, and baking soda until smooth.
- Pour into a greased 10 x 15 x 1-inch baking pan.
- Bake at 375° 20 to 22 minutes or until cake is golden brown and tests done.
- Cool for 20 minutes.

Frosting:
- Combine butter and milk in a saucepan. Bring to a boil.
- Remove from heat; add sugar and extract and mix well.
- Stir in walnuts; spread over warm cake.

Usually Texas cake is chocolate. This fabulous variation is a great party dessert! Very moist.

CARROT CAKE

Yield: 12 servings

2	cups **flour**
2	teaspoons **baking powder**
1½	teaspoons **baking soda**
1	teaspoon **salt**
2	teaspoons ground **cinnamon**
1½	cups vegetable **oil**
2	cups **sugar**
4	**eggs**
2	cups grated **carrots**
1	8-ounce can **crushed pineapple** with juice
¾	cup chopped **pecans**

Icing:

1	8-ounce package **cream cheese**, softened
1	cup (2 sticks) **butter**, softened
1	16-ounce box **powdered sugar**
2	teaspoons **vanilla**
½	cup chopped **pecans**
1	8-ounce can **crushed pineapple**, drained

- Sift all dry ingredients together and set aside.
- In a large mixing bowl, mix oil, sugar, and eggs, beating after each egg.
- Add dry ingredients to mixture. Mix well.
- Add carrots, pineapple, and nuts.
- Grease and flour three 9-inch round cake pans.
- Bake at 325° for 40 minutes.

Icing:

- Beat all ingredients well.
- Spread on cooled cake.

CHOCOLATE-RASPBERRY POUND CAKE

Yield: 8 to 10 servings

1   16-ounce store-bought
     frozen **pound cake**
1½   cups **raspberry jam**
1   12-ounce package **semi-
     sweet chocolate chips**
     (2 cups)
1   cup dairy **sour cream**
1   teaspoon **vanilla**
2   teaspoons **framboise** or
     kirsch liqueur (optional)

- While pound cake is still frozen, use a serrated knife to slice it horizontally into 5 or 6 thin layers. (This is more difficult with a thawed cake.)
- Generously coat each cake layer with raspberry jam, stacking layers evenly on top of one another.
- To make frosting, in a double boiler over hot water, melt chocolate chips with sour cream.
- Remove from heat; stir in vanilla. Stir in liqueur.
- Cool frosting slightly.
- Reserve ⅔ cup of frosting for decoration later.
- Spread remaining frosting over top and sides of cake. Refrigerate cake.
- Just before serving, use a pastry bag and pipe decorations on cake with the reserved frosting.

This is a very special and delicious dessert—easy to prepare and no baking! Keeps well in refrigerator.

SUPER CHOCOLATE ROLL

Yield: 8 to 10 servings

Cake:

5	**eggs**, separated
1	cup sifted **confectioners sugar**
3	tablespoons **cocoa**
1	teaspoon **vanilla**

Filling:

1	cup **whipping cream**
2	tablespoons **confectioners sugar**
1	teaspoon **vanilla**

Sauce:

½	cup (1 stick) **butter**
4	squares **unsweetened chocolate**
1	cup **milk**
3	cups **confectioners sugar**
1	tablespoon **vanilla**

Cake:

- In a small bowl, beat egg yolks; set aside.
- In another bowl, beat egg whites, adding sugar gradually, until stiff.
- Fold in 3 tablespoons cocoa, beaten egg yolks, and vanilla.
- Prepare a jellyroll pan by lining it with greased foil.
- Spread batter evenly in pan.
- Bake at 350° for 20 minutes.
- Remove cake from oven and cover with a damp towel for 5 minutes to remove heat.
- Sprinkle remaining cocoa on a clean linen towel and invert cake onto towel.
- Carefully remove foil from cake.
- Roll cake in towel, jellyroll fashion, while cake is warm.
- Cool completely.

Filling:

- Whip cream, gradually adding sugar and vanilla.
- Unroll cake and spread evenly with filling.
- Roll again and refrigerate.

Sauce:

- In a large saucepan, melt butter and chocolate over low heat.
- Add milk and bring to a boil. Remove from heat.
- Add confectioners sugar and beat 5 minutes with a wire whisk. Add vanilla.
- Serve with Chocolate Roll.

This delicious dessert makes an elegant pinwheel presentation and it melts in your mouth!

HEAVENLY HASH CAKE

Yield: 12 servings

12 ounces **chocolate chips**

4 **eggs**, separated

2 teaspoons **sugar**

2 cups **whipping cream**

1 cup **pecans**

1 teaspoon **vanilla**

½ teaspoon **salt**

1 large **angel food cake**

- Melt chocolate over low heat; beat egg yolks and add to chocolate.
- In another bowl, beat egg whites; add 2 teaspoons sugar.
- In another bowl, beat whipping cream; set aside.
- Add egg whites to chocolate and egg mixture. Stir and add pecans, vanilla, and salt.
- Fold in whipped cream.
- Break cake in chunks.
- Cover bottom of large greased bowl or angel cake pan.
- Cover with half of chocolate mixture. Add cake and remaining mixture for second layer.
- Refrigerate overnight.

RICH & SINFUL CAKE

Yield: 12 servings

1 18½-ounce **chocolate cake mix**

½ cup (1 stick) **margarine**, melted

4 eggs

1 cup chopped **nuts**

1 16-ounce package **confectioners sugar**

1 8-ounce package **cream cheese**, softened

- Combine cake mix, melted margarine, and 2 eggs.
- Pat into 9 x 13-inch pan (mixture will be thick).
- Sprinkle nuts over the top.
- Mix together confectioners sugar, 2 eggs, and cream cheese and spread over nuts.
- Bake at 350° for 40 minutes.

A rich, sweet dessert. Cut into 2 x 2-inch bars.

CHOCOLATE SYRUP CAKE

Yield: 12 servings

½ cup (1 stick) **margarine**, room temperature
1 cup **sugar**
4 **eggs**
1 cup **flour**
1 teaspoon **baking powder**
¼ teaspoon **salt**
1 16-ounce can **chocolate syrup**
1 tablespoon **vanilla**

Topping:
½ cup (1 stick) **butter** (no substitute)
1 cup **sugar**
⅓ cup **Carnation®** **evaporated milk**
½ cup **chocolate chips**
1 cup chopped **pecans** (optional)

- In a large bowl, cream together margarine, sugar, and eggs.
- Add flour, baking powder, salt, chocolate syrup, and vanilla. Beat well.
- Pour batter into greased and floured long 3-quart glass baking pan (or 9 x 13-inch).
- Bake at 325° for 30 minutes.

Topping:
- In a saucepan bring butter, sugar, and milk to a rolling boil.
- Stir only once while on the stove.
- Remove from heat and stir in chocolate chips.
- Pour over the hot cake.
- Sprinkle nuts on top, if desired.

APRICOT KIFLES

Yield: 4 dozen

Filling:

18	ounces dried **apricots**
3	cups **water**
½	cup **granulated sugar**

Dough:

1	pound **butter**, softened
12	ounces **cream cheese**, softened
4	cups **flour**
	Powdered sugar

Filling:

- Put apricots and water in large saucepan.
- Heat to boiling and simmer for about 35 minutes.
- Add sugar and simmer for another 5 minutes.
- Stir well to cause apricots to break apart.
- Cool and set aside.

Dough:

- Cream butter and cream cheese with electric mixer.
- Add flour by hand until well mixed.
- Roll dough into approximately 16 balls and refrigerate until well chilled.
- Let dough warm slightly until workable and roll with rolling pin in powdered sugar.
- Cut dough into circles with large (approximately 4 inches in diameter) cookie cutter,
- Fill circles with 1 to 2 tablespoons of apricot filling; roll up and place on cookie sheet.
- Bake at 400° for 12 to 15 minutes until lightly browned.

An old Hungarian holiday treat. Absolutely delicious!

APRICOT-ALMOND BARS

Yield: 6 dozen bars

Crust:

2	cups **flour**
½	teaspoon **salt**
¾	cup (1½ sticks) **butter**, softened
¾	cup **powdered sugar**
1	teaspoon **vanilla**
1	12-ounce jar **apricot preserves**

Topping:

1½	cups **flour**
1½	teaspoons **baking powder**
½	teaspoon **salt**
¾	cup (1½ sticks) **butter**, softened
⅔	cup **granulated sugar**
⅔	cup firmly packed **brown sugar**
¼	teaspoon **almond extract**
3	**eggs**
1	cup chopped toasted **almonds**

- Preheat oven to 350°.
- To make crust, mix flour and salt in bowl.
- In another bowl, beat butter, sugar, and vanilla until fluffy.
- Gradually add flour, beating well (dough will be crumbly).
- Press evenly into greased 10 x 15 jellyroll pan.
- Bake 20 minutes, or until golden.
- Spread preserves over crust and cool.
- To make topping, mix flour, baking powder, and salt in bowl.
- In another bowl, beat butter, sugars, and almond extract until light and fluffy.
- Add eggs one at a time, beating well after each addition.
- Beat in dry ingredients until combined.
- Stir in almonds.
- Spread topping evenly over crust.
- Bake 30 minutes.
- Cool completely on wire rack.
- Cut into 2 x 1-inch bars.

BETTER THAN PECAN PIE COOKIES

Yield: 3 dozen cookies

Dough:

2½	cups unsifted **flour**
1	cup (2 sticks) **butter**, softened
½	cup **sugar**
½	cup **dark corn syrup**
2	**eggs**, separated (reserve whites)

Filling:

½	cup **confectioners sugar**
¼	cup (½ stick) **butter**
3	tablespoons **dark corn syrup**
½	cup finely chopped **pecans**

- Combine all dough ingredients, using only the egg yolks from the eggs; blend.
- Chill dough in refrigerator at least 4 hours.
- Meanwhile, combine in a saucepan all filling ingredients except pecans.
- Cook filling over medium heat, stirring occasionally, until it reaches a boil. Remove from heat and stir in pecans.
- Chill filling mixture until ready to place in cookie centers.
- Beat egg whites.
- Roll chilled dough into 1- to 1½-inch balls; brush with egg white.
- Place balls on ungreased cookie sheet and bake in preheated 375° oven for 5 minutes.
- Remove cookies from oven; dough in centers will be soft. Indent centers and fill each cookie center with ½ teaspoon of the filling mixture.
- Bake cookies 5 minutes more until bottoms of cookies are light brown.

A traditional Southern recipe, especially popular at holiday time.

GINGERBREAD COOKIES

Yield: 3 to 4 dozen

¾ cup **shortening**
¼ cup **light molasses**
1 **egg**
1 cup **sugar**
2 cups **flour**
½ teaspoon **salt**
2 teaspoons **baking soda**
½ teaspoon ground **cloves**
½ teaspoon ground **ginger**
1 teaspoon ground **cinnamon**

- Melt shortening in oven-safe bowl. Add molasses and egg.
- Mix in remaining ingredients.
- Chill dough in freezer for 15 minutes or until stiff enough to roll out and cut.
- Place cut-out cookies on greased baking sheet.
- Bake at 375° for 10 to 12 minutes.
- Top with sugar, if desired, or decorate with icing or red hots.

Very easy to make. Great for gift giving.

BROWN SUGAR BUTTER BITES

Yield: 2 dozen

1 cup (2 sticks) **butter**
¾ cup **brown sugar**
1 **egg yolk**
2 cups **flour**

- In a large bowl, beat butter until consistency of whipped cream.
- Add brown sugar and egg yolk; beat well.

- Gradually add flour, beating until very smooth.
- Roll dough into small balls and place on ungreased cookie sheet.
- Flatten balls with fork, or imprint a design with a stone cookie press.
- Bake at 375° for 8 to 10 minutes until lightly brown.
- Store cookies in a sealed container.

Wonderfully rich shortbread cookies that melt in your mouth!

WORLD'S BEST SUGAR COOKIES

Yield: 7 dozen

1   cup (2 sticks) **butter**, softened
1   cup **vegetable oil**
1   cup **granulated sugar**
1   cup **powdered sugar**
2   **eggs**
1   teaspoon **vanilla**
1   teaspoon **baking soda**
4¼ cups **flour**
1   teaspoon **cream of tartar**
1   teaspoon **salt**

- Thoroughly cream butter, oil, and both sugars.
- Add eggs and vanilla.
- Sift dry ingredients. Stir in and blend with creamed mixture.
- Chill dough about 1 hour.
- Preheat oven to 350°.
- Roll soft dough into 1- to 2-inch diameter balls.
- Flatten balls on ungreased cookie sheet, using flat-bottomed glass dipped in sugar.
- Bake 8 to 10 minutes.

CHOCOLATE CHIP COOKIES

Yield: 2 dozen cookies

½   cup (1 stick) **butter**, softened
½   cup **brown sugar**
¼   cup **granulated sugar**
½   teaspoon **vanilla**
1   **egg**, beaten
1   cup sifted **flour**
½   teaspoon **baking soda**
½   teaspoon **salt**
6   ounces **chocolate chips**
½   cup chopped **pecans** (optional)

- In a large bowl, beat well butter, sugars, and vanilla.
- Add egg and beat again. Add flour, baking soda, and salt.
- Blend in chips and pecans.
- Refrigerate dough overnight for best results (dough may be refrigerated several days).
- Drop by spoonfuls on greased cookie sheet.
- Bake at 375° for 8 to 10 minutes (until edges are golden brown).
- Let stand before removing.
- Cool on cookie racks before storing.

ICED CHOCOLATE COOKIES

Yield: 3 dozen

2   squares **unsweetened chocolate**
½   cup **vegetable oil**
1½ cups **brown sugar**
1   **egg**
½   cup **buttermilk**
1   teaspoon **vanilla**
2   cups **flour**
½   teaspoon **baking soda**
½   teaspoon **salt**

Icing:

½   cup (1 stick) **butter**, softened
1   pound **powdered sugar**
2   tablespoons **shortening**
2   tablespoons **cocoa**
1   teaspoon **vanilla**
    Milk

- Blend together cookie ingredients.
- Drop by tablespoonfuls onto ungreased cookie sheet.
- Bake at 350° for 10 minutes. Cookies will be soft.
- Let cookies cool for a moment on the sheet.
- Remove cookies from the cookie sheet.
- Meanwhile, combine icing ingredients with enough milk to make a smooth spreading consistency.
- When cookies have cooled completely, spread with icing.

Soft and almost cake-like, these yummy cookies are always a hit!

GRANDMA'S COOKIES

Yield: 3½ dozen

1   cup (2 sticks) **butter**, softened
½   pound crushed **pecans**
¾   cup **sugar**
1   teaspoon **vanilla**
2   cups **flour**
2   cups **confectioners sugar**

- Combine all ingredients in mixing bowl until well blended.
- Roll into small crescents or balls.
- Bake on ungreased cookie sheet at 350° for 18 to 25 minutes.
- Roll cookies in confectioners sugar.

An old family recipe that continues to receive rave reviews.

CREAMY CHOCOLATE WAFERS

Yield: 2 dozen

Brownie Layer:

4   ounces **unsweetened chocolate**

1   cup (2 sticks) **butter**

4   **eggs**

2   cups **sugar**

1   cup **flour**

Vanilla Buttercream Layer:

½   cup (1 stick) softened **butter**

4   cups **confectioners sugar**

¼   cup **cream**

1   teaspoon **vanilla**

Chocolate Glaze:

4   ounces **semisweet chocolate**

4   tablespoons **butter**

Brownie Layer:
- Melt chocolate and butter in top of double boiler. Cool slightly.
- In a separate bowl, beat eggs until light and lemon-colored.
- Gradually add sugar to egg mixture. Add butter and chocolate; stir in flour.
- Pour batter into a greased and floured 15½ x 10½-inch jellyroll pan.
- Bake at 350° for 15 to 20 minutes, or until toothpick inserted in the center comes out clean.
- Cool and chill in refrigerator.

Vanilla Buttercream Layer:
- Cream butter thoroughly with electric mixer.
- Gradually add confectioners sugar alternately with cream. Add vanilla and beat until very light and fluffy.
- Spread batter evenly over cooled Brownie Layer.
- Chill in refrigerator at least 10 minutes.

Chocolate Glaze:
- Melt chocolate and butter together in top of double boiler. Beat well.
- Drizzle over the chilled buttercream in a lacy pattern.
- Chill 1 hour or longer.
- Cut into squares and serve.

Wickedly rich and delicious!

Chewy Chocolate Cookies

Yield: 4 dozen

1¼ cups (2½ sticks) **butter** or **margarine**, softened
2 cups **sugar**
2 **eggs**
2 teaspoons **vanilla**
2 cups all-purpose **flour**
¾ cup **cocoa**
1 teaspoon **baking soda**
½ teaspoon **salt**
1 cup finely chopped **nuts** (optional)

Vanilla Glaze:
1 cup **confectioners sugar**
1½ tablespoons **milk**
1½ teaspoons **butter** or **margarine**, softened
¼ teaspoon **vanilla**

- In a large mixing bowl, cream butter and sugar until light and fluffy. Add eggs and vanilla; beat well.
- In a separate bowl, combine flour, cocoa, baking soda, and salt; gradually blend into cream mixture. Stir in nuts, if desired.
- Drop by teaspoons onto an ungreased cookie sheet.
- Bake at 350° for 8 to 9 minutes or until almost set.
- Cool slightly on cookie sheet.
- Remove from cookie sheet; cool completely on wire rack.
- Drizzle with Vanilla Glaze.

Vanilla Glaze:
- Combine all ingredients in small mixing bowl; beat until smooth.

ChocoNut Caramel Bars

Yield: 12 servings

1   11½-ounce package
     (2 cups) **Nestle® milk
     chocolate chips**

2   tablespoons **vegetable
     shortening**

14   ounces **caramels**

5   tablespoons **butter** or
     margarine

2   tablespoons **water**

1   cup coarsely chopped
     peanuts

- Melt milk chocolate chips and shortening in double boiler over hot, not boiling, water.
- Stir until mixture is smooth. Remove from heat.
- Pour half of chocolate mixture into an 8-inch foil-lined square pan and spread evenly.
- Refrigerate until firm (about 15 minutes).
- Return remaining chocolate mixture to low heat.
- Combine caramels, butter, and water in a small microwave mixing bowl. Microwave, stirring every 1 to 2 minutes, until melted and smooth.
- Stir in nuts and pour over chocolate-lined pan. Spread evenly.
- Refrigerate until tacky (15 minutes).
- Top with remaining chocolate mixture and spread evenly.
- Refrigerate for 1 hour.
- Cut into squares.
- Refrigerate until ready to serve.

ACKNOWLEDGEMENTS

We would like to express our sincere appreciation to all of the volunteers and committee members who worked so willingly on *Saint Louis Days... Saint Louis Nights* and especially to Ida Early and Dorcas Dunlop for their vision and support throughout.

A very special thank you goes to Marta Hawthorne Wolfe, Bob Prow, and Steve Wienke at Hawthorne/Wolfe Corporate Communications Consultants, Inc.; to Susan Garson, who created the cover plate for the cookbook; to James Huber, food stylist for the cookbook; and to John Watson, who supplied the beautiful photography included in its pages.

We would also like to thank the Junior League of St. Louis members and friends who submitted more than 2,500 recipes and the 300 volunteers who triple-tested each recipe until the final 343 were ultimately selected. We regret that we were unable to use all of the recipes received.

Finally, we would like to thank our families for being so supportive and patient from beginning to end.

Linda Fendler Sperberg
Chair

Dorothy Markwort Rhodes
Editor

Mary Lagen Corrigan
Vice Chair

Sharon Etzel Boranyak
Associate Editor

John Watson is a commercial photographer who specializes in food and beverage photography. His clients include Ralston Purina Co., Anheuser-Busch, Pet Incorporated, Robert Mondavi Winery, Monsanto, and Glen Ellyn Winery. An Iowa native and a graduate of Southern Illinois University at Carbondale, Watson has made his home with his wife, Marcy, in St. Louis for the past eight years. Watson shares his photography studio with partner Michael Feher in a renovated firehouse in the historic Soulard neighborhood.

Susan Garson is an artist living in Boulder, Colorado with her husband, Tom Pakele, a ceramic artist, and their two sons. They have been collaborating and selling their ceramic pieces in galleries and museums all across the United States for the past ten years. The American Craft Museum, New York; Kohler Art Center, Sheboygan, Wisconsin; National Museum of American Jewish History, Philadelphia; and Craft Alliance, St. Louis, are among the places where their work is shown. They both received M.F.A. degrees at UCLA. Susan enjoys working in many media, including watercolor and etching.

COMMITTEE MEMBERS

Distribution

Renee Bailey
Elizabeth Braznell
Sarah Christian
Pam Farris
Claire Jablonski
Missy Kent
Beth Newhouse
Erin Olschansky
Cele Schnoebelen
Robin Walsh
Debbie Williams
Elizabeth Williams

Editorial Committee

Betty Amelotti
Donna Auld
Jennifer Burke
Gretchen Davis
Terry Eckles
Linda Finerty
Julie Gaebe
Susan Gausnell
Mary Hannig
Randi Hanpeter
Cathy Marshall
Lisa Marstiller
Darlene Miller
Cindy Schnabel
Julie Spitzfaden
Liz Sprague

Internal Public Relations

Angie Bernardi
Susie Blatt
Terese Boveri
Julie Dobbs
Madonna Doheny
Mary Beth
   Hammack
Kay Harbison
Sandra Hayes
Mary Henges
Karyn Koury
Krista Kudla
Elizabeth Kurila
Shelley Lange
Barbara Manthe
Susan Miller
Leslie Niemoeller
Gale Oertli
Beth Recar
Kim Rist
Eleanor Simpson

Publicity

Katie Barry
Mary Beth Engler
Elisabeth Farrell
Mary Hannig
Karen Horstmann
Diana Kohn
Kim Kolman
Ann Lucas
Loren Ludmerer
Julie Mentel
Darlene Miller

Susan Miller
Monica Nabholz
Peggy Newsham
Laura Ponte
Andrea Tramelli
Pam Tvedt
Amy White
Pam Wingbermuehle

Recipe Steering Committee

Celeste Kennedy
Darlene Miller
Gay Moppert
Patricia Seeler
Beth Ripley

Sales Committee

Betty Amelotti
Stephanie Garland
Cynthia Garrett
Joan Hagedorn-Ball
Mary Hannig
Sydney Hiatt
Jeannie Citerman-
   Kraeger
Elizabeth Kurila
Myra Lincoln
Linda Mace
Tracy McMonigle
Angela Montgomery
Deborah Williams

RECIPE TESTERS

Mary Adkins
Lynne Allenspach
Neal Alster
Patricia Alster
Gina Altoiles
Betty Amelotti
Marta Anglim
Patty Arnold
Dale Auffenberg
Donna Auld
Jo Axelrod
Joan Hagedorn-Ball
Liz Basler
Debbie Battocletti
Diane Beaver
Tom Beaver
Joan Birchler
Sharon Boranyak
Kay Brassey
Kristyn Brennan
Ann Bresnahan
Janet Brobeck-
    Jones
Kathi Broughton
Cindy Brown
Judy Bruton
P. J. Burnette
Kathy Bussman
Moira Byrd
Barb Calkins
Diana Calkins
Jane Card
Vicki Carius
Margie Carlson
Letah Carruthers
Emily Castle
Letah Chambers
Anne Chivetta
Janet Ciapciak
Mary Cobb

The Junior League of St. Louis would like to thank those whose culinary skills and energy made the selection of recipes for Saint Louis Days...Saint Louis Nights *possible.*

Bob Cocking
Sam Cocking
Judi Coleman
Bonnie Coleman
Kate Convy
Christine Covert
Midge Crider
Maureen Crowley
Karen Crum
Nancy Davidson
Gretchen Davis
Kathy Dessent
Doris Devereux
Claire Devoto
John Devoto
Debbie Dillon
Julie Dobbs
Madonna Doheney

Kathi Doisy
Libby Donnell
Barb Donohue
Mary Jane Driscoll
Amy Drummond
Dorcas Dunlop
Ida Early
Janice Eickhorst
Pam Farris
Linda Finerty
Peggy Finn
Jan Fishman
Joan Flynn
Peggy Fonke
Bob Fournie
Kate Fox
Carla Freund
Kathy Frost
Cindy Fry
Judy Gallaher
Chris Garcia
Chris Gardiner
Stephanie Garland
Cindy Garrison
Pat Gates
Mary Gatz-Meiners
Susan Gausnell
Jane Geer
Kay Genevose
Debbie Genung
Tracy Gildehaus
Eileen Gilleland
Cindy Gillentine
Liz Gladney
Rhonda Goedeker
Sally Gordon
Nancy Grable
Susie Graham
Laura Grant

Jessica Greenhall
Barb Greteman
Sally Griesedieck
Mike Grimes
Nancy Grimes
Carolyn Guest
Ellen Gunn
Karleen Hagan
Becky Hallemeier
Susan Haller
Mimi Hammack
Sue Hammann
Mary Hannig
Randi Hanpeter
Lisa Hansen
Kay Harbison
Laura Haskins
Cyndy Haumesser
Sandra Hayes
Anne Hegeman
Mary Henges
Cindy Henges
Cara Henke
Nancy Herzog
Sallie Herzog
Mrs. John Hicks
Joan Hicks
Kathy Hill
Tendai Hilliard
Winston Hilliard
Stephanie Hof
Gina Hoiles
Susie Holman
Tracee Holmes
Susie Holthaus
Angela Hoops
Celia Hosler
Sally Hovater
Mary Howe

Gloria Hutchison
Monique James
Lisa Jennings
Susan Johnston
Julie Jostrand
Margi Kahn
Mike Kahn
Peggy Kahle
Karen Kane
Joan Kaufman
Christine Kaufman
Paula Kaufman
Barb Kemery
Celeste Kennedy
Missy Kent
Mary Beth Kinsella
Mary Ellen
   Klostermeyer
Anne Kniffen
Sandy Knott
Krista Kudla
Betsy Landman
Shelley Lange
Jennifer Langford
Heather Lankford
Meg Lauber
Kitten Lawless
Sally Ledbetter
Kelly LeGard
Patti Leonard
Mary Beth Leritz
Susie Linebroker
Steffie Littlefield
Kim Livingston
Deb Lohmuller
Suzanne Lohnes
LaVerne Lorenzini
Paula Lorio

Terry Lucas
Monica Mach
Kit MacNee
Kathy Maher
Meg Maher
Susan Maher
Sherri Manion
Barbara Manthe
Shawn Marhefka
Tara Markenson
Martha Markwort
Cathy Marshall
Peggy Martin
Diane Martin
Jeff McCullough
Jacque McCullough
Susan McCusker
Mary Lou McGuire
Cathie McLead
Tracy McMonigle
Terry Meiners
Kathy Meiners
Margaret Merkel
Cindy Meyer
Bette Miller
Anne Miller
Susan Miller
Darlene Miller
Renee Montgomery
Liz Moore
Ellie Moreland
Anna Morgan
Bette Mueller
Dave Mueller
Genie Mueller
Judy Mueller
Dale Naas
Jeri Neumann
Mary Newmaster
Peggy Newsham

Christy Nicklin
Julie Nies
Donna Nonnenkamp
Nancy Novak
Karen Noyes
Casey O'Brien
Leigh Ann O'Neil
Sheila O'Toole
Gail Oertli
Beth Olin
Carol Oliverio
Erin Olschansky
LaWanda Oswald
Jane Overton
Patty Padawer
Nancy Pautler
Wendy Perry
Laurie Peters
Jean Marie Petersen
Sally Petty
Mary Beth Placht
Susan Pohrer
Trisha Polluck
Angie Power
Yvonne Pratte
Jan Proctor
Jeanne Pyzdrowski
Lisa Ragan
Nancy Rambaud
Jenny Rapp
Peggy Rassieur
Barbara Ravenscraft
Beth Raymond
Peggy Reardon
Deanie Reis
Tracey Rhea
Krista Richardson
Beth Ripley
Kim Rist
Beth Rogers

JoAnn Rull
Lynne Rutledge
Val Rutterer
Claire Schenk
Kim Scherer
Judy Schiff
Rick Schiff
Cindy Schnabel
Nancy Schnarre
Cele Schnoebelen
Nancy Schnuck
Sally Scott
Pat Seeler
Lori Shanfeld
Jane Sharp
Annette Shroyer
K. C. Shute
Katie Simoneit
Suzie Sivewright
Peggy Sizemore
Pat Slay
Susan Smith
Julie Smith
Sally Snavely
Penny Snellings
Melissa Snodsmith
Michelle Sokol-
    Dean
Mary Lee Sonderman
Vicky Sonnenberg
Susie Spence
Linda Sperberg
Liz St. Cin
Sally Stephen
Max Steward
Maxine Stewart

Patti Stoddart
Mary Stowe
Gigi Strauss
Michelle Sullivan
Tari Suter
Sally Taylor
Kathy Tessier
Dawn Thomas
Rita Throgmorton
Becky Toman
Lynn Tomiello
Pam Tvedt
Diane Upchurch
Lucy Volding
Caren Vredenburgh
Jim Vredenburgh
Debbie Von
    Doersten
Mary Alice Wack
Ann Walter
Mary Bridget Ward
B. Lynn Webster
Gail Weller
Ann White
Amy White
Maury Whitelaw
Sue Wickenhauser
Lottchen Wider
Barbara Wilcher
Genie Wilhelm
Heather Winsby
Barb Wittich
Ann Wyrick
Janet York
Mary Ann Zehnder
Stephanie Zornes
Nancy Zwiener

RECIPE CONTRIBUTORS

We would like to thank our many members and friends who have so graciously shared their favorite recipes.

Beverly Wade Aach
Louise Akers
Dorothy Allan
Yvonne Allen
Lynne Allenspach
Betty Amelotti
Beth Amend
Sharon Anderson
Lenwood Anthon
Barbara Archer
Mrs. James Audrain
Donna Auld
Mrs. Nancy Auld
Ann Flachman
   Babington
Renee Bailey
Janice Baker
Rita Baker
Joan Hagedorn Ball
Vicky Balore
Sharron Barker
Desirée Barnett
Catharine Barron
Charlotte Barteau
Susan Bartlett
Mrs. Dudley Batchelor
Beth Beattie
Gail Beck
Darlene Becker
Rika Beckley
Doelling Haus Bed
   & Breakfast
Barbara Bell
Jane Berkmeyer
Honey Bernstein
Barbara Bettonville
Karen Blumeyer
Vicky Bolan
Matthew Bolton
Sharon Boranyak
Diane Bordeaux
Margaret Boveri
Nancy Bowe
Carole Brandt
Kathleen Brennan
Kristyn Brennan
Irene Brooks
Kathryn Brooks

Mary Ruth Brown
Charla Bruce
Jennifer Bryant
Patti Bubash
Kaye Burns
Beth Burst
Sarah Butler
Mrs. W. Butterworth
Denise Butts
June Bux
Moira Byrd
Frances Byrnes
Karen Calabria
Vicki Carius
Annalou Carrier
Carmen Cervantes
Carolyn Chapman
Katherine Chapman
Margaret Chatham
Jean Chouquette
Sarah Christian
Mrs. R.B. Clark III
Loris Clifford
Mary Ann Clifford
Sam Cocking
Virginia Coleman
Suzanne Collins
Kirby Colson
Anne Connell
Martha Conzelman
Barb Cook
Georgia Cooke
Janet Cordes
Micki Costello

Mary Ellen Cotsworth
Mrs. George Cottrill
Audrey Coyle
Jan Craig
Midge Crider
Peggylynne Cupp
Lorayne Curtis
Nancy Czajkowski
Karen Dahman
Jane Daniel
Jackie Danis
Shirley Dauzat
Gretchen Davis
Jeaneane Davis
Mrs. Hugo Davis
Sue Davis
Pat Deming
Mimi Denes
Claire Devoto
Pam DeWitt
Maria Diekneite
Carol Doelling
Kathi Doisy
Eugina Doll
Judie Donohue
Bill Dooley
Joan Dowell
Dorcas Dunlop
Mary Dwivedy
Chris Earls
Diane Easton
Trish Eaton
Mimi Edlin
Ella Edwards
Anita Eftimoff
Christy Ehrenreich
Janice Eickhorst
Ann Eisel
Dollye Elliott
Natalie Elliott
Becky Engelbrecht
Mary Beth Engler
Linda Estell
Kathleen Evans
Elizabeth Eversman
Stephanie Faron
Mrs. Web Federspiel
Danae Fendler

Christine Ferrer-Garcia
April Fey
Linda Finerty
Marianne Finnegan
Judith Firth
Cam Fischer
Carol Fisher
Gretta Forrester
Kathleen Fothergill
Bob Fournie
Marianne Fournie
Ann Frawley
Lynn Froeber
Cyndy Fry
Margo Funkhouser
Megan Galgano
Tracey Gans
Kathy Gardner
Stephanie Garland
Cindy Garrison
Delphine Gatch
Pat Gates
Susan Gausnell
Betty Gaydos
Agnes Gear
Jane Geer
Debbie Genung
Barbara George
Alice Gerdine
Beth Goad
Shirlee Goeckel
Mary Goedde
Rhonda Goedeker
Elizabeth Gorder
Nancy Gorder
Sam Gould
Mrs. C.E. Grable
Nancy Grable
Laura Grant
Mrs. Russell Grass
Jessica Greenhall
Col. William Gregory
Debbie Grelle
Kelly Griswold
Mrs. Robert Ground
Dudley Grove
Angela Grupas
Peggy Gundlach

Suzy Gunter
Mary Jo Hamilton
Sue Hammann
Linda Hammond
Bonnie Hana
Jeannette Hanke
Clare Hanlon
Mitch Hanneken
Mary Hannig
Randi Hanpeter
Lynn Hansen
Maureen Hanson
Tammy Hardesty
Marie Harrington
Henrietta Harris
Jane Harris
Michelle Harris
Mrs. Chester Hart
Marianne Haskins
Cyndy Haumesser
Mrs. Joseph Haupt
Anne Hegeman
Laurie Hegeman
Vicki Henderson
Mrs. E.C. Henderson, Jr.
Marlene Hennessey
Nancy Herzog
Mrs. Elsie Hey
Margaret Hickey
Mrs. John Hicks
Lissa Hildreth
Mrs. Jack Hipps
Jean Hobler
Karen Hoeman
Kippy Hoene
Mary Louise Hoevel
Tina Hogan-Shannon
Mary Hoke
Tracee Holmes
Christine Homan
Barbara Homeier
Debbie Hoosack
Janet Hopkins
Rosanne Horan
Lorraine Hornung
Donna Hostetter
Mrs. Paul Houston
Mrs. James Howe, III

Mary Beth Hughes
Jane Hull
Dixie Hummel
Susan Hummel
Elsa Hunstein
Lerinda Ingraham
Debbie Jacobson
Gay Jarrett
Judith Jensen
JLSL
Mildred Johnson
Susan Johnson
Mrs. Myra Johnston
Susan Johnston
Ann Jones
Gretchen Jones
Helen Jones
Mary Jotte
Dee Joyner
Mrs. Franck H. Kaiser
Joni Karandjeff
Mrs. Fred Karches
L. A. Kelly
Barbara Kemery
Missy Kent
Mary Beth Kinsella
Deb Klarfeld
Melinda Klinghammer
Hazel Knapp
Diana Kohn
Caroline Komyati
Mrs. Alice Kopsky
Elizabeth Kramer
Rita Kubitschek
Kathy Kugman
Rachel Kunstman
Elizabeth Kurila
Reba Lacey
Betsy Landman
Berry Lane
Michelle Lange
Jennifer Langford
Heather Lankford
Jo Larsen
Julie Latz
Laura Laughlin
Madonna Lawton
Florence Leavy

Sally Ledbetter
Kelly LeGard
Noel Leicht
Jessie Leutwiler
Mrs. Charles Lewis
Marcella Leydig
Mrs. Nancy Lich
Nancy Lillenberg
Helen Lindenmann
Kim Lindley
Joyce Littlefield
Steffie Littlefield
Stephen Littlefield
Allison Livesay
Emily Long
Jessica Long
Susie Loomis
Robyn Loomstein
Caroline Loughlin
Rachel Lovitt
Cynthia Lund
Jane Lutz
Barbara MacCarthy
Kit MacNee
Mrs. Guy Magness
Kathy Maher
Julie Maire
Debbie Mallory
Debbie Maly-Schneider
Barbara Manthe
Kimberley Marchant
Tara Markenson
Martha Markwort
Joyce Marsh
Cathy Marshall
Terri Marx
Lisa Mastorakos
Steve Mattis
Nancy Maupin
Ellen Maxfield
Beth McCann
Aldena McCormack
Claire McCown
Donna McKinney
Mason McMullin
Cynthia McNeill
Maura McShane
Helen McWhorter

Blythe Meisinger
Pam Melvin
Christina Merriman
Diane Metz
Lisa Meyer
Helen Meyers
Anne Michener
June Middlebrooks
Janet Mika
Darlene Miller
Denise Miller
Joan Miller
Mrs. Craig Miller
Susan Miller
Estelle Mills
Karen Mills
Alta Moore
Liz Moore
Pat Moore
Ellie Moreland
Arthur Morgan
Cissy Morgan
Lea Morris
Mrs. Robert Morrow
Rita Morton
Gregory Mosberger
Genie Mueller
Jane Mulkey
Katy Mullins
Jeanette Myers
Susan Myers
Gladys Myles
Dale Naas
Doreen Nersesian
Stacy Neuman
Nellie Nicholson
Kathy Novelly
Mrs. Edward Nusrala
Ann O'Brien
Sally O'Halloran
Leigh Ann O'Neil
Sue Oertli
Helen Oetter
Beth Olin
Cathy Oliver
Erin Olschansky
LaWanda Oswald
Lori Overmyer

Patty Padawer
Virginia Pankey
Jenny Pappas
Ashley Parriott
Irene Patton
Nancy Pautler
Anne Pellett
Mrs. Norman Penkert
Peri Pepmueller
Wendy Perry
Gini Peterson
Hester Peterson
Janice Peterson
Mrs. Norman Peukert
Sharon Phelan
Kristen Pierce
Nell Pinckert
Margaret Poggemeier
Katherine Pope
Angie Power
Anne Probst
Jan Proctor
Evelyn Pronko
Susan Pruchnicki
Rosemary Quigley
Lisa Ragan
Rebecca Randolph
Renee Raponi
Barbara Ravenscraft
Beth Raymond
Marla Reece
Naomi Reed
Ruth Reidenbaugh
Mrs. Wilbur Reinhart
Jeana Reisinger
Peggy Renshaw
Susan Reynolds
Suzanne Reynolds
Tracey Rhea
Allison Ricks
Alexandra Riddle
Beth Ripley
Nancy Rife
Leslie Rives
Lynette Roccia
Beth Rogers
Katina Rogers
Deborah Romo

Anne Rosenberg
Bernice Rosenow
Deborah Ross
Jody Ross
Judy Ross
Carol Rosse
Mary Ellen Roth
Dotty Roy
Judith Rubenstein
Susan Ruble
Jennifer Rudloff
Cookie Ruis
Pam Ryan
Sharon Schaefer
Claire Schenk
Kim Scherrer
Elizabeth Schmidt
Wilma Schmitz
Cindy Schnabel
Nancy Schnarre
Nancy Schnuck
Kathi Schoene
Ruth Schomburg
JoAnne Schranck
Mabel Schray
Barbara Schukar
Ann Sedgwick
Pat Seeler
Ruth Selfridge
Karen Serra
Pat Sewell
Pat Shaver
Vicki Sheehan
Eleanor Sheppard
Mrs. John Shillington, Jr.
Louise Shore
Anita Siegmund
Joan Silber
Joan Siler
Katie Simoneit
Jean Sippy
Susie Sivewright
Susan Slattery
Becky Smith
Connie Smith
Audrey Smith-Deglman
Mary Beth Soffer
Michelle Sokol-Dean

Donna Sondag
Helen Southworth
Linda Sperberg
Ginny Starke
Lisa Stein
Mimi Stephens
Julie Stephenson
Christine Sterkel
Randall Sterkel
Stephanie Sterkel
Fran Sternberg
Lynne Stevenson
Agnes Stewart
Margaret Stock
Suzanne Stolar
Anne Stoltz
Mrs. L. Keever
Stringham
Mrs. W. Stanley Stuart
Charlotte Sulltrop
Julie Swanston
Judy Swearingen
Keri Sweet
Helen Tasch
Tina Tebbe
Elizabeth Telthorst
Mrs. Dorsey Thomas, Jr.
Carol Thompson
Diane Thompson
Laura Thompson
Teresa Thompson
Jean Tilden
Terri Todt
Lynn Tomiello
Betsy Tracy
Ann Travis
Ardeen Tucker
Lynne Turley
Pam Tvedt
Doris Tyler
Louise VanLandingham
Susan Vatterott
Kathy Vertucci
Cristin Viebranz
Freda Vollmar
Mary Jo VonAllmen
Liz VonRohr
June Vouga

Dianne Waldron
Robin Walsh
Doris Waltz
Connie Ward
Virginia Wasiuk
Mary Wasserman
Teri Webster
JoAnn Wegman
Betty Weitzman
Gail Weller
Mrs. John Welty
Davin Wenner
Edward Wetzel
Nancy Wetzel
Amy White
Molly Wight
Debbie Williams
Margie Williams
Linda Willman
Betty Wilson
Jane Wilucki
Heather Winsby
Francine Wishart
Bette Wolf
Kathleen Woodworth
Ann Wyrick
Lynn Yaeger
Janet York
Mary Ann Zehnder
Katherine Ziegler
Stephanie Zornes

*We would like to thank those whose
contributions have helped support the project*
Saint Louis Days...Saint Louis Nights

Cookbook Stars

Mrs. Frederick S.
   Anheuser
Barbara C. Archer
Virginia Batson
Elizabeth Bohlman
Mrs. Patricia Bollozos
Jane Daniel Bryan
Mrs. Thomas F. Cline
Mary Lagen Corrigan
Mrs. George W. Cottrill
Vicki Cutting
Sandra Crawford Dillard
Judy Andrews Fierstein
Judith Kuelker Firth
Mrs. Lillian Fischer
Mrs. August John Furla
Georgianna Jacobs Gerber
Mrs. Marguerite Giese
Mr. & Mrs. Michael
   Hammack
Mrs. F. Lee Hawes
Vicki L. Henderson
Mrs. Jack K. Higgins
Becky B. Hubert
Mary Beth Hughes
Mrs. Neona Karches
Betty K. Kruse
Valerie Lawlor
Connie Lohr
Frances S. MacNaughton
Mrs. John W. Marsh
Mrs. R.U. Meckfessel
Gay Moppert
Genie Mueller
Tina Niemann
Laura Ponte

Mrs. Phyllis Paulson
   Rainwater
Jeana Barnes Reisinger
Allison S. Ricks
Mrs. T. C. Rischbieter
Mrs. Margaret W. Rosenthal
Martha Rounds
Mrs. Owen Rush
Anne F. Ryan
Jane Hoyt Sanders
Jean W. Sippy
Virginia C. Sodemann
Patricia Green Stabler
Mrs. A. Hamilton Strong
Mrs. Gale Swango
Shirley Sweet
Barbara B. Taylor
Mrs. Thomas A. Taylor
Mrs. Sylvia Tober
Lucie Vassia in memory
   of Rose Marie Vassia
Cristin Viebranz
Mrs. William L. Weiss
Peggy Weltmer
Marie R. Zimmerman

Cookbook Sponsors

Maggie Albers
Anne O'C. Albrecht
Mrs. Vern Ambach
Betty Amelotti
Lori Aston
Joan Hagedorn-Ball
Marilyn E. Baumann
Christine Bell
Jane Berkmeyer
Terry R. Bettendorf

Mrs. Raymond H.
   Bialson
Mrs. Lillian H. Biggs
Judy Brown
Laura Mae Brown
Kathleen T. Burns
Sarah Butler
Frances A. Byrnes
Mrs. Graham M. Carroll
Mrs. Alfonso J. Cervantes
Elizabeth D. St. Cin
Mary Ann Clifford
Mrs. Robert Cochran
Sam Cocking
Allison Hawk Collinger
Michaela Costello
Christine M. Covert
Sheila Creecy
Gretchen Davis
Sue Davis
Jeaneane K. Davis
Connie Diekman
Dorcas Dunlop
Ida H. Early
Terry Eckles
Mrs. J. Robert Edwards
Anita K. Eftinoff
Mrs. Rey Eilers
Mrs. Edwin Ellston
Dr. & Mrs. Robert J. Fallon
Elisabeth C. Farrell
Edie Fay
Lillian Federspiel
Linda Finerty
Dr. & Mrs. Michael
   S. Flom
Marianne S. Fournie

273

Mrs. Charles D'Arcy Fox
Ann Lieb Frawley
Betty Gaydos
Barbara Gervais
Catherine H. Gidcumb
Mrs. Milton W. Gruber
Randi Hanpeter
Mrs. Robert H. Harper
Mr. & Mrs. Shawn Hayes
Mrs. J. York Hewitt
Lucy Hicks
Jacquelyn Hinkamp
Jane R. Huey
Jeannette R. Huey
Sally Jones
Mrs. Endsley Jones
Joni Karandjeff
Mrs. Franck H. Kaiser
Mrs. Frank Key
Mrs. Edward D. Kinsella
Peggy A. Kleffner
Becca Klingler
Carolyn Kolman
Jacqueline F. Kwon
JoElissa Larsen
Laurie Laughlin
Margie Kranzberg Lazarus
Sally Ledbetter
Mrs. Jack (Nancy) Lich
Margrit M. Lorenz
Peggy Luth
Julie H. McGoogan
Jennifer Miller/
   Miller-Page Insurance
Angela Ginger Montgomery
Mary Jane Muschany

Mrs. Marion Oertli
Helen Oetter
Elly Painter
Irene W. Patton
Mrs. Myron Peterson
Mrs. Vernon W. Piper
Marjorie Rister
Judy L. Ross
Mrs. Angela Sanders
Sharon Schaefer
Kim Scherrer
Deby Schlapprizzi
Kathleen S. Schoene
Mrs. Don S. Schomburg
Marilyn M. Schuermann
Ms. Ann Sedgwick
Anita Siegmund
Eleanor P. Simpson
Mrs. Russell J. Sims
Jessie H. Slaughter
Donna M. Sondag
Linda Sperberg
Marjorie E. Stauss
Mrs. W. Stanley Stuart
Mrs. Mead Summers
Keri Sweet
Sondra L. Thomas
Laura Thompson
Linda Tracy
Elaine W. VanderSchaaf-
   Zgdowska
Debbie Watkins
Gail Weller
Debbie Wilhelm
Phebe Ann Williams
Marion Wilson

Janet I. York
Dorcas Dunlop
   Tribute to:
   Randi Hanpeter &
   Linda Sperberg

In-Kind Donations

Blue Water Grill
Brown Shoe Company
Cardwell's
A Change of Taste
J.Cira's Beauty Salon
Gloria Jean's Coffee Bean
Gourmet in a Flash
Hank's Cheesecakes
Hawthorne/Wolfe
   Corporate Communi-
   cation Consultants, Inc.
Marcella Borghese
Paper Patch
Plaza Frontenac
Prescriptives
The Ritz Carlton St. Louis
St. Louis Marriott
   Pavilion Hotel
Sayers Printing Company
The Studio at St. Albans
Mary Tuttle's Flowers
Unisource Paper Company
Vincent's Jewelers
John Watson Photography
YSL

INDEX

MAIL TO: *Saint Louis Days...Saint Louis Nights*

10435 Clayton Road, St. Louis, Missouri 63131 (314) 569-3117

Please send _____ cookbooks   @ $22.95 _____

      Postage and handling: Total for 1 book $4.50 _____

                      Total for 2-6 books $8.00 _____

                             GRAND TOTAL _____

❑ Check   ❑ Money Order   ❑ Visa or MasterCard *(see over)*

Make check or money order payable to: **Junior League of St. Louis Cookbook**

Name _____

Address _____

City _____ State _____ Zip _____

MAIL TO: *Saint Louis Days...Saint Louis Nights*

10435 Clayton Road, St. Louis, Missouri 63131 (314) 569-3117

Please send _____ cookbooks   @ $22.95 _____

      Postage and handling: Total for 1 book $4.50 _____

                      Total for 2-6 books $8.00 _____

                             GRAND TOTAL _____

❑ Check   ❑ Money Order   ❑ Visa or MasterCard *(see over)*

Make check or money order payable to: **Junior League of St. Louis Cookbook**

Name _____

Address _____

City _____ State _____ Zip _____

MAIL TO: *Saint Louis Days...Saint Louis Nights*

10435 Clayton Road, St. Louis, Missouri 63131 (314) 569-3117

Please send _____ cookbooks   @ $22.95 _____

      Postage and handling: Total for 1 book $4.50 _____

                      Total for 2-6 books $8.00 _____

                             GRAND TOTAL _____

❑ Check   ❑ Money Order   ❑ Visa or MasterCard *(see over)*

Make check or money order payable to: **Junior League of St. Louis Cookbook**

Name _____

Address _____

City _____ State _____ Zip _____

IF USING VISA OR MASTERCARD, PLEASE FILL IN THE FOLLOWING:

Name _____

Address _____ Phone ( ) _____

City _____ State _____ Zip _____

Charge to my: ☐ Visa   ☐ MasterCard

Account Number: _____

Expiration Date: _____

Customer's Signature: _____

- -

IF USING VISA OR MASTERCARD, PLEASE FILL IN THE FOLLOWING:

Name _____

Address _____ Phone ( ) _____

City _____ State _____ Zip _____

Charge to my: ☐ Visa   ☐ MasterCard

Account Number: _____

Expiration Date: _____

Customer's Signature: _____

- -

IF USING VISA OR MASTERCARD, PLEASE FILL IN THE FOLLOWING:

Name _____

Address _____ Phone ( ) _____

City _____ State _____ Zip _____

Charge to my: ☐ Visa   ☐ MasterCard

Account Number: _____

Expiration Date: _____

Customer's Signature: _____